Marsh's Library, Dublin

For Ian Hunter
With best wishes
Muriel. Marsh's Library.

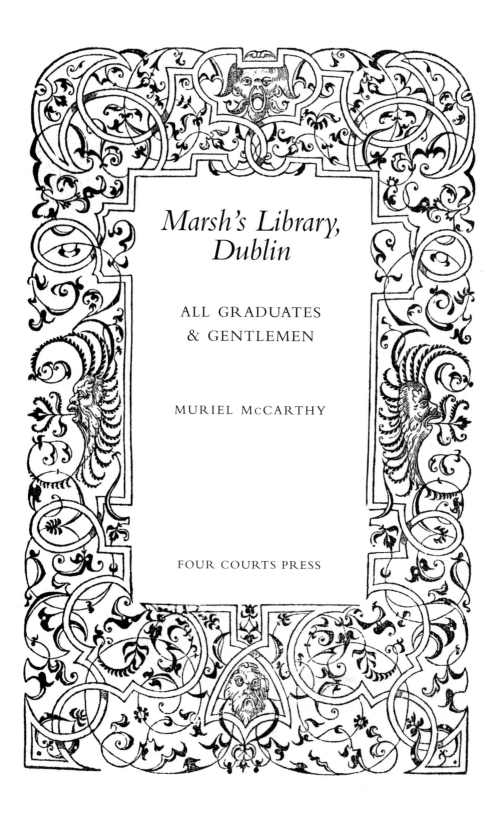

Marsh's Library, Dublin

ALL GRADUATES
& GENTLEMEN

MURIEL McCARTHY

FOUR COURTS PRESS

Typeset in 11.5 pt on 15 pt Bembo by
Carrigboy Typesetting Services, County Cork for
FOUR COURTS PRESS LTD
7 Malpas Street, Dublin 8, Ireland
e-mail: info@four-courts-press.ie
and in North America for
FOUR COURTS PRESS
c/o ISBS, 920 N.E., 58th Avenue, Suite 300, Portland, OR 97213.

© Muriel McCarthy 2003

The author would like to express her gratitude to Ann Simmons
for all her help in the preparation of this edition.

A catalogue record for this title is available
from the British Library.

ISBN 1–85182–730–7 hardback

The title-page uses a border that appears on the title-page of
Carolus Stephanus, *Dictionarium historicum ac poeticum*, [Paris], 1567.
The endpapers carry a plate, 'A Dance in Otaheite' from James Cook,
A Voyage to the Pacific Ocean [c.1784].

The first edition of this book was published in Dublin
in 1980 under the title of *All graduates and gentlemen*,
ISBN 0–905140–55–9.

Printed in Ireland
by ßetaprint Ltd., Dublin.

Contents

ACKNOWLEDGMENT

The author and publishers gratefully acknowledge a grant in aid of publication provided by Mr Patrick C. Kilroy and Mrs Dorothy Kilroy.

Illustrations

Plates appearing between pp 160 and 161

Credits for plates

4 National Gallery of Ireland; 2, 3, 6, 7, 8 John Reid/Fennell Photography.

Abbreviations

Abbott	T.K. Abbott, *Catalogue of fifteenth-century books in the Library of Trinity College, Dublin, and Marsh's Library, Dublin.* Used only for author and title.
Alden	John Alden, *Bibliographica Hibernica: additions and corrections to Wing.*
Aldis	H.G. Aldis, *A list of books printed in Scotland before 1700.*
A & R	A.F. Allison and D.M. Rogers, *A catalogue of catholic books in English printed abroad or secretly in England 1558–1640.*
Brunet	J.C. Brunet, *Manuel du libraire et de l'amateur de livres.*
Campb.	M.F.A.G. Campbell, *Annales de la typographie Néerlandaise au XVe siècle.*
CHEL	*The Cambridge history of English literature.*
DNB	*Dictionary of national biography.*
Dix	E.R.McC. Dix, *Catalogue of early Dublin-printed books 1601– 1700.*
Gesamtkatalog	*Gesamtkatalog der Wiegendrucke, vols 1–8.*
H.C.	Hain's *Repertorium,* with Copinger's *Supplement.*
Hoskins	Edgar Hoskins, *Horae beatae Mariae virginis, or, Sarum and York primers, with kindred books and primers of the reformed Roman use.*
JRSAI	*Journal of the Royal Society of Antiquaries of Ireland.*
Lowndes	W.T. Lowndes, *The bibliographer's manual of English literature.*
Madan	Falconer Madan, *The early Oxford press.*
PRIA	*Proceedings of the Royal Irish Academy.*
Ramage	David Ramage, *A finding-list of English books to 1640 in libraries in the British Isles.*
STC	A.W. Pollard and G.R. Redgrave, *A short-title catalogue of books printed in England, Scotland and Ireland and of English books printed abroad 1475–1640.*
Teerink	Herman Teerink, *A bibliography of the writings of Jonathan Swift.*
Walsh	M.ON. Walsh, *Irish books printed abroad 1475–1700.*
Wing	Donald Wing, *Short-title catalogue of books printed in England, Scotland, Ireland, Wales, and British America and of English books printed in other countries 1641–1700.*

corr.	corrected.
enlar.	enlarged.
rev.	revised.
repr.	reprinted.
s.a.	*sine anno*, undated.
s.l.	*sine loco*, no place of publication.
s.n.	*sine nomine*, without name of printer or publisher.

Introduction

n 2001 Marsh's Library celebrated its tercentenary. On 9 July 1701 the dean and chapter of St Patrick's Cathedral gave a grant to Archbishop Narcissus Marsh 'to build erect and place several pillars under the aforsaid Library of lyme and stone ... Granted because of the public advantage of so great a work'.

The library was until recently almost a forgotten institution, due to the fact that so few people knew about it. But when Marsh's opened to the public in the early eighteenth century it was a popular library and was much used by scholars and some distinguished writers. Its popularity began to change when the Royal Irish Academy, National Library, Royal Dublin Society and other libraries opened to members and the public. The fact that in the late eighteenth century, and until recently, the area around Marsh's had become run down did not help. Another factor which made it unpopular was the unfortunate entrance, which was through a walled passage in the grave-yard of St Patrick's Cathedral. (The entrance was changed and the library was restored by Sir Benjamin Lee Guinness and his family in 1865.)

Another reason for the lack of use made of Marsh's was the fact that there were no printed catalogues. It was not until Canon G.T. Stokes' lectures were published in 1900 that some information on the library and the books became generally available. In the early part of the twentieth century Newport J.D. White published catalogues of the French and English books and short lives of Narcissus Marsh and Elias Bouhéreau. He also published *An account of Archbishop Marsh's Library, with a note on autographs*, written by his nephew, Newport Benjamin White (Dublin, 1926). *A catalogue of the manuscripts* was compiled by John Russell Scott and edited by Newport J.D. White (Dublin, [1913]). This was the first time that the small but very important collection of manuscripts was made known. Another significant contribution was the catalogue of printed and manuscript music compiled by Richard Charteris and published by the Boethius Press in 1982. In recent years a series of exhibitions, together with illustrated catalogues and numerous articles in journals, magazines and newspapers have helped to promote the library and its collections.

But one of the most exciting recent contributions was an anonymous donation to computerise our catalogues. This has now been completed, and the entire catalogue of printed books and manuscripts can be consulted on our website at www.marshlibrary.ie.

Apart from the publication of the catalogues, some earlier and significant generous donations have improved and promoted the library. In 1980 the late United States ambassador to Ireland, Professor William Shannon, visited Marsh's and suggested that the American Ireland Fund might be interested in assisting it with a refurbishing programme. The American Ireland Fund (now Ireland Funds) carried out superb restoration, and provided badly needed facilities for scholars and visitors. The programme included security systems, lighting, complete redecoration of the library and the conversion of a totally derelict area into a reading/lecture room. Then, in 1988, an American couple, Jean Paul and Gladys Delmas, built a new addition to the library. This consisted of an entirely new building designed by Dr Arthur Gibney as a conservation bindery. As well as working on our own books, this conservation workshop repairs and restores books, manuscripts, prints and drawings for national institutions and private collectors.

In 1997 another major development took place. This was the suggestion by the government to the governors and guardians of the library that they might consider broadening the membership of the board by accepting two government appointees for five-year terms. The governors and guardians agreed, and the government nominated the two new members. This change was included in the National Cultural Institutions Act, 1997.

Another exciting change occurred in 2001 when the minister for Arts, Heritage, Gaeltacht and the Islands, Ms Síle de Valera, and the Department of Finance, agreed to maintain the library. A planned programme of conservation and maintenance by the Office of Public Works has already begun, and Marsh's Library can now look forward to its next 300 years.

Chapter 1

Archbishop Narcissus Marsh (1638–1713)

ARCISSUS MARSH was born on St Thomas' Eve, 20 December 1638, in a village called Hannington near Highworth in the north part of Wiltshire. He wrote in his diary[1] that he was of 'honest parents'. His father's name was William Marsh and his mother's Grace Colburn. Narcissus was the youngest of his family. He had two brothers and two sisters.[2] His 'honest parents' must have been a little unusual since they selected some rather extraordinary names for their children. The name Narcissus is certainly uncommon, but his brothers were given the names of Epaphroditus and Onesiphorus. We were curious to see if we could possibly find a reason for such names and the only tentative explanation which we can give is that Narcissus' father may have been an admirer of St Paul; all three names are

---

1 Diary of Archbishop Narcissus Marsh from 1690 to 1696. The diary in the library is a nearly contemporary transcript of the original (Marsh pressmark Z2.2.3b). It was printed in the *British Magazine* for July–August 1845 with notes by Dr James Henthorn Todd. It was reprinted in the *Irish Ecclesiastical Journal*, v, 1848–9, pp 51, 132, 148. A life of Archbishop Marsh with some extracts from his diary by 'Omicron' was published in the *Christian Examiner and Church of Ireland Magazine*, September, 1831, pp 645–50. Biographical details of Marsh are contained in *The whole works of Sir James Ware concerning Ireland*, Dublin, 1739, edited by Walter Harris, i, pp 358–2, 449–50 and 487. For a more detailed history see G.T. Stokes, *Some worthies of the Irish church*, edited by H.J. Lawlor, London, Hodder & Stoughton, 1900, pp 65–111, and N.J.D. White's *Four good men,* (3) Narcissus Marsh, Dublin, Hodges Figgis, 1927, pp 42–55, and Muriel McCarthy, 'Archbishop Marsh and his Library', in *Dublin Historical Record*, xxix, no. 1, Dec. 1975, pp 2–23. See also *DNB* and C.B. Fry, *Hannington: the records of a Wiltshire parish*, Gloucester, 1935.   2 Marsh's brother Onesiphorus was steward to Anthony (Ashley-Cooper) Lord Ashley (afterwards the famous earl of Shaftesbury). He died unmarried at Wimborne St Giles in England and was buried there on 20 May 1668. G.E.C. [i.e. George E. Cokayne] Compiler, *Some notice of various families of the name of Marsh*, Exeter, W. Pollard, 1900 [*The Genealogist*, n.s., vol. 16, suppl.], pp 34–42. His brother Epaphroditus came to Ireland and lived at Mobarane near Fethard, Co. Tipperary. He was elected a burgess for the borough of Fethard and sat as an MP for Fethard 6 Sept. 1703 and 2 Nov. 1715. He died in 1719 and is buried in Archbishop Marsh's tomb. 'Extracts from the minutes of the Corporation of Fethard, Co. Tipperary', by the Revd W.G. Skehan, ed. M. O'Donnell, *Irish Genealogist*, 4, no. 2, pp 87 and 203. I am grateful to the librarian of the County Library in Tipperary, Ms Guinan-Darmody, for sending me information on Epaphroditus Marsh and for notes from a local historian. Marsh's sisters were called Grace and Deborah. Grace Marsh was born in about 1630 and died in 1645. She is buried at Hannington in Wiltshire. Deborah came to Ireland and was married to

mentioned by St Paul in his Epistles. Onesiphorus and Epaphroditus both brought help to St Paul when he was in prison and St Paul in his Epistle to the Romans says: 'Greet them that be of the household of Narcissus which are in the Lord.'[3]

Marsh went to five local schools; first to Mr Lamb's school in the parish, then to Mr Virgil Pleydall at Lyshill, and next to Mr Dudley, a minister at Highworth, where Marsh was taught Latin. He was then sent to a Mr Crouch, minister of Hannington, and finally to Mr Thomas Hedges, minister of Rodburne in Wiltshire. Marsh wrote proudly in his diary, 'in all which schools I never was so much as once whipt or beaten'.[4]

When Marsh was sixteen he was entered as a commoner at Magdalen Hall in Oxford. He describes his studies as 'old Philosophy, Mathematicks and oriental languages, and before Lent 1658 (when I took my degree of Batchelor of arts) I had made good progress in them all'. Marsh then added, 'I constantly kept an entire fast every week from Thursday six a Clock at night untill Saturday eleven at Noon.' It is not altogether clear from this remark whether Marsh kept this fast throughout the year or not; presumably it was during Lent; even so it was a remarkable act of voluntary penance and reflected Marsh's deeply sincere religious beliefs.

When Marsh received his degree of bachelor of arts he was elected to a Wiltshire fellowship at Exeter College. The fellowship was partly due to his academic abilities which had also impressed some influential friends including a particularly good friend whom he mentions briefly in his diary, a Mr John Jenner. Subsequently Mr Jenner got into serious financial difficulties and Marsh very generously came to his rescue.

In 1660 Marsh took his degree as master of arts and in 1662 he was offered the living of Swindon in Wiltshire. Dr Skinner bishop of Oxford ordained him deacon and priest in King Henry VII's chapel, Westminster, even though he was under age for the priesthood. Marsh was unhappy about this as he wrote in his diary: '… the Lord forgive us both, but then I knew no better but that it might Legally be done'.

Marsh at this time became chaplain to the bishop of Exeter, taking up residence in Swindon. He then discovered to his horror that in return for

the archdeacon of Cashel, William Williams. He died in 1693. Deborah Williams died in 1697, aged 65, and is buried in the Church of Ireland church at Leixlip.   **3** Dom Augustin Calmet, *Dictionary of the holy Bible*, 3 vols, translated into English by Samuel D'Oyly and John Colson, London, 1732, Onesiphorus, ii, p. 317, Narcissus, ii, pp 262–3, and Epaphroditus, ii, p. 511.   **4** Details from his diary in

his appointment he was expected to marry a friend of the persons responsible for his preferment. But Marsh refused to marry. We gather from his diary that he had in fact no intention of ever getting married, but on this occasion he offered the reason that his father was opposed to the marriage and that he had no wish to disobey him. He left Swindon and returned to Oxford. The bishop of Exeter was furious and demanded Marsh's resignation as his chaplain.

Marsh thanked God for delivering him

> out of the snare that they had laid for me, & if I have done amiss in that affair, I beg thy pardon, I beg their pardon & am ready to make my satisfaction & O Lord pardon them I beseech Thee for what they designed & what they acted (not agst me I do think) but agst the intent & purpose of my heart to render Thee & thy holy Church such service as in a marry'd state I could not be able to do, wch is ye only reason why I have hitherto kept myself a single man.

It seems that Narcissus was a handsome man and had many difficulties escaping from matrimony. He writes many amusing accounts of his narrow escapes. He said he had many 'advantageous offers' which included substantial dowries. One lady had £800, another £1,500, and another £2,400, and, he noted, they were 'all very desirable … beautiful, lovely persons'. But Marsh was not tempted. He continued with his studies in Oxford and in 1665 was made chaplain to Lord Chancellor Hyde, before whom he preached in Worcester House in May and in Berkshire House the following February. In 1667 he took the degree of bachelor of divinity; he was then about 29 years old. In the year 1671 he began to study for his doctorate of divinity. These studies were delayed by reason of his undertaking, at the request of Dr Fell, the bishop of Oxford, to advise the notes and supervise the printing of the translations of Balsamon and Zonaras' 'Comments on the canons of the Greek councils', which Mr Beveridge was then printing at the Theatre in Oxford. This monumental task took almost a year but Marsh had some earlier experience with this type of work; he revised and altered Du Trieu's *Logick* (Oxford, 1662)[5] and when he became provost in Trinity College he had it printed for the use of

Marsh's, Z2.2.3b.   **5** Philippus Du Trieu, *Manuductio ad logicam*, Oxoniae, 1662 (*Wing* D 2909).

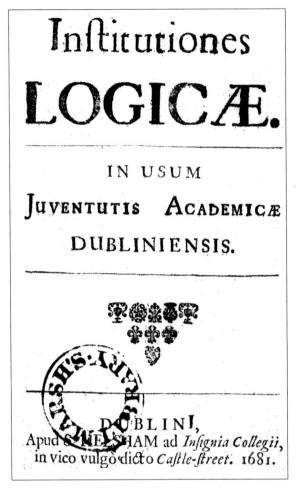

1 Title-page of [Narcissus Marsh], *Institutiones logicae* (Dublin, 1681).

the students in the university. It was entitled *Institutio logicae in usum juventutis academicae Dubliniensis* when it was published in 1679.[6] Miss Constantia Maxwell says that the 'Logic' of Dr Marsh was on the course till about 1782 when it was replaced by the text book of Dr Richard Murray.[7]

One of the most interesting entries in Marsh's diary deals with his love of music; it also gives a valuable account of the musical events held in

---

6 The copy in Marsh's own collection in the library is the second edition printed in 1681. It has been annotated and corrected by Marsh. For further information on the bibliographical problems of the first unrecorded edition of 1679 see Miss M. Pollard's article, 'The Provost's Logic: An unrecorded first issue' in *Long Room: Bulletin of the Friends of the Library of T.C.D.*, no. 1, 1970. (n.s.).   7 Constantia Maxwell, *A history of Trinity College, Dublin 1591–1892*, Dublin, The University Press Trinity College, 1946, pp 73 and 149. (Came to be known among the students as 'The Provost's Logic'.)

TENORE

DI M· FILIPPO DI MONTE
MAESTRO DI CAPELLA
DELLA S. C. MAESTA DELL'IMPERATORE
MASSIMILIANO SECONDO.
Il Terzo Libro delli Madrigali, à Cinque voci, Con uno à sette nel fine

Nuouamente posto in luce.

IN VINEGIA,
APPRESSO GIROLAMO SCOTTO
M D LXX.

2 Title-page of Filippo di Monte, *Il terzo libro delli madrigali* (Venice, 1570).

Oxford at this period. Marsh played the bass viol and lute and he wrote a tract entitled 'Essay touching the sympathy between lute or viol strings', which was printed by Robert Plot in his *Natural history of Oxfordshire* (1676).[8] Although this was his only relaxation he was not happy about it; he said, 'After the Fire of London, I constantly kept a weekly consort (of Instrumental musick & sometimes vocal) in my Chamber on Wednesday in the afternoon, & then on Thursday, as long as I lived in Oxford.' And then Marsh added, 'Yet O Lord, I beseech thee to forgive me this loss of time and vain Conversation.'

Marsh was next appointed principal of St Alban Hall in Oxford by the duke of Ormond who was chancellor of the university. He made a great success of this position and it was no doubt his administrative and organisational ability which encouraged the bishop of Oxford, Dr Fell, and the duke of Ormond to suggest a more important appointment for Narcissus Marsh – the provostship of Trinity College, Dublin.

Marsh accepted the position, and was sworn and invested provost on 24 January 1679.[8a] But Marsh seems to have been unhappy in Trinity. He wrote in his diary:

> But finding this place very troublesome partly by reason of ye multitude of business & impertinent [useless, trivial, irrelevant] Visits the Provost is obliged to, & partly by reason of the ill Education that the young Scholars have before they come to the College, whereby they are both rude & ignorant; I was Quickly weary of 340 Youngmen & boys in this lewd debauch'd town; & the more so because I had no time to follow my allways dearly beloved studies.

This constant complaint continues throughout Marsh's diary. He was basically a scholar. He disliked 'worldly business', and was devoted to prayer and study. He loved working out mathematical problems and wrote, 'Thy name be praised O Lord for all thy mercies, this Evening I invented a way to find out the Moons distance from the Center of the Earth without the help of its Parallaxe.'

Nevertheless, while he was in Trinity he played a major part in the preparation for printing of Bishop William Bedell's Irish translation of the

---

8 Robert Plot, *The natural history of Oxfordshire*, Oxford, 1677 (*Wing* P2586, 2nd ed in Marsh's), pp 289–99.   **8a** See S. Ó Seanóir and M. Pollard, 'A great deal of good verse' in *Hermathena*, nos. cxxx and cxxxi, 1981, pp 7–36.

Old Testament. Bishop Bedell had supervised the translation of the Old Testament into Irish before 1641 but it had never been printed.[9]

With the help of Dr Andrew Sall and a transcriber called Denine and some others, Marsh prepared the transcripts which they then sent to the Hon. Robert Boyle in London.[10] Marsh gives an interesting description of how they carried out their work:

> when a quantity of sheets were transcrib'd I got Dr Sall ... Mr Higgins, Mr Mullen, and the Transcriber (& sometimes some other Gentlemen well skill'd in Irish) to compare the Transcript with the originall copy, to find whether they agreed, then to render the Irish into English, whilst I had the Polyglott Bible before me to observe whether it came up to the originall [Hebrew] & where any doubt did arise (which was very seldom) after a Debate upon the true import of the words, and their agreem[t] upon a more proper expression, 'twas written in the margin & left to Mr Boyle to advise with Mr Reily thereupon, but I think very few alterations were made in the Impression.

The Irish translation of the Old Testament was printed in London in 1685.

It was a fine achievement, but Marsh was not content. He discovered that under the statutes of the college 30 of the 70 scholars chosen each year had to be natives of Ireland.[11] Marsh noticed that while these thirty scholars could speak Irish they could not read or write it. He was determined to rectify this situation and he employed, at his own expense, a former Catholic priest, Paul Higgins, to teach Irish to the students and to preach an Irish sermon once a month. He then insisted that no Irish scholar should be chosen unless he could read and write Irish. The sermons and lectures were very popular. The attendance was never less than 300 people at the sermons

9 *Two biographies of William Bedell bishop of Kilmore*, ed. with notes by E.S. Shuckburgh, Cambridge, at the University Press, 1902, pp 55–6.   10 A detailed version of how Marsh arranged Bedell's manuscript is contained in Marsh's letter to his friend Dr Thomas Smith (original kept in the Bodleian Library) printed in the *Christian Examiner*, no. xxiv, vol. ii, November 1833, pp 761–72. Further information contained in Ms Z4.4.8 in Marsh's Library. This includes copies of 20 original letters from the Hon. Robert Boyle to Narcissus Marsh, while he was provost of TCD, and bishop of Ferns and Leighlin, 1682–4. See also Deasún Breathnach, *Bedell and the Irish version of the Old Testament*, Baile Atha Cliath, Clódhanna Teo, 1971, and see also *The works of the Hon. Robert Boyle*, London, A. Millar, 1744, v, pp 602–14, which contains letters from Narcissus Marsh and Dr Andrew Sall on this subject.   11 *Christian Examiner*, p. 768.

LEABHUIR

na

Seintiomna

ar na

Ctairings go gaiblis tre curam 7 ditras an Doctúir

UILLIAM BEDEL,

Roime ro Earbug Chille móire a Néirin,

Agur anoir ar na cour a celó cum maitior prbliohe na Tirerin.

The BOOKS of the

OLD TESTAMENT

Tranflated into IRISH by the Care and Diligence of

Doctor WILLIAM BEDEL,

Late Bifhop of *Kilmore* in *IRELAND*,

AND,

For the publick good of that Nation,

Printed at *London*, Anno Dom. MDCLXXXV.

3 Title-page of *Leabhuir na Seintiomna* (London, 1685).

and 80 students came to the lectures. Marsh as provost himself set a fine example by attending both lectures and sermons.[12] He was severely criticised by the lord primate and many important people in the government for promoting the Irish language. He was told by the lord primate that there was an act of parliament the object of which was to abolish the Irish language. Marsh ignored their warnings and continued with his work.[13] While he was undoubtedly interested and enthusiastic about the Irish language for its own sake, and tried for many years to produce an Irish grammar, his main purpose was to communicate with the majority of the Irish people in order to propagate the reformed religion.

This study and promotion was not his only contribution to Trinity College. He began building the new college hall and chapel[14] and, according to J.W. Stubbs, it was under Marsh's provostship that the professorship of mathematics, established during the Commonwealth, was united with the Donegal lectureship.[15] Marsh had received a letter from his friend Dr Thomas Smith in England, which had contained severe criticisms of the poor state and neglect of the library in Trinity College.[16] He replied explaining the reasons for this neglect and how he had set about reorganising it.[17] Because of the rebuilding programme the students had been forced to eat in the library, and the books had been moved elsewhere. But now the buildings were finished, and the books were back. Unfortunately they had no library keeper, but one of the junior fellows was chosen every year and was paid only six pounds annually. Marsh checked and revised the regulations; he ordered tables to be drawn up and hung at the end of each classis (division) of the books, containing the shelves and numbers and names of all the books on every shelf, the books likewise being numbered and figured. Marsh then insisted that when the new library keeper was appointed all the books in his care should be accounted for, and the next year, when a new library keeper was appointed, he insisted that the new man should check all the books, requiring the old library keeper to replace the missing books or pay for them.

Although Marsh was able to reorganise the running of the library, he was unable to change the statutes of the college which entitled only the provost and fellows to study in the library.[18] The students had to be accompanied by

12 Ibid., p. 769.   **13** Ibid.   **14** Ibid., p. 763.   **15** John William Stubbs, *The history of the university of Dublin*, Dublin, Hodges Figgis, 1889, p. 115. Stubbs, however, gives no authority for this statement. **16** *Christian Examiner*, footnote on p. 762.   **17** Ibid., p. 764.   **18** Ibid.

either the provost or one of the fellows who was also obliged to remain in the library with the reader. Marsh also noted that the booksellers' shops were furnished with 'new Triffles and Pamphletts, & not well with them also'. Marsh concluded, ''twas this, & this consideration alone yt at first mov'd me to think of building a library in some other Place (yn in the College) for publick use, where all might have free access, seeing they cannot have it in the College'.[19]

Marsh's next appointment was to the bishopric of Ferns and Leighlin, with the rectory of Killeban *in commendam*.[20] He was consecrated bishop in Christ Church Cathedral on 6 May 1683. He took up residence in his diocese, but he did not stay for long. King James was on the throne, and these were difficult days for a Protestant bishop in the Irish countryside. Marsh was subjected to various threats and there were several incidents which made his position impossible.[21] He returned to Dublin and stayed in the provost's house and a short time later left for England.

Marsh says in his diary that when he returned to England he was 'kindly received' by many of his friends and by the English bishops. He was presented to the vicarage of Gresford, Flint, by Bishop Lloyd of St Asaph and was made canon of St Asaph. In 1690 Marsh went to London and preached before the queen at Whitehall. After the battle of the Boyne Marsh left almost immediately for Ireland. On the journey back he had a very lucky escape from drowning when his ship ran aground on a sandbank.

Before Marsh fled to England in 1688 he had become one of the first members of the Dublin Philosophical Society.[22] He contributed an early paper to that society, called 'An introductory essay to the doctrine of sounds, containing some proposals for the improvement of acousticks'. This was printed in *The Philosophical Transactions*. (According to E.W. Rosenheim Marsh's 'Essay' was parodied by Swift.)[23] K. Theodore Hoppen in his book *The common scientist in the seventeenth century* says the Oxford Society thought

---

19 Ibid. **20** Marsh's diary, p. 16. **21** Ibid., p. 16. For further details of Marsh's ill treatment see MS Z1.1.16 (1) in the library which contains a letter from Bishop Marsh to the lord chancellor giving details of this event. **22** Marsh's diary, p. 16. It is interesting to note that when Marsh came to Dublin in 1679 he kept in constant touch with his friends in England. He begged them to keep him informed about 'what's doing abroad in the learn'd world'. Marsh explained that in Dublin 'we live here in profound ignorance'. He was, I think, exaggerating the lack of learning in Dublin. The Dublin Philosophical Society, which he had joined, included some notable figures such as Robert Huntington, William Petty, Archbishop William King and George Berkeley. **23** *Philosophical Transactions*, February 20, 1683/4, no. 156, vol. xiv, Oxford, 1684, pp 471–88. See also E.W. Rosenheim, *Swift and the satirist's*

Marsh's article of 'great consequence'.[24] Hoppen maintains however that the paper had few original conclusions but it was remarkable because of Marsh's use of three new words. He used 'diacoustics' to describe the study of refracted sound, 'catacoustics' for that of reflected sound and, most important of all, he was the first scientist to use the word 'microphone'.[25] He was deeply interested in comets and in scientific instruments.[26] When Marsh's friend, William Molyneux, the founder of the Dublin Philosophical Society, developed the 'Dublin hygroscope', an instrument for indicating the moisture in the air, Marsh suggested as an improvement the substitution of a lute string for the more fragile whipcord which Molyneux had been using.

Marsh also invented a new lamp to enlighten a large hall or church.[27] Hoppen says that Marsh's knowledge of insects, and particularly of caterpillars, was zoologically up to the mark. He was acquainted with the researches of Johann Goedart, whose major work Martin Lister had published in English translation in 1682. Hoppen said that

> Marsh tried to discover some reliable and logical method of insect classification – one of the perennial problems of contemporary zoology – and his proposals were not without merit, for they incorporated the suggestion of classification by follicles and aurelias.[28]

Hoppen explained that

> Bishop Marsh, after a perfectly sound and scholarly account of the caterpillar, somewhat nervously concluded that 'all this is conjectures and wants to be confirmed by experiments'.[29]

Many years later when Marsh became primate, he was made vice-president of the Dublin Philosophical Society.[30]

---

art, University of Chicago Press, 1963, p. 76.   **24** K. Theodore Hoppen, *The common scientist in the seventeenth century*, London, Routledge & Kegan Paul, 1970, p. 126.   **25** Ibid., p. 126. See also G.T. Stokes, *Some worthies of the Irish church*, p. 138. (Additional note on the Dublin Philosophical Society added by Professor S.P. Johnston.)   **26** Letters from John Wallis in Oxford to Marsh dated June 16, August 17 & 18, 1681. In Royal Irish Academy MS12/D/34, pp 1–19.   **27** T. Birch, *History of the Royal Society*, iv (1757) pp 448–9. A letter of Mr St George Ashe dated at Trinity College Dublin, 16 Sept. 1685 … mentioned a new lamp invented by the bishop of Ferns to enlighten a large hall or church. See also Marsh's notebook in Royal Irish Academy MS12/D/34,44. Marsh's drawing of a double-pile house, as well as other designs.   **28** K.T. Hoppen, op. cit., p. 141.   **29** Ibid., p. 76.   **30** Ibid., p. 193.

Marsh's diary is fascinating in the insight it gives into his character. He gives detailed accounts of various dreams which he had. In one account he was in Rome, and was watching the pope being carried into St Peter's on men's shoulders, before whom all fell on their knees as he passed by. But, Marsh says, 'I shifted from place to place in the church to avoid it & being taken notice of.' Marsh was noticed, however, and left the church and entered a nearby house where he became involved in a scholarly argument on religion. He says that in this dream he replied

> with so much subtilty & maintained the dispute with so much dexterity (defending truth & yet giving them no advantage against me) that when I awaked I did much admire myself for the subtileness & acuteness of my Answers which I did then remember perfectly well, being able to do nothing like it when I was Waking.[31]

In December 1690 Marsh was promoted archbishop of Cashel. To Archbishop William King[32] and to the bishop of Oxford, Narcissus Marsh appeared to be too modest and unacquainted with the world, and the bishop of Oxford[33] also felt that if Marsh met with opposition he would lack sufficient courage to assert his authority. This may have been true as far as state affairs and duties were concerned (as Marsh himself said 'worldly business is that which above all things I do hate')[34] but it was certainly not true in regard to the church. When Marsh went to take out his patent for his new promotion as archbishop of Cashel, in March 1691, he learned that Sir Charles Porter, one of the lords justices and lord chancellor, had raised the fees for passing the 'broad seal'. Marsh was outraged at the increase in 'those miserable times' and was determined to petition the king and ordered the proceedings for his own promotion to be stopped. Marsh records in his diary how he was circumvented by a man called Richard Jones of Bride Street who 'went fraudulently & laid down the fees'.[35] This of course set the

31 Marsh's diary, pp 24–5. 32 Richard Mant, *History of the Church of Ireland*, London, J. W. Parker, 1840, ii, p. 91. Letter from Bishop King to Sir Robert Southwell, 29 April 1697, in which King refers to Archbishop Marsh as follows: 'The Archbishop of Dublin (though an excellent person and a scholar) yet is too modest and unacquainted with the world to make a great bustle, without which I am informed little is done there.' 33 *Church of Ireland Gazette*, 9 December, 1927, p. 714. In a reference to Marsh the bishop of Oxford's opinion is quoted describing Marsh as 'a man of learning, virtue, gravity and diligence', though he honestly confesses his fear that if Marsh meets with faction and opposition 'he may want courage to vindicate himself and assert his authority'. 34 Richard Mant, op. cit., Letter from Marsh to Dr Thomas Smith dated 4 May 1700, ii, p. 109. 35 Marsh's diary, p. 33.

precedent for the payment of all future fees. Marsh said he would have been content to have given up his bishopric and his life rather than pay the increased fees. On another occasion there was a proposal to promote Dean Synge to a bishopric and the views of many of the bishops were sought. Marsh vigorously opposed the dean's promotion and similarly admonished the bishop of Ferns and Leighlin for ordaining clergy outside his own diocese without letters dimissory. Marsh on two occasions in his diary refers to Dean Synge as a man of 'ill fame'[36] and in fact Dean Synge was never promoted. When the bishop of Clonfert, William Fitzgerald, was consecrated in Christ Church, Marsh thanked God that he had taken no part in the ceremony.[37] A few years earlier, when Marsh was in Trinity, he had deprived the vice-provost of his fellowship because he had got married.[38] The obligation to celibacy among the fellows in Trinity was not removed by statute until 1840. Nor were the students immune from Marsh's disciplinary regulations. Shortly after Marsh's arrival as provost there are accounts in the general registry of penalties being imposed on the students for breaches of discipline and indeed in some instances they were expelled.[39] This strict keeping to the rules made Marsh many enemies, and Hely Hutchinson said they called him 'Reverend Log'.[40]

Although Marsh was archbishop of Cashel through one of the saddest and most turbulent times in Irish history, in his diary he records very little about these great events. However, he strongly disapproved of the treaty of Limerick and he wrote:

> Spare us good Lord & bring not thy heritage in this kingdom to confusion, we beseech thee, tho our sins have deserved it & the times threaten it & 'tis to be feared that 'twill be the effect of the unhappy conditions that (I know not how or why) have been granted to a rebelious people.[41]

Earlier he had written that he spent

36 Ibid., pp 57–8 and 60.   37 For an account of William Fitzgerald's character see Mant, op. cit., Letter from Archbishop King to Archbishop Wake, July 1722, ii, p. 380.   38 Constantia Maxwell, op. cit., p. 151.   39 TCD general registry, 1697, pp 202–33, Mun V.5.2.   40 Constantia Maxwell, op. cit., p. 74. 41 Marsh's diary, p. 42. See also J.G. Simms, *The treaty of Limerick*, Dundalk, Dundalgan Press for the Dublin Historical Association, 1965, p. 12.

many days in hard study, especially in Knotty Algebra to divert
melancholy thoughts these sad calamitous times wherein I am forced
to live from home; & do hear almost every day of the murther of some
or other Protestant, yet my heart & hope is always steadfastly fixed
on the Lord my God & I trust it shall, never be moved. I am thine
O Lord save me for thy mercies sake. [42]

He also mentions in his diary and in his correspondence the work he was
engaged in as a member of several committees in the house of lords.[43] Marsh
was a member of the committees for religion and grievances and was chairman
of the committee for temporary acts. He also records his visitations throughout
his diocese and the work which he did. It was while he was on a visitation
in Cork that he received news of his promotion to the see of Dublin.[44]
Marsh was enthroned as archbishop of Dublin in St Patrick's Cathedral on
26 May 1694. He worked incredibly hard in his dioceses. He gives an account
of the long difficult journeys which he undertook with great diligence. He
never spared himself and he visited all his clergy and parishes.[45] When he
first heard the news of his new appointment he wrote, 'O Lord, thy ways are
wonderful, & as this is thy sole doing, so I beseech thee to grant me
sufficient assistance of thy holy spirit to enable me to perform the work
which Thou hast assigned me. Amen. Amen.'

While Marsh was archbishop of Dublin and living as an old bachelor in
the Palace of St Sepulchre, his niece, young Grace Marsh, came to stay with
him. Grace was only nineteen and probably found the archbishop's lifestyle
and strict discipline rather depressing. On 10 September 1695, this rather sad
entry appears in his diary:

> This Evening betwixt 8 & 9 of the Clock at night my Niece Grace
> Marsh (not having the fear of God before her eyes) stole privately
> out of my house at St Sepulchers, & (as it is reported) was that night
> marryd to Chas Proby Vicar of Castleknock in a Tavern & was
> bedded there with him – Lord Consider my affliction.[46]

Grace lived to be 85 years old and it is nice to know that she was, after her
death, buried in the same tomb with her uncle the archbishop.[47] This

42 Marsh's diary, pp 36–7.   43 Ibid., pp 50–4.   44 Ibid., p. 65.   45 Ibid., pp 66–7.   46 Ibid., p. 69.
47 *Parish Register Society of Dublin. The Registers of St Patrick, Dublin 1677 to 1800*, transcribed by C.H.P.

elopement has of course given rise to the ghost story: that Grace regretted her elopement and left a letter for Marsh in one of his books which he could not find. His ghost still haunts the library searching through the books for Grace's letter. There is one fascinating memento of Grace Marsh in the library. Amongst Marsh's own books is a curious book entitled, *Lachrimæ lachrimarum or the spirit of teares distilled for the vn-tymely death of the incomparable prince Panaretus*. It was written by Joshua Sylvester and printed in London in 1613. This work is a grim funeral elegy on the death of Prince Henry. The title-page is in black with the title shown in white, the head and tail of many pages have deep black borders with the sides illustrating skeletons and emblems of death. There is a signature on the endpapers: 'Grace Marsh Her Booke 1689'. It is quite possible that the archbishop gave his young niece some improving literature and it might well have been one explanation for her subsequent elopement.

Marsh was many times one of the lords justices; the lords justices were the virtual rulers of the country during the absence of the lord lieutenant, a fairly frequent occurrence.[48] In 1697 the primate was ill, and Marsh had to undertake his work.[49] The lord primate according to Archbishop William King 'is the chief member of the Church under his Majesty, and a great minister of state'.[50] But for Marsh this was the 'worldly business' which he hated so much.[51] It involved work for the church which was then in a particularly bad way. Indeed, Queen Mary in 1690 had written to King William when he was in Ireland asking him to 'take care of the church in Ireland, everybody agrees that it is the worst in christendom'.[52] In a letter dated October 13th 1697 Marsh wrote to his friend Dr Smith complaining about the amount of public business he had on hand, preparing bills to be passed into acts of parliament for the better establishment of this poor distressed church.[53] It was in the parliament of 1697 that the following acts

Price, edited by J.H. Bernard, Dublin, Alex Thom, 1907, ii, p. 68.   **48** Payments to Archbishop Marsh for acting as lord justice appear in the *Calendar of treasury books*, Sept 1698 to 31 July 1699. Prepared by William A. Shaw, London, 1934, xiv. See Royal Warrant, June 1, 1699, p. 378. See also *Calendar of treasury papers*, March 31, no. 134, pp 334–5. Letter from Mr Southwell to Mr Taylor, dated, Dublin, March 31, 1705. P.S. 'Pray let me desire you to further the Primate's request about getting £500 in order for buying Dr Stillingfleet's library unless you are afraid we should grow too learned.' It would appear from this letter that Marsh also tried to get money from the government to help with the purchase of Edward Stillingfleet's library.   **49** Richard Mant, op. cit., ii, p. 72. (Letter from Marsh to Dr Smith, Oct. 1697.)   **50** Ibid., Letter from William King to Lord Harcourt, p. 410.   **51** Ibid., Letter from Marsh to Dr Smith, May 1700, p. 109.   **52** John D'Alton, *The memoirs of the archbishops of Dublin*, Dublin, Hodges & Smith, 1838, pp 288–9.   **53** Richard Mant, op. cit., Letter from Marsh to Dr Smith, p. 72.

were passed: the banishment act;[54] an act for the confirmation of the articles
of Limerick; and an act to prevent Protestants inter-marrying with papists. One
year later, in 1698, the woollen act, to prohibit export of Irish woollens, was
passed. It does seem that Archbishop Marsh took a leading part in the
drafting of these acts.

The proposal to prohibit the export of Irish woollens occurred when an
influential group of English clothiers, alarmed at the success of Irish woollen
exports, lobbied the English government to introduce an act to impose a
duty on Irish woollen exports and develop the linen manufacture. While
this act was being discussed in parliament Archbishop Marsh wrote to his
friend Dr Smith in England. He began, as he usually did, by complaining
about the 'worldly business' he was engaged in. He said,

> I am forct to divert mostly to the Politicks, especially at this time agst
> the sitting of our Parliament we are endeavouring to please England
> all we can, by effectually setting up the Linnen Manufacture (if an
> Act of Parliament that we are preparing can do it) & discouraging
> the woollen; though really Ireland is in too poor & low a condition
> at this time to raise any jealousie in England. The raising our mony
> a fifth part hath made every man loose so much of his Estate; now
> the great scarcity & dearness of all sorts of grain & hay (which are
> now three times as dear as they use to be at this time of the year,
> new hay being here at fifty shillings a tun; old was sold 3 months ago
> at four pounds a tun) this scarcity I say will also soon raise the price
> of Beef & Mutton & make it very hard for men to live, when our
> trade shall be sunk. Pray God preserve us all. I am, Rev.d Sir, your
> affectionate brother & humble servant Narcissus Dublin. I may truly
> say, that the plenty of Ireland is turn'd to scarcity & am certain that
> a man may live cheaper in London, than in Dublin & yet as well.[55]

Marsh's agreement with the proposed legislation to impose a duty on the
woollen exports and develop the linen manufacture was in complete
contrast to Bishop William King's reaction.[56] King regarded the proposal as

---

54 9th of William III 1697. (i) An act for banishing all papists exercising any ecclesiastical jurisdiction,
and all regulars of the popish clergy out of this kingdom. *The statutes at large passed in the parliaments held
in Ireland*, Dublin, Boulter Grierson, 1765, chap. I, pp 339–53.   **55** Letter to Dr Smith, 30 August 1698.
Bodleian Library, Smith 45. Microfilm in Marsh's Library.   **56** See Philip O'Regan, *Archbishop William*

grossly unfair because he knew that if the linen industry became as successful as the woollen industry England would undoubtedly impose a duty
on it. But this was not the only reason for Bishop King's misgivings. As an
astute politician he knew that the Ulster Presbyterians would benefit most
and as a result there might be an increase in the Presbyterian population and
this could become a serious threat to the Church of Ireland.

Again Archbishop Marsh, unlike Bishop King, was prepared to assist the
government with the legislation for the penal laws. The banishment act was
one of the most severe of the many penal laws passed in this period and
meant that all Catholic archbishops, bishops, vicars general, deans, friars, and
many other religious had to leave Ireland. The transportations began in 1698
and the Catholic Church, which had already suffered so much, was
eventually left with only two bishops in Ireland.

It is almost three hundred years since the penal laws were passed and it is
interesting to read what modern Irish historians have written about them,
particularly such a fine expert as Maureen Wall.[57] She wrote:

> Although the Irish Parliament passed the various Popery Acts it had
> no power to enforce those laws ... The executive in Dublin Castle
> ... was under the direct control of the ministry in England and it
> depended to a great extent on that ministry whether or not the
> popery laws were to be enforced at any particular time.

These laws did not receive the support of a great section of public opinion
and even those officials who might have been interested in the pursuit of friars
and bishops had to contend with a very efficient warning system. Bishop
William King considered the passing of these bills had nothing to do with
religion and said they were passed 'on pretence of weakening the Popish
interest ... [T]here is not the least consideration of religion at the bottom and
we must learn from this not to judge according to appearance.'[58] W.D. Killen
in his *Ecclesiastical history of Ireland* said that '[Marsh] might have been much
better employed than in concocting the penal laws'.[59] Presumably he meant
the urgent reform of the abuses in the Church of Ireland. Since Bishop

King of Dublin (1650–1729), Dublin, 2000, pp 112–16. **57** Maureen Wall, *The penal laws, 1691–1760*, Dundalk, Dundalgan Press for the Dublin Historical Association, 1967, pp 24–5. **58** Richard Mant, op. cit., Letter from William King to his friend the bishop of Waterford, Oct. 1697, pp 95–7. **59** W.D. Killen, *The ecclesiastical history of Ireland*, London, Macmillan & Co., 1875, ii, p. 185.

King did not consider they were for the benefit of the Church of Ireland it seems more likely that they were passed for political motives and were initiated by the Protestant laity for their own purposes.

The reforms needed in the Church of Ireland were obvious to everybody: the scandalous number of pluralities, the bishops who were non-resident in their dioceses, and the ordination of unworthy men for the church. Although Marsh, according to his letters to his friend Dr Thomas Smith, worked hard for these reforms, they were not very effective as far as Bishop King was concerned. King, who had been dean of St Patrick's and later bishop of Derry, succeeded Marsh as archbishop of Dublin in 1703. When he took up his appointment as archbishop of Dublin he described the condition of his diocese to a friend and said, 'it was in worse circumstances (both in respect to discipline and attendance of the cures) than most others in the kingdom'. He thought Marsh 'though an excellent person and scholar yet is too modest and unacquainted with the world to make a great bustle, without which I am informed little is done there [Dublin]'. The bishop of Oxford described Marsh as a man of 'learning, virtue, gravity, and diligence', though he honestly confessed his fear that if Marsh 'meets with faction and opposition he may want courage to vindicate himself and assert his authority'.[60] The opinions of Marsh's contemporaries indicate that while he was sincerely concerned with reforms in the Church of Ireland he was far too much of an academic and was not vigorous enough to carry them out. He was however, in great contrast to many of his fellow bishops, an exemplary prelate, pious and sincere, if not effective as a reformer. But Archbishop Marsh's earlier letters to the archbishop of Canterbury give a different view of the conditions in the Dublin diocese. It seems possible that both may have been exaggerating in order to impress the English hierarchy. Some years later when the convocation of the Church of Ireland was held in Dublin in conjunction with the meeting of parliament, Archbishop King was distressed at the inadequate amount of business which had been transacted. In fact King was so angry at Marsh's ineptness as chairman of convocation (the primate was apparently the traditional chairman) that he went to England and tried to persuade the authorities to address the queen's licence to himself as archbishop of Dublin and not Primate Marsh. But

---

60 Richard Mant, op. cit., William King's letter to the bishop of Norwich, Dr John Moore, August 1704, p. 132, and letter to Sir Robert Southwell, p. 91. See also *Church of Ireland Gazette*, 9 December 1927, p. 714.

Marsh was informed about King's visit and wrote a protest to the archbishop of Canterbury.[61] On 5 October 1703 he warned the archbishop that King would try to get the queen's licence addressed to himself (King) by pretending that the archbishop of Dublin sometimes presided in convocation even when the primate was present. Marsh said, 'For I must not easily quitt the privileges belonging to my See which have been endeavoured to be invaded now four manner of waies that hath created me no small trouble.' A few months later Archbishop King wrote some bitter remarks which would seem to refer to Marsh. He wrote, 'Some men are very dexterous at doing nothing; I wish those of that temper would keep out of places that require something to be done.'[62]

Marsh's protest to the archbishop of Canterbury did not prevent Archbishop King from ignoring him again. In 1709 King solicited the government to recall convocation for another session. King's second attempt to usurp the prerogative of the primate infuriated Marsh. He wrote a letter of protest to the government. But Marsh's letter was regarded as too drastic and he was eventually forced to seek the queen's pardon.[63]

Archbishop King's opinion of Marsh must be taken a little cautiously however. He was the complete opposite of Marsh: he was a fine writer and a fine administrator, but he was inclined to be aggressive and somewhat hasty. His prolonged and unedifying law case against Christ Church Cathedral's authorities was not very prudent and did harm to the church. To Lord Deputy Capel, King was 'a little too hot'[64] and to Sir Robert Southwell 'a mighty positive man'.[65] Nevertheless while Marsh was occupied with parliament throughout 1697 the bishops did not hold their customary meetings at the archbishop's (that is, Marsh's) house.[66] Bishop King also noted that there was not any effective committee for religion in the house of lords. But later Marsh did take the significant step of calling for a provincial synod.

---

61 H.J. Todd, *A catalogue of the archiepiscopal manuscripts in the library at Lambeth Palace*, London, printed by Law and Gilbert, 1812. Codices manuscripti, Edmundi Gibsoni, episcopi Londinensis (929–943). Letter from the archbishop of Armagh about convocation business, and his own right of presiding in convocation, Dublin, Jan. 16, 1704–5, no. 56, p. 200. See also Bodleian Library, Ms Rawl. C. 983.
62 Richard Mant, op. cit., Letter from William King to bishop of Cloyne, June 26, 1705, p. 178.
63 Nicholson album (extract), Petition of Narcissus Marsh archbishop of Armagh to the earl of Wharton lord lieutenant to intercede with her majesty for a pardon for the former's late miscarriage in the upper house of convocation. Sept. 1709. National Library, microfilm, N 153, p. 348. See also, Philip O'Regan, *Archbishop William King of Dublin*, p. 168.   **64** C. Beckett, 'The government and the Church of Ireland under William III and Anne' in *Irish Historical Studies*, Dublin, 2, no. 7, March 1941, p. 291.   **65** J.C. Beckett, op. cit., p. 295.   **66** Ibid., p. 290.

The parliament of 1697 passed without anything being done for the reform of the abuses in the Church of Ireland. This parliament, apart from the passing of the penal laws, was remarkable because of the dispute between many of the bishops in regard to one particular piece of legislation. This was 'An act for the better security of his majesty's person and government'. John D'Alton in his *Memoirs of the archbishops of Dublin* said the house of lords, including Bishop King, considered the provisions of the bill so unjust and oppressive that they voted against it.[67] Dr Andrew Carpenter in his thesis 'Archbishop King and Dean Swift' explains that 'according to this bill, any two justices of the peace could force anyone to take an oath swearing loyalty to the king and denying the doctrine of transubstantiation; if he refused, he could suffer imprisonment and even possibly execution'.[68] King objected strongly to 'persecuting any upon mere conscience'. And many other members of the house of lords agreed with King and the bill was thrown out. Archbishop Marsh was furious at the objections. He took an entirely different view and he and thirteen other peers protested against their refusal to pass the bill.[69] John D'Alton again commented on Marsh and the other peers' objections and he wrote, 'certainly it is not a record of their christian charity'.[70]

While Marsh was not as active in the reform of pluralities and other abuses as Bishop King and some of the other bishops would have liked, many of the clergy themselves were not committed to reform. Indeed some of the worst offenders were the bishops themselves. Nor were the Protestant laity much help. Maureen Wall said,

> the spirit of monopoly and exclusiveness was stronger by far in the members of the Irish Protestant ascendancy than the desire to spread what they considered to be the true faith among the people in general. Protestant ascendancy, as applied to a small privileged group, must disappear if the whole population were to become Protestant.[71]

While Archbishop Marsh, Bishop King and Bishops Foley and Foy did their utmost to reform and improve the established church in Ireland they were not very successful. In 1712 Archbishop King complained that 'there

---

67 John D'Alton, op. cit., p. 294.   **68** Andrew P. Isdell-Carpenter, 'Archbishop King and Dean Swift' (unpublished PhD thesis), 2 vols, Dept. of English, University College, Dublin, i, pp 247–8. **69** Richard Mant, op. cit., pp 82–5.   **70** John D'Alton, op. cit., p. 294.   **71** Maureen Wall, op. cit., p. 7.

were eight of the Irish bishops in England; … and there was not one bishop in the province of Ulster'. Again in 1714 he said, 'There had not been more than one bishop at a time in that province for several years.'[72]

It is perhaps a little ironic that with all the penal laws enacted against Catholics, the Catholic Church not only survived, but actually thrived and eventually became the dominant religion in Ireland. Mrs Wall commented that because of the penal laws the Catholic bishops abstained from politics, and stayed at their posts, and lived without pomp and splendour. The diocesan clergy by their concerted refusal to take the oath of abjuration in 1710 preserved the unity of the Catholic Church. Mrs Wall concluded,

> as a result of the popery laws the Catholic Church, by 1760, had more freedom to work out its destiny in Ireland than it had in many of the countries of Europe where Catholicism was the State religion, and where Catholic rulers constantly intervened in church appointments and in church policy.[73]

While many historians agree with Mrs Wall's view that the effect of the penal laws was exaggerated, it is also clear that the Catholic Church did experience great difficulty during the later part of the seventeenth century. The banishment act in particular was certainly effective as far as the regular clergy were concerned. Many of the priests in the religious orders were forced to leave Dublin.[74]

As far as the penal laws are concerned, Archbishop Marsh may well have been used by the politicians for their own purposes. But it was also at this period of the passing of the penal laws that Marsh and the Church of Ireland were faced with another fundamental but very different religious problem. This occurred when John Toland published his book *Christianity not mysterious* (London, 1696). Toland, who was from the Inishowen peninsula off Co. Donegal, was born a Catholic and became a Protestant. Toland's book was regarded as religiously subversive and was denounced for its pseudo-deist philosophy. His attack on Christian mysteries and his defence of natural or deistic religion represented a fundamental challenge to the ascendancy establishment. As David Berman has pointed out, Toland

---

72 J.C. Beckett, op. cit., pp 298–9.   **73** Maureen Wall, op. cit., p. 67.   **74** See James Kelly, 'The impact of the penal laws' in *History of the Catholic diocese of Dublin*, ed. James Kelly & Dáire Keogh, Dublin, Four Courts Press, 2000, pp 144–74.

believed that 'if there were no Christian mysteries then there could be nothing to separate the rival Christian religions or sects. And then there could be no basis for the Penal Code.'[75]

Archbishop Marsh and the clergy were outraged at Toland's attack on the Christian mysteries and his defence of natural or deistic religion. Marsh sent a copy of *Christianity not mysterious* to Peter Browne, who was a senior fellow of Trinity College, and requested him to reply to it. Browne's reply, *A letter in answer to a book entitled Christianity not mysterious* (Dublin, 1697) was not regarded as a particularly good reply but it seems to have pleased Marsh. The copy in his collection in the library bears his imprimatur and he wrote on the title-page 'Ex dono Authoris. N. Dublin 1697'. More interesting, however, are Marsh's scathing comments in his copy of Toland's book. When Toland wrote, 'That nothing ought to be called a Mystery, because we have not an adequate Idea of all its Properties, nor any at all of its essence', Marsh described this chapter as 'very weak'. Beside Toland's idea that '*Eternity* therefore is no more above Reason, *because it cannot be* imagin'd, than a Circle, *because it may*; for in both Cases *Reason* performs its Part according to the different Natures of the Objects, whereof the one is essentially imaginable, the other not', Marsh wrote, 'very well! Eternity is not above Reason, because Reason performs its part about it. You speak like a man that both knows & useth Reason indeed such as it is, that is very weak, as yet as the whole book declares, being very weakly written.' When Toland summed up his ideas at the end of the book he said, 'This I stand by still, and may add, I hope, that I have *clearly* prov'd it too.' Marsh sarcastically replied in the margin, 'You have often said it indeed, but yet prov'd nothing, unless saying a thing is so, be proving it to be so.'

The committee on religion in the Irish house of commons condemned Toland's book and the house of commons ordered it to be burnt. It was burnt in front of the Parliament House and outside the Tholsel on 11 September 1697. Toland, who was in Dublin at this time, managed to evade arrest by fleeing to England. Marsh must have been relieved at Toland's departure. Peter Browne was richly rewarded for his reply to Toland. Archbishop Marsh recommended him for the provostship of Trinity College and afterwards for the bishopric of Cork. It is interesting to note that

---

75 David Berman, 'The Irish freethinker', in *John Toland's Christianity not mysterious*, ed. P. McGuinness etc., Dublin, 1997, pp 221–2, note 21.

European philosophers took a totally different view of Toland's ideas. He was highly regarded as a pioneer of free thought and the Enlightenment.

There are, however, other instances of Marsh's harsh behaviour in what he considered were threats to his own church, and this is illustrated by his attitude towards a sect called the Muggletonians. When four Muggletonians arrived in Dublin Marsh wrote to the archbishop of Canterbury and told him that they were trying to get converts for their 'senceless Doctrine'.[76] Marsh said, 'I will watch very narrowly to find if the law can lay hold of them.' The Muggletonians were not much of a threat to Marsh and the establishment; they were a tiny harmless sect who made only a few converts in Dublin and Cork. Another example of Marsh's intolerance is his harsh treatment of Mr Thomas Emlyn, who was the first minister to introduce Unitarian principles into Ireland.[77]

Thomas Emlyn was one of the Presbyterian ministers to the Wood Street congregation. When Emlyn's Unitarian views were discovered he was deposed by the Presbyterians. Emlyn then published a book explaining his beliefs and this led to a charge of publishing a blasphemous book. After a disgraceful and humiliating trial Emlyn was sentenced to one year in prison, fined £1000 and not to be released until the fine was paid. When Emlyn had spent two years in prison, his friends petitioned the government for a reduction in the fine. The petition was successful and the fine was reduced to £70. But Marsh, who sat on the bench at Emlyn's trial, demanded a shilling in the pound of the whole fine as the queen's almoner. Poor Emlyn believed that the church would at least be as merciful as the state and reduce their fee proportionately. After much pleading and negotiation Marsh was persuaded to reduce his fee and accepted £20. Philip McGuinness has suggested that the reason for Marsh's severe treatment of Thomas Emlyn was because Emlyn might well have been at the receiving end of the backlash that followed the publication of *Christianity not mysterious* six years earlier.[78] Another case with which Marsh was concerned was that of Mr Fleming, a Presbyterian in Drogheda, which Professor J.C. Beckett says Marsh personally instituted.[79] It became a *cause célèbre* because the government of

---

76 Archbishop Marsh to the archbishop of Canterbury, Apr. 1697. Photocopy in Marsh's Library. 77 Clarke H. Irwin, *A history of presbyterianism in Dublin*, London, Hodder & Stoughton, 1890, pp 19–21. 78 Philip McGuinness, 'John Toland and Irish politics', in *John Toland's Christianity not mysterious*, ed. P. McGuinness etc., pp 261–92. 79 J.C. Beckett, op. cit., p. 300. See *The thirtieth report of the deputy keeper of the public records and keeper of the state papers in Ireland*, 14 May 1898. On page 55 of

the day had a policy which was sympathetic to dissenters and had the case withdrawn.

Jonathan Swift, who had a poor opinion of Marsh, did support him in his opposition to dissenters. Swift noticed that Marsh had been attacked in an English whig publication which he described as 'that paltry rascal of an Observator' for his persecution of the missionary of Drogheda. Swift defended Marsh and said 'our excellent primate was engaged, and did nothing but according to law and discretion'.[80] While Marsh held the view that Presbyterians and Unitarians as well as Catholics should be dealt with severely, shortly after the Drogheda case he appears to have developed a more tolerant attitude towards the Presbyterians. It could also be that without the support of the government Marsh was not prepared to undertake any more persecutions, and this seems to be borne out by Marsh's very different treatment of Mr Fleming's successor in Drogheda, Mr William Biggar.

Mr William Biggar was prosecuted by the mayor of Drogheda and Dean Cox and was confined to prison for six weeks. Both the mayor and Dean Cox used Marsh's name and certificate as the authority for the proceedings. John D'Alton says that when Marsh discovered what had happened he was extremely annoyed and said 'such severity against his dissenting brethren, was both against his principles and his inclination'.[81]

Archbishop Marsh did, however, deal much more sympathetically with Huguenots than with Catholics. With the Huguenots he showed great skill and understanding. At that time they worshipped in the Lady Chapel of St Patrick's Cathedral and they were bound by the discipline and canons of the Church of Ireland. The French congregation prepared their own discipline and this was a more liberal interpretation of conformity than that which was required of them as a condition of their use of the Lady Chapel. They submitted their new discipline to Archbishop Marsh, who approved and praised it. Mr T.P. Le Fanu said, 'full credit to Archbishop Marsh for his moderation'.[82] It was also a shrewd move. The Huguenots, unlike the other groups, gradually merged into the Church of Ireland.

this report, 'Narcissus, Archbishop of Dublin in 1708'. Marsh was at this date archbishop of Armagh and primate. (Narcissus Marsh has often been confused with his predecessor Francis Marsh, who was also archbishop of Dublin, but no relation.) **80** Sir Charles Simeon King, *A great archbishop of Dublin, William King, 1650–1729*, London, Longmans Green, 1906, p. 276. **81** John D'Alton, op. cit., p. 298. See also [James Kirkpatrick], *An historical essay upon the loyalty of presbyterians*, [Belfast, James Blow] 1713, pp 512 and 521. **82** Thomas Philip Le Fanu, 'Archbishop Marsh and the Discipline of the French Church of St Patrick's', Dublin, 1694. Reprinted from the *Proceedings of the Huguenot Society of London*, xii, No.

Marsh also showed great caution and moderation when he had to deal with differences within the established church itself. On the question of the wearing of surplices by the clergy in the diocese of Armagh Marsh said the practice should be introduced gradually, 'For the parishioners will be apt to mutiny if the thought of paying for a surplice should be laid on them in these calamitous times'.[83]

Archbishop Marsh was promoted to the primacy of Armagh in February 1703. But he seems to have been unhappy about his promotion. It would appear that although he was promoted to the primacy in January his patent was not dated until some weeks later.[84] Consequently Marsh did not receive the quarter's rent due to the see of Armagh. (In fact some of the rent had been paid by the crown to the Blue Coat Hospital in London.) Marsh because of his financial difficulties became so depressed that he considered retiring from the primacy and opening a private school in order to earn his living. But he did receive part of the quarter's rent some months afterwards.[85]

Although Marsh as the new primate had difficulty receiving the rents due to him in Armagh he had no difficulty being recognised by the city of Dublin. In January 1707/8 at a meeting of the city council it was ordered on the lord mayor's warrant that Primate Marsh should receive his freedom in a gold box.[86]

While he was in Armagh, he repaired the cathedral, and rebuilt many churches in his archdiocese entirely at his own expense. He bought in impropriations and restored them to the church. But that was not all. He instituted and largely endowed the almshouses for the widows of clergymen who had served cures in the Armagh diocese, and he provided the widows with pensions.[87] He contributed large sums of money to the missionaries who worked for the Society for the Propagation of the Gospel in Foreign Parts.[88]

4, London, Spottiswoode, Ballantyne & Co Ltd, 1922, p. 16.   **83** [Narcissus Marsh], 'State of the province of Armagh', 1706 (Lambeth Palace, Gibson Papers, MS 929, f. 41).   **84** Letter from Bishop of London, to Ld (High Treasurer) respecting the circumstances of the archbishop of Armagh, *Calendar of Treasury Papers, 1702–1707*, prepared by Joseph Redington, London, 1874. See vol. lxxxvi, July 1 & 11, no. 107, 1703, pp 174–5. See also two letters in the *Church of Ireland Gazette*, 30 August 1935, p. 563.   **85** *Calendar of treasury books, April 1705 to Sept 1706*. Treasury Warrants, Treasury Minutes, prepared by William A. Shaw, London, 1952. See vol. xx, pt II, April 30, 1705, p. 239.   **86** John T. Gilbert, *Calendar of ancient records of Dublin*, vi, p. 380.   **87** William King, *The remembrance of the righteous in a sermon preach'd at the funeral of … Narcissus [Marsh] … November 6th, 1713*, Dublin, Andrew Crooke, 1714, p. 34.   **88** H. Vere White, *Bishop Berkeley as a missionary: a paper*, Dublin, Office of the Irish Auxiliary of the S.P.G. in Foreign Parts, 1900, Appendix B, p. 36.

Marsh carried on his good work for four years and then the first hint of a serious illness appeared in a letter to his friend Dr Smith. Marsh complained about the amount of parliamentary work which he had to do, and which left him no time to write to his friends. But it would appear that he had suffered a mild stroke from which he recovered.[89] In 1711 Archbishop King wrote to Swift complaining about how difficult it was to complete the business of convocation because of Marsh's illness. Marsh apparently was determined to attend the sessions and act as chairman.[90] Earlier the duke of Ormond told Swift that Marsh was hardly able to sign a paper. Swift answered that 'everyone knew he was a dying man this twelvemonth past'.[91]

Primate Narcissus Marsh died on 2 November 1713 and is buried in the churchyard of St Patrick's Cathedral. The monument to Marsh was first erected by the west wall of his library. In 1728 the governors and guardians of Marsh's Library noticed that the monument was 'too much exposed to the weather' which then appeared to them to 'damnify it very much'. They decided to have it moved into the cathedral where it was placed in one of the arches of the southern nave arcade. In the nineteenth century it was moved to its present position, at the eastern end of the south wall of the south transept. Marsh's monument was recently identified by Dr Edward McParland as 'the most important surviving work by Grinling Gibbons in Ireland'.[92]

We have already quoted the bishop of Oxford and Archbishop William King on Marsh's character. But when Archbishop King preached the funeral sermon in St Patrick's Cathedral he was a little more generous. He said:

> Though a strict and rigid Adherer to the Service of our Church, yet so far as I could observe, neither *Dissenters* nor *Roman Catholicks* did ever complain of him: on the contrary they looked on him as a mild and merciful Adversary that rather chose to Convert than hurt them. In his Family he was an indulgent Master, beloved of his Servants, and ready to his Power to do good Offices not only to them, but to all Men … The frequent Addresses to him by Petitions and other Applications were so many, that one would wonder he had any thing to spare for other occasions … These acts of Charity were Privately done without Noise or Ostentation … such as the

89 Richard Mant, op. cit., Letter from Marsh to Dr Smith, September, 1707, ii, p. 181.   **90** Ibid., Letter from Archbishop William King to Jonathan Swift, Oct. 27, 1711, p. 227.   **91** Ibid., p. 262. (Duke of Ormonde told Dr Swift, that …)   **92** Edward McParland, 'A monument to Grinling Gibbons', in *Irish*

relieving Fifty Widows every first *Friday* of the Month together with many Private Pensions regularly paid the Necessitous … Nor did he forget his private *Relations* or *Friends* to whom he left good Legacies, that amount to *Eight* or *Nine* Thousand Pounds.[93]

But one great Irishman, Jonathan Swift, did not share Archbishop King's charitable opinion of Narcissus Marsh. Swift blamed Marsh for his having to write the famous 'penitential letter' and for his lack of promotion in the Church of Ireland; he also held Marsh responsible for removing him from the management of the petition for the first fruits for the Church of Ireland at the very moment when he had almost brought it to a successful conclusion.[94] He never forgave Narcissus Marsh and wrote the spiteful 'A Character of Primate Marsh' about three years before Marsh's death. Swift wrote:

Marsh has the reputation of most profound and universal learning; this is the general opinion, neither can it be easily disproved. An old rusty iron-chest in a banker's shop, strongly lockt, and wonderful heavy, is full of gold; this is the general opinion, neither can it be disproved, provided the key be lost, and what is in it be wedged so close that it will not by any motion discover the metal by the chinking. Doing good is his pleasure; and as no man consults another in his pleasures, neither does he in this; … without all passions but fear, to which of all others he hath least temptation, having nothing to get or to lose; no posterity, relation, or friend to be solicitous about; and placed by his station above the reach of fortune or envy … He is the first of human race, that with great advantages of learning, piety, and station ever escaped being a great man … He is so wise to value his own health more than other mens noses, so that the most honourable

Arts Review, 1993, pp 108–9.   **93** William King, *The remembrance of the righteous*, pp 27–34. See also G.E.C. [i.e. George E. Cokayne] Compiler, *Some notice of various families of the name of Marsh*, Exeter, W. Pollard, 1900 [*The Genealogist*, n.s., vol. 16, suppl.], pp 37–42. The legacies which he left to his family included four thousand pounds to his brother Epaphroditus. He also asked his brother to 'be kind to his only daughter, my niece'. It would appear from this instruction that Archbishop Marsh had forgiven Grace Marsh for the great distress which she caused him when she eloped with the Revd Charles Proby in 1695. He was also generous to Grace. He left her all his jewels, rings, plate and musical instruments in his houses in Dublin, Drogheda and Johnstown. He left the residue of his estate to his domestic chaplain, the Revd Benjamin Huson, and money to Benjamin Huson's children.   **94** Muriel McCarthy, 'Swift and the Primate of Ireland (Marsh's Library in the early eighteenth century)', in *Dublin Historical Record*, xxvii, no. 3, June 1974, pp 109–12.   **95** Jonathan Swift, *Miscellanies X* (1745),

place at his table is much the worst, especially in summer ... No man will be either glad or sorry at his death, except his successor.[95]

Bitter words indeed. But perhaps it would be more fair to end this account of Primate Narcissus Marsh with part of the sermon which Marsh himself gave at his primary visitation held in St Patrick's Cathedral on 27 June 1694. He was speaking about popish, recusant and all other dissenters and he said,

> That, we have a love to their Souls; that what we do is with a design to save them, and to make them happy forever; and that our only endeavour is to put them in the right way to Heaven; and if possible to bring them thither. For which purpose we must, always treat them with the *Spirit of Meekness* and of *Love*: else our labour will be but lost upon them. For *Haughtiness* and *Bitterness of Spirit* do but incense and provoke, and is rather apt to drive men out of the Church, than to bring any into it.[96]

Archbishop King, the bishop of Oxford and Jonathan Swift may all have had their own opinions, charitable, spiteful or otherwise, but Marsh, whatever his personal failings, left one noble tribute to his memory – the first public library in Ireland, built entirely at his own initiative and expense.

pp 169–71.   **96** Narcissus Marsh, *The charge given ... to his clergy at his primary visitation held in the cathedral church of St Patrick, in Dublin, June 27th 1694*, Dublin, Joseph Ray, 1694, p. 13.

Chapter 2

The Library

RCHBISHOP NARCISSUS MARSH began building his library about 1701. Most of the information concerning the library is contained in a series of letters which Marsh wrote to his friend Dr Thomas Smith in England to which we have already referred. They were published in Richard Mant's *History of the Church of Ireland* and in the *Christian Examiner*.

As we have seen, the idea of a library had first occurred to Marsh when he was provost of Trinity College and observed how difficult it was to use the library there.[1] It was open only to the provost and fellows and, as Marsh said,

> the booksellers' shops are furnished with nothing but new trifles; so that neither the divines of the city, nor those that come to it about business, do know whither to go to spend an hour or two upon any occasion at study.[2]

The first letter[3] about the library from Narcissus Marsh to Dr Smith is dated 4 May 1700 and Marsh seeks Dr Smith's assistance in 'recommending to him choice books'. He tells Dr Smith he intends leaving all his oriental manuscripts to the Bodleian Library and as for the rest of his books, to dispose of them thus. He intends building a public library and he explains that the Archbishop's House, St Sepulchre's, where Marsh lived,

> though it may well be called a palace for the stateliness of all the publick rooms of reception, yet hath it no chapel nor library, belonging to it, nor indeed any convenient room to hold an ordinary study of books, so that mine lay dispersed in three distant rooms.

The chapel he intended for the archbishop's own use.

---

1 *Christian Examiner*, no. xxiv, vol. ii, Nov. 1833, p. 764 and pp 762–72.   2 Richard Mant, *History of the Church of Ireland*, London, J. W. Parker, 1840, ii, p. 111.   3 Ibid.

Marsh decided to build the library on ground which he held by reason of his being archbishop of Dublin but the site extended into the churchyard, for which the dean and chapter of St Patrick's gave formal permission[4] in July 1701.

The library was designed[5] by Sir William Robinson, the surveyor general of Ireland. Robinson had already designed the Royal Hospital which Marsh was familiar with; as archbishop of Dublin he was automatically a governor.[6] There is still a fine portrait of him there. The library was beautifully designed and is now one of the very few eighteenth-century buildings left in Dublin which is still being used for its original purpose. It is an L-shaped building, the lower storey being designed as a residence for the librarian, although Marsh hoped that eventually the whole building would become a library. The library is furnished with magnificent dark oak bookcases each with carved and lettered gable topped by a mitre. The first gallery is approximately 60 feet long and the second gallery approximately 76 feet long. At the end of the second gallery are three wired alcoves, usually called 'the cages'. They were intended by Marsh for the protection of the smaller more valuable books. Over the years the rather charming tradition developed that 'the cages' were used to lock students in so that they could not steal the books. The design and arrangement of the library was obviously influenced by the design of part of the Bodleian Library, judging from Marsh's many references to it.[7] The first gallery and the reading room were completed by 1703.[8] The rules of the library are also similar to those of the Bodleian. It is particularly interesting that because the library has changed so little internally the books which the first librarian, Dr Elias Bouhéreau, catalogued and which both he and the archbishop placed on the shelves in the first gallery are still in those same places with the same shelf numbers three hundred years later.

---

4 Calendar of leases 1546–1776, no. 59 (10) 1701, Marsh's Library. The Calendar is kept in the records in St Patrick's Cathedral.   5 Richard Mant, op. cit., letter from Marsh to Dr Thomas Smith, 26 Jan. 1703, p. 113.   6 See E.S.E. Childers and Robert Stewart, *The story of the Royal Hospital, Kilmainham*, London, Hutchinson, 1921, pp 56 and 74. See also article by W.G. Strickland on Sir William Robinson, in *JRSAI*, liii, no. xiii, 1923, p. 103. See also Rolf Loeber, *A biographical dictionary of architects in Ireland 1620-1720*, London, John Murray, 1981.   7 *Christian Examiner*, letter from Marsh to Dr Thomas Smith, 19 Jan. 1705–6, p. 764. And Richard Mant, op. cit., p. 113 'the upper part, that is contrived like the cross part of the Bodleyan [*sic*] Library'. Marsh was probably referring to the Seldon end, the architectural counterpart of the Arts end, the Duke Humphrey library forming the connecting gallery to both. 8 *Church of Ireland Gazette*, 9 Dec. 1927, p. 713. Copy of letter from Marsh to Bishop of London, 7 June 1703, and see Richard Mant, op. cit., letter from Marsh to Dr Thomas Smith, 26 Jan. 1703, p. 112.

Marsh having built the library and furnished it with books was anxious to have it and its government incorporated in an act of parliament.[9] The act which he drew up was called 'An Act for Settling and Preserving a Publick Library for ever'. The act vested the house and books in the following dignitaries and officials (and their successors) as governors and guardians: the Church of Ireland archbishop of Armagh, the lord chancellor of Ireland, the archbishop of Dublin, the lord chief justice of Queen's Bench, the lord chief justice of Common Pleas, the lord chief baron, the dean of Christ Church, the dean of St Patrick's and the provost of Trinity College. Of these the archbishop of Dublin is the most important. He directs meetings to be summoned and he and two other governors constitute a quorum for business purposes; if he is not present there must be five governors. The legal governors and the lord chancellor's office became extinct on the formation of the Irish State in 1922. The governors of Marsh's were anxious to have the chief justice made a governor of the library but there was a legal difficulty which was not overcome until 1970 when to the governors' great satisfaction Chief Justice Cearbhaill Ó Dalaigh became a governor *ex officio*.

The act of 1707 incorporating Marsh's Library as a public library gives details about the foundation and the contents. The building was exempted forever from all manner of taxes, and from all chimney money, hearth money, and lamp money and from all manner of taxes or charges 'hereafter to be imposed by Act of Parliament'.

An income had to be provided for the librarian.[10] Archbishop Marsh purchased land[11] in Co. Meath from which, however, no income would arise until the death of Lady Tyrconnell, who was a beneficiary for life. Marsh also

9 Act of parliament, chap. XIX of the 6th Queen Anne. In the *Statutes at large, passed in the parliaments held in Ireland*, Dublin, Boulter Grierson, MDCCLXV, pp 169–79. **10** Payments to Dr Elias Bouhéreau and references to his position as keeper of Marsh's Library appear in the *Calendar of treasury papers, 1697–1701–2* and *1708–1714*. Also in the *Calendar of treasury books, 1704–1705, 1708–1709*. **11** *Irish Record Commissioners' Reports 1821–5*, p. 373. (This appears to be the land Marsh purchased.) The following are abstracts of the trustees' conveyances: To Sir John Dillon of Lismullen, Co. Meath: Little Finlaghtowne and Creroge 240 acres, Grangeboyne 279 acres, barony of Deece, Newtown and Clunbrun 620 acres, barony of Navan. Estate of Richard, earl of Tyrconnell attainted; granted to Henry, Viscount Sidney and by him conveyed to Sir John Dillon for £1724 0s. 8d.; conveyed by trustees for forfeited estates to Dillon for £4907 10s. on 17 March 1702. (Grant cancelled by English parliament's Act of Resumption 1700.)• Lady Tyrconnell's life interest secured by private act of English parliament (I Anne, stat. I, c.4) 30 March 1702. • The Revd G.T. Stokes, op. cit., p. 114 also referred to the *Record Commissioners' Reports*, vol. iii, p. 373, no. 6, and wrote: 'It appears that the lands which Marsh bought originally formed part of the forfeited Tyrconnell estates, and that they had been sold for £4,907.10s. to Sir John Dillon in June 1703'. Stokes also quoted from Marsh's will which said: 'That Samuel Dopping, Joseph Deane,

wished to provide for his brother Epaphroditus.[12] (Epaphroditus appears to have got into debt in England and been deprived of his lands.) Consequently under the act a temporary arrangement was made until such time as this income would become available. The act provided that the librarian should have conferred on him the precentorship or treasurership of St Patrick's Cathedral, whichever might first become vacant, and would therefore hold office as a 'presbyter of the Church of England or Ireland as by law established', and an MA of any university in England or Ireland, the nomination to be in

Edmond Stafford, Stephen Ludlow, Thomas Tilson, senior, Thomas Tilson, junior, and Francis Burton Esquires, by their Deeds of Lease and Release bearing date 18th and 19th days of March 1708, did grant and convey unto [Marsh] … the Towns and Lands of Little Finlaghtown alias Little Finglastowne and Creroge containing 240 acres … Grangeboyne containing 270 acres … in the barony of Deece and County of Meath and also … the towns and lands of Newtown and Clonbrun … containing 620 acres … in the Barony of Navan'. • W.M. Mason in his *History of St Patrick's Cathedral*, pp 11–14 gave details regarding the foundation of Marsh's Library and said that Marsh in his will 'bequeathed the above mentioned lands to Marmaduke Coghill and the Rev John Stearne, Dean of St Patrick's Cathedral, their Heirs and Assigns for ever, as Trustees, to the intent that his Brother Epaphroditus Marsh should enjoy the issues and profits for and during his life, but after his decease and the decease of the Lady Tyrconnell, "who at that time received the said rents", he declared it to be his will that the said Trustees should ever after pay to the Governors of the Library, out of the first rents and profits of the premises above named, the yearly sum of £250.0.0. for ever, over and above all taxes or contributions, the said payments to be made quarterly, and the first payment to commence in the first quarter after the death of Epaphroditus Marsh and Lady Tyrconnell; this sum was to be appropriated by the Governors in the manner following, viz.: £210.0.0. per annum to the said Library-Keeper, "to assist him to keep, support and maintain said Library and the Buildings thereof in good and sufficient repair, as required by said Act"; £30.0.0. per annum to an Assistant Librarian and £10.0.0. per annum to buy books. The residue of the issues and profits from these lands the Most Rev Prelate appropriated to the maintenance of certain widows houses which he had built in Drogheda.' • The money from the land purchased by Archbishop Marsh appears to have been paid directly to the keeper of the library. This annuity which amounted to £230 sterling was redeemed in 1929 for £4609 Irish 4½ land bonds which yielded £207 per annum. In 1980 the library's income consisted of approximately £800 per annum. This included the rents from the flats, the income from a holding of land bonds and consols representing the original endowments and a further endowment made by Sir Benjamin Lee Guinness in 1856 and a small annual government grant towards the assistant librarian. In 1997 the government, under the National Cultural Institutions Act, appointed two new governors to the board of Marsh's Library. They also increased the funding to the library.   **12** From *Calendar of treasury books*, xiv, 1 Sept. 1698 to 31 July 1699. Prepared by William A. Shaw, London, 1934. Royal Warrants. Treasury Warrants, p. 170. 'Same to Sir Thomas Trevor, Attorney General, of the petition of Patience Bond widow, shewing that Epaphroditus Marsh being indebted £200.00 to her husband she sued him to an outlawry and thereby certain lands in Hannington Co. Wilts., of which he held a 99 years' term were seized into the hands of the Crown therefore praying a grant to the King's interest therein.' And from page 212, 'same to same for a grant to Patience Bond widow and executrix of John Bond, of all the Crown's title to the extended lease of a messuage and certain parcels of land in Hannington which vested in Epaphroditus Marsh for the lives of him, Narcissus Marsh and Henry Marsh and which upon the outlawry of the said Epaphroditus on a plea of debt on a bond of £400.00 for £200.00 owing by him

the hand of the archbishop of Dublin. (Originally Marsh hoped to unite forever either the treasurership or chantership of St Patrick's Cathedral to the office of Marsh's librarian. But Archbishop King would not consent to that arrangement.)[13] Thus the first librarian, Dr Elias Bouhéreau, was made precentor of St Patrick's Cathedral at an income from the state of £200 per annum. The act however went on to provide that should a person endow the librarianship with £150 per annum at least, then the two offices of precentor (or treasurer) and librarian were to be separated and that the librarian thereafter would be elected by the governors and need not be a presbyter. The separation did not take place until 1762 when John Wynne, the third librarian, died, although Marsh's endowment became available on the death of Lady Tyrconnell in March 1730. (Epaphroditus Marsh died in 1719.)[14] In 1762 the governors for the first time used their powers of election, and appointed Thomas Cobbe LLD, the first layman to hold office.

Archbishop Marsh left strict instructions to the governors of the library on the qualifications he expected the librarians to have. He also required the librarians to take a solemn oath promising not to give away, lend, or embezzle any of the books in the library. Marsh also included rules for readers in the library,[15] which said that

> All Graduates and Gentlemen shall have free access to the said Library on the Dayes and Houres before determined, Provided They behave Themselves well, give place and pay due respect to their Betters, But in case any person shall carry Himself otherwise (which We hope will not happen) We order Him to be excluded, if after being admonished He does not mend His manners.

Rather surprisingly, the act setting up Marsh's Library met with some opposition in Ireland; although in England, Marsh said, 'It met with great applause, if I may say so.'[16] The opposition in the Irish house of lords was

---

to the said John Bond was on May 16 last seized into the King's hands on a *capias utlagum*'. **13** H.J. Todd, op. cit., Letter from Archbishop Marsh to Archbishop Tenison 16 Oct. 1703. MS 929/89, p. 200. **14** *Parish Register Society of Dublin. The registers of St Patrick, Dublin 1677 to 1800*, p. 25. **15** Visitation book of Marsh's Library. This 'fair Vellom Book' was given by Narcissus Marsh to the library. It contains the act of parliament, a map or plan of the ground of the library, and all rules and orders made by the governors and guardians. It also includes accounts of all the visitations and meetings held in the library from 1707 to 1924. **16** Richard Mant, op. cit., Marsh's letter to Dr Thomas Smith, undated, probably near the end of 1707 and letter from Marsh to Dr Smith 13 Dec. 1707, pp 115–16.

really intended for Marsh personally and came, as he described it, 'by men of mine own coat'. Four bishops opposed the act and said it contained simony, sacrilege and perjury. Mant in his *History of the Church of Ireland* suggests that this opposition came from Bishops Lloyd of Killala, Hartstong of Ossory, Lindsay of Killaloe and Pooley of Raphoe.[17] These dissenting lords entered their protests against the bill. But the house of lords disapproved greatly of this opposition and at the next session voted that the opposers should be sent prisoners to the Castle unless they withdrew their opposition. That apparently ended that. The house of commons passed the bill *nemine contradicente*, and a committee of eight members was appointed to give Marsh the thanks of the house for his benefaction. The lower house of convocation, which was meeting at the same time as the parliament, also voted their thanks to Marsh, although there had been some opposition to parts of the bill which many of the clergy including Jonathan Swift had a voice in.[18]

Marsh was deeply upset by this opposition. He wrote to his friend:

> By this you will perceive how difficult a matter it is for a man to do any kindness to the people of this country. If he will be a publick benefactor, he must resolve to fight his way through all opposition of it; it being a new and unheard-of-thing here, that certainly hath some secret design in it to subvert the Church ... I confess this opposition has struck a great damp upon my spirits.[19]

The opposition to Marsh's Library bill in the Irish house of convocation of the Church of Ireland came from the same bishops who had earlier opposed the bill in the house of lords. This opposition had as much to do with the bishops' and clergy's different views on political and church politics as with personal spite towards Marsh who had on many occasions punished and disciplined the clergy.

The political differences arose because Archbishop Marsh and Archbishop William King were regarded as the leaders of the whigs or 'low church' group in convocation, while the bishops who opposed Marsh – John Hartstong of

---

17 Ibid., p. 119.   18 Louis A. Landa, *Swift and the Church of Ireland*, Oxford, At the Clarendon Press, 1954, p. 51. See also Muriel McCarthy, 'Swift and the Primate of Ireland, Marsh's Library in the early eighteenth century' in *Dublin Historical Record*, xxvii, no. 3, June 1974, pp 109–12.   19 Richard Mant, op. cit., Marsh's letter to Dr Thomas Smith, 13 Dec. 1707, p. 116. See also Louis A. Landa, op. cit., p. 51, and Muriel McCarthy, op. cit.

Ossory, Thomas Lindsay of Killaloe and John Pooley of Raphoe – were strong tories and were influenced by their friend the English clergyman, the Revd Francis Atterbury. Atterbury held strong anti-Erastian views and tried to uphold and preserve the rights of the clergy against the secular power. Atterbury was using his Irish friends in the convocation in order to pursue his own juridical and political views for the English convocation of Canterbury. Archbishop Marsh disagreed with Atterbury and became so angry with his Irish followers that he instructed his chaplain, the Revd William Tisdall, to denounce Bishops Lindsay and Hartstong as 'the incendiaries of the upper house'.[19a] This led to another vociferous row when Marsh as primate and chairman of convocation used his position to adjourn the upper house. This raised the issue as to whether the lower house could continue to meet in intermediate sessions. The Revd Francis Atterbury believed that the English bishops could not terminate the sittings of the lower house by an adjournment and this view also influenced some of the Irish clergy.

These disputes over ecclesiastical procedures led to a series of pamphlets from both sides. The issues and arguments became so complicated that they have been described as 'a tangled web'.

The poisoned atmosphere and spite towards Marsh in the convocation did not help to promote the passing of his Library bill. And Marsh seems to have been unaware of the strength of feeling and hostility towards him. It is interesting to look back at contemporary accounts of the chief protagonists, Bishops Pooley, Lindsay and Hartstong. The chief secretary, Addison, said Pooley was 'a man of ungovernable passions … and generally passes for mad'.[20] Swift called him 'an old, doating, perverse coxcomb'.[21] Irvin Ehrenpreis described Lindsay as 'the feckless Lindsay'[22] and 'a weak character'[23] and he also said that he was 'chiefly remembered for the splendour of his funeral'.[24] Swift in his *Journal to Stella* wrote, 'Stella is in the right; the bishop of Ossory [Hartstong] is the silliest, best-natured wretch breathing, of as little consequence as an egg-shell.'[25]

Jonathan Swift also objected to Marsh's Library bill. Swift had developed a poor opinion of Archbishop Marsh and, as we have already said, blamed him for his lack of promotion in the Church of Ireland.

19a D.W. Hayton, 'The High Church Party in the Irish Convocation, 1703–1713'; see note 27.
20 Irvin Ehrenpreis, *Swift: the man, his works and the age*, London, Methuen, 1983, ii, p. 263.
21 Jonathan Swift, *Journal to Stella*, ed. Harold Williams, Oxford, Clarendon Press, 1948, i, p. 354.
22 Irvin Ehrenpreis, op. cit., iii, p. 355.   23 Irvin Ehrenpreis, op. cit., ii, p. 718.   24 Ibid., p. 717.
25 Jonathan Swift, op. cit., ed. H. Williams, ii, p. 424.

The most serious cause of objection to the Library bill was Marsh's proposal to annex the librarian's job to that of the treasurership or precentorship of St Patrick's Cathedral. Marsh said that Archbishop King refused to agree to this arrangement because he believed that the archbishop of Dublin would be responsible for the upkeep of the library. Archbishop King had other reasons. He did not want the precentorship and the librarian's job amalgamated in case it might prevent him from bestowing the precentorship on someone of his own choice.

But there was another serious problem as far as Archbishop King and the clergy were concerned. The proposed board of Marsh's Library was to consist of four clerical governors, the provost of Trinity College and four legal governors. If the provost was a layman, then it might happen that a majority of laymen on the board would have authority over an important officer of the cathedral. This of course was unacceptable to Archbishop King. Eventually he agreed to the arrangement that the appointment of the librarian should be in the gift of the archbishop of Dublin and that the librarians should be responsible for the upkeep of the library. He was obviously impatient with Archbishop Marsh and told him he 'ought to endow the Library'.[26] Archbishop King was equally impatient with the members of the lower house of convocation who objected to some of the proposals in the Library bill. He sent a furious message to them, 'Convocation has medeled with matters that do not belong to them, and they shall soon know it and tell them so from me'.[27]

It is interesting to discover that when the first librarian, Dr Elias Bouhéreau, died in 1719, the autocratic Archbishop King quickly appointed his own nephew, Dr Robert Dougatt, to the position. Archbishop King and his nephew appear to have had similar litigious tendencies. At this period they were both involved in long acrimonious legal battles with the dean and chapter of Christ Church Cathedral.

Jonathan Swift agreed with Archbishop King and the clergy that the Library Act was dangerous as far as the cathedral was concerned. But when

26 Letter Oct. 16, 1703, no. 89, Marsh to Archbishop of Canterbury.   27 A short account of the Proceedings in the lower house of convocation in relation to my Lord Primate's Library Bill, 18 December 1707, Bodleian Library, Ballard 36. F 45 & 43. [W. Percival.] To Revd Dr Charlett, Master of University College, Oxford. See also Hayton, D.W., 'The High Church Party in the Irish Convocation 1703–1713' in Real and Stöver-Leidig, ed., *Reading Swift: Papers from the Third Münster Symposium on Jonathan Swift*, Munich, 1998, pp 117–39.

resolutions were proposed protesting against the act and the lower house of convocation voted to keep the resolutions on the records of convocation as a permanent protest, Swift dissented and he entered into the records a notarised statement of his disagreement. According to Louis Landa, Swift's position was that the final action to keep them there was unnecessary. It was therefore a technicality concerned with procedure.

The earlier hostility shown by Bishop Pooley to Marsh had an amusing sequel a few years later when Marsh was on his visitation of the diocese of Raphoe. In a letter to the archbishop of Canterbury, Thomas Tennison, Marsh said that Bishop Pooley had told all the clergy that Marsh had no power to visit Raphoe and that he would oppose him. But after Marsh's vicar general put pressure on Pooley, he weakly conceded and, according to Marsh, 'appeared at my visitation & submitted without showing the least sign of opposition'.[27a]

But fortunately for Ireland in spite of all opposition the act incorporating Marsh's Library as a public library was passed in 1707.

The library cost Marsh £5000 and he intended spending another £500 on it.[28] The first part of the library seems to have been completed by midsummer 1703. Marsh had hoped it would have been built earlier and complained about the delay, because 'Sir William Robinson, who is my architect, had not stayed so long in London the last year'.[29] Marsh wondered about an additional building or, as he said in his letters, 'the present be carried on, as is designed, I fear that I shall not find room in it to place any more books'. This raises an interesting point about the second gallery. Some architects believe that because the woodwork in the second gallery is not as elegant as the woodwork in the first gallery, the second gallery may not have been designed by Sir William Robinson. But in a letter written by Bishop William King in Derry on 16 March 1702/3 to Narcissus Marsh in St Sepulchre's Palace,[30] King, who had been promoted in Marsh's place as new archbishop of Dublin and who was very anxious to move into the palace, wrote,

> I hope I may lodge all my servants & will need nothing but to put the publick rooms in order and I hope your Grace will go on with the Library & forward the Gallery you intend, for I can't well order the room I intend for myself till I fully understand your Grace's design.

27a Sept 12, 1706; (photocopy in the library).   28 Richard Mant, op. cit., Marsh's letter to Dr Smith, 13 Dec. 1707, p. 116.   29 Ibid., letter from Marsh to Dr Smith, 26 Jan. 1702/3, pp 112–13.   30 Trinity College Dublin, MS N3.2b., letter from William King to Marsh, 16 March, 1702/3, p. 173.

King again wrote to Marsh on 23 March 1702/3.[31] He was clearly impatient at Marsh's reluctance to move out of St Sepulchre's and said,

> [I] am sorry your Grace should be disappointed as to a house[32] but there are enuf in Dublin and therefore I hope the hardship will not be great. As to the door of the Gallery if I were there I must be governed by your Grace and also Wm. Robinson. I intend the room within the drawing room for my bed Chamber and so it be left large enuf for that purpose I care not how the Gallery be Continued.

But it seems possible that William Robinson did not entirely complete the whole building. In another letter nearly seven years later King said,

> I have pressed Captain Burgh to make me a moddel for the Porch of the Library towards St Patrick's Church but he is [so thoroughly] engaged in the arsenall that I could not prevail with him yet to prepare it, but he promises to have it very speedily for me.[33]

It is a curious letter, and is obviously a reply to an accusation by Marsh that King had taken some of the library's ground, which King denied and he said he had 'given four times as much on the other side where the Old Tower stood'. Since there was already at that time a tower belonging to the library where the private passage from the archbishop's palace came into the back of the library, it would seem as if there might have been an older tower facing St Patrick's. It raises an interesting point about the design of the library and the surrounding area. The tower which was part of Marsh's Library was definitely removed in 1833,[34] and the door through which the archbishops came through the private passage from St Sepulchre's was

31 Ibid., letter dated 23 March 1702/3, pp 181–2. See also TCD, The Lyons collection of the correspondence of Abp. William King, MS 1995–2008 a–g, no. 1011, Marsh to King, 26 April 1703. 32 Marsh seems to have lived or stayed in several places around Dublin. A note in MS Z4.4.8 (in the library) says Marsh when he was Provost of TCD lived 'in the old house in Drumcondra'. In TCD MS 1995–2008 a–g op. cit., letter No 1011, Marsh to King, the address is Rathbeal. In Dr Bouhéreau's diary, MS Z2.2.2 (in the library) p. 112 the following entry appears: '17 May, 1704, J'ay ete, avec Mr Quartier, voir My Lord Primat a Rathbeale, Maison ou il se retire de tems en tems, a sept Miles de Dublin'. In another letter in TCD, MS 1995–2008 a–g op. cit., written by Marsh to King dated 8 March 1705/6 the address is Johnstown. (Dr J.G. Simms informed me that this was Colonel Moore's house near Finglas.) 33 Trinity College Dublin, MS N2.27, No. 208, letter from King to Marsh, 9 Oct. 1710. (There is a copy of this letter in the archives box in Marsh's Library.) 34 Newport J.D. White, An account of Archbishop Marsh's Library, Dublin, Dublin, Hodges Figgis, 1926, p. 7. See also William Seynol's

hidden by a bookcase containing books in the Everth collection. When the Everth collection was removed to the new seminar room in 1985, the door was again revealed.

The library was now erected and the most important task began. Marsh began looking for books, and wrote to Dr Smith saying that he was 'indeed earnestly pressed to buy Dr Stillingfleet's library'.[35] Edward Stillingfleet (d.1699) had been dean of St Paul's and later bishop of Worcester.[36] He was one of the best known preachers and writers of his day; his famous controversy with Locke on the doctrine of the Trinity and his books against Socinians and Catholics had aroused great interest. Pepys in his diary records that he went to hear Stillingfleet preach at Whitehall. Stillingfleet was also known for his good looks and was nicknamed 'the beauty of holiness'. More important he was a superb book collector; indeed he had continued to collect books to within a few weeks of his death. John Evelyn had described Stillingfleet's library as the best private library in England.[37] Dr Richard Bentley, master of Trinity College, Cambridge, and royal librarian, tried to get William III to buy it and said of it 'the like of which was not anywhere else in the world'.[38] Thomas Hearne regretted that like Dr Isaac Vossius' books Stillingfleet's books were allowed to go out of England 'to the eternal scandal and reproach of it'.[39] Ninian Wallis after the Stillingfleet library had come to Ireland referred to it as 'this Golden Fleece'.[40]

Curiously when Marsh received the Stillingfleet catalogue before he decided to purchase the books, he did not find the collection particularly impressive.[41] In fact, he wrote to his friend Dr Smith, 'there must of necessity be many *insignificant* books in it',[42] and again, 'The collection is great; but, as far as I can yet discern, is on some subjects superfluous and redundant.'[43] But

accounts for repairs to the library in 1833. (In archives box.) **35** Richard Mant, op. cit., letter from Marsh to Dr Smith, 5 July 1704, p. 113. **36** Information on Bishop Edward Stillingfleet from *DNB* and Revd James Nankivell's lecture, 'Edward Stillingfleet', a lecture to the Worcestershire Archaeological Society, Dec. 1946, (s.l.). See also George Sampson, *The concise Cambridge history of English literature*, Cambridge, At the University Press, 1941, p. 441. **37** James Nankivell, op. cit., p. 15. **38** Ibid., pp 15–16. **39** Newport J.D. White, op. cit., p. 8. **40** Ninian Wallis, *Britannia libera*, Dublin, S. Powell, 1710 (Epistle dedicatory, p. 9). **41** It seems likely that Dean Stearne (later Bishop of Clogher) may have acted and advised Marsh with the negotiations and arrangements for the purchase of the Stillingfleet collection. See remains of letter from Dr Bouhéreau to Archbishop William King in Trinity College, MS 1995–2008 a–g., letter no. 2395, c.July 1705. (Bouhéreau wrote this letter in English.) See also letters from Dean Stearne to William King. Letters no. 1349, 1350, 1352 in this collection. Dean Stearne also discusses suitable books for Archbishop King's own library. **42** Richard Mant, op. cit., letter from Marsh to Dr Smith, 5 July 1704, p. 113. **43** Ibid., letter from Marsh to Dr Smith, 7 Sept. 1704, p. 114.

when Marsh bought the books, and when they arrived in Dublin he was delighted and said, 'I am very well pleased with the purchase, there being very many excellent books amongst them, and most very well bound and of the best editions.'[44] He thanked Dr Smith for all his assistance. But Marsh was not satisfied even with this great purchase. He was determined that the library would continue to be useful, and he again asked Dr Smith's assistance in suggesting new purchases and better editions of books.[45]

The Stillingfleet collection is the most important in the whole library. It contains almost 10,000 books and cost Marsh £2500, quite a large sum of money in 1705.[46] It contains books on a wide range of subjects, including theology, history, the classics, law, medicine and travel. Many of Stillingfleet's books were owned by famous people and many had belonged to well-known English book-collectors and were bought at the earliest auctions held in England.

There are books which belonged to Richard Smith (d.1675) and there are examples of his handwriting in his books.[47] Smith was a compiler (one of his books is in Marsh's collection, and bears Marsh's motto) and had been admitted to the office of secondary of the Poultry compter (that is, an assistant to the sheriff with his office in the court in the Poultry); this office was apparently worth about £700 a year. Wood says, 'he was constantly known every day to walk his rounds among the booksellers' shops (especially in Little Britain) in London, and by his great skill and experience he made choice of such books that were not obvious to every man's eye'. Richard Smith died in 1675 and left his books to his daughter who afterwards sold the collection to Richard Chiswell, and eventually they were sold at the famous auction held in 1682. The sale began on Monday 15 May 1682, at the Swan in Bartholomew's Close, and it lasted for twenty-four days.[48] Another English book-collector represented in the Stillingfleet collection is Humphrey Dyson.[49] Gordon Duff said that the majority of the rare books in Smith's collection were obtained from the library of Humphrey Dyson,

44 Ibid., 3 Nov. 1705, p. 114.   **45** Ibid.   **46** Newport J.D. White, op. cit., p. 8.   **47** Identified by Professor T.A. Birrell in Abraham Bucholcerus, *Index chronologicus*, Frankfurt, 1634 and in the *Book of Common Prayer*, E. Whytchurche, 1553?   **48** E.G. Duff, 'The library of Richard Smith' in *The Library*, second series, no. 30, viii, April 1907, pp 113–33. Further information on Richard Smith contained in *DNB*. See also W.Y. Fletcher, *English book collectors*, ed. Alfred Pollard, London, Kegan Paul, Trench, Trübner, 1902, pp 93–6 and John Lawlor's *Book auctions in England in the seventeenth century 1676–1700*, London, Elliot Stock, 1898.   **49** W.A. Jackson, 'Humphrey Dyson's library, or, some observations on the survival of books' (1949) no. 10. *Records of a bibliographer*, ed. W.H. Bond, Harvard University Press,

4 An illustration from *Here after folowith the boke callyd the Myrroure of oure lady*,
sometimes attributed to T. Gascoigne (London, R. Fawkes, 1530).

'a person,' says Hearne, 'of a very strange, prying and inquisitive genius in the
matter of books, as may appear from many libraries; there being books,
chiefly in old English, almost in every library, that have belonged to him
with his name upon them'.[50] Dyson was a notary public who died in 1632.
He collected books mainly relating to the history of church and state and
there are about ten of these in the library which also have his signature on
the title-page. When Gordon Duff visited Marsh's in 1903[51] he noticed that
a book relating to Mary, queen of Scots, and printed in 1584 also had
Humphrey Dyson's printed book-stamp which Gordon Duff had not seen
anywhere else. Duff said that this book was sold with others for 10s. 2d. at
Richard Smith's sale to 'Mr Patrick', the name used by the buyer for Edward
Stillingfleet at the auction. The copy of the Richard Fawkes *Myrroure of oure*

1967, pp 135–41.   **50** E.G. Duff, 'The library of Richard Smith', pp 117–18.   **51** E.G. Duff, 'Notes on
a visit to Archbishop Marsh's Library, Dublin' (in July 1903). Reprinted from vol. VI of the *Publications
of the Edinburgh Bibliographical Society*, Edinburgh, MCMVI.

lady dated 1530 also belonged to Dyson, who had originally paid five shillings for it, and was later bought by Richard Smith and similarly sold to Edward Stillingfleet in 1682. Hilsey's *Primer* of 1539 printed at London by John Mayler for John Wayland, Andrew Hester, and Michael Lobley also belonged to Dyson who paid 2s. 6d. for it. It was catalogued Lot 51 at Richard Smith's auction.

There are at least forty books in the library which belonged to Edward Gwynn (*d*.1649?). These are bound in calf and have his name stamped in gold on the upper covers, and his initials on the lower covers.[52] But not all Edward Gwynn's books are in the Stillingfleet collection. Two Gwynn books belonged to Archbishop Marsh and have his motto on them, and another book has the bookplate of Bishop Stearne. Although very little is known about Edward Gwynn, to judge from his books he was a most impressive collector. Indeed Professor Birrell has pointed out that one book in the Stillingfleet collection by Petro Albino entitled *Novae Saxonum historiae progymnasmata* (Wittenberg, 1585) owned by Gwynn was bought by Richard Smith in June 1652 from the London bookseller, Cornelius Bee.[53] This confirms, I think, the origin of many of the books in the different collections as having been bought from the London booksellers. Archbishop Marsh in his correspondence[54] mentions Mr Brabazon Aylmer at the Three Pigeons on Cornhill and Mr Leigh at the Rose and Crown in St Paul's Churchyard. He also refers to Mr Churchill. These were all well-known London booksellers. (Marsh also bought books from a French bookseller called Mr Paul Vaillant.) This view is, I think, confirmed to some extent by an annotation in a mathematical book by Christopher Clavius which belonged to Archbishop Marsh. The annotation is written on the upper endpapers and reads, 'I warrant these 3 Volumes of Clavius his workes to be perfect 12 Decmb 1648 John Fosbrose Servant to Mr Cornelius Bee'. Cornelius Bee was also the bookseller that Stillingfleet bought books from.[55] As well as this interesting annotation the book bears the signature of a former dean of St Patrick's Cathedral, Michael Jephson. Jephson died in

52 W.A. Jackson, 'Edward Gwynn' (1934) no. 8, *Records of a bibliographer*, ed. W.H. Bond, Harvard University Press, 1967.   **53** Information supplied by Professor T.A. Birrell. But see also *Totius orbis ... descriptio*, Leody, 1643. The following annotation appears on the endpaper: 27.5.55 C.B. (Cornelius Bee) £0. 6s. 2d.   **54** Now available on microfilm in Marsh's Library. Narcissus Marsh's letters to Dr Smith are preserved in the Bodleian Library in Oxford.   **55** Bishop Stillingfleet also purchased from another bookseller (?) Robert Scott (1661–91). In a copy of Claudius Salmasius, *Plinianae exercitationes*, Paris, 1629, the following annotation reads, 'I doe warrant this booke perfect and compleat. Robert Scott'.

1694 and Marsh apparently bought Jephson's books, as many of the books in Marsh's collection have Jephson's signature as well as Marsh's motto on them. Another annotation in an English-French legal dictionary, again with Jephson's signature and Marsh's motto, possibly supports this view. It reads inside the upper cover: '£278.18.9 from A:B: this 13th July 1694'. It could be the amount Marsh paid for these books since Marsh was at the time archbishop of Dublin and would naturally have known the dean of St Patrick's Cathedral. I think both Marsh and Jephson as well as buying books in London would have bought good books when available in Ireland.

At least fifteen books in the library belonged to Lazarus Seaman DD, the master of Peterhouse, Cambridge.[56] The majority are in the Stillingfleet collection, but there are two in the Stearne collection. Edward Stillingfleet may also have bought books at the great auction of Dr Francis Bernard's famous library held in London in 1698. In the copy of the sale catalogue of Francis Bernard's books many of the items are marked with a cross and some of these are in the Stillingfleet collection.

Professor T.A. Birrell recently discovered twelve books which originally belonged to John Morris in the Stillingfleet collection.[57] John Morris (d.1658) was in 1640 ranked as one of the second wealthiest group of inhabitants in London, and Birrell described him as 'a wealthy dilettante' who collected interesting books.

As well as famous English book-collectors represented in the library there are many notable autographs and among the most important are those of William Laud, Hugh Latimer, Joseph Justus Scaliger, Isaac Casaubon and William Camden. Interesting sixteenth-century autographs include those of Myles Blomfielde, Lord Burghley, Ben Jonson, Dr John Dee, John Foxe, Lord Lumley, Nicholas Udall (who wrote the first English comedy *Ralph Roister Doister*) and John Donne whose beautiful Italian motto, which appears in one of his books, was translated by Mr John Sparrow as 'I have served for Rachel and not for Leah'. Mr Sparrow explained that in medieval symbolism Rachel stood for the contemplative, Leah for the active. There is a book stamped with the arms of Sir Christopher Hatton. Of the seventeenth century, the names of Sir Kenelm Digby, Bishop Richard Montague and Sir Philip Warwick are the most important. Of Irish interest are the names of

56 *DNB*. See also John Lawlor, op. cit., p. 185. **57** T.A. Birrell, *The library of John Morris: the reconstruction of a seventeenth-century collection*, London, British Museum Publications, 1976, p. 66, X9–X20.

per Rachel hò scritto & no f lui

DE
LA LIBERTE
ANCIENNE ET
CANONIQVE DE
l'Eglise Gallicane,

Aux Cours souueraines de France,

Par IAQVES LESCHASSIER
Aduocat en Parlement.

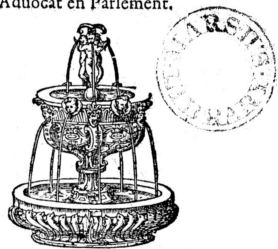

A PARIS,

Chez CLAVDE MOREL, ruë sainct
Iaques, à la Fontaine.

M. DCVI.

AVEC PRIVILEGE DV ROY.

5 Title-page of Jaques Leschassier, *De la liberté ancienne et canonique
de l'Eglise Gallicane* (Paris, 1606); John Donne's copy.

Adam Loftus, Sir H. Bourchier (earl of Bath), Arthur Annesley (earl of Anglesey), James Barry (Lord Santry); and of the nineteenth century, Thomas Davis, Richard Lalor Sheil and the infamous Leonard MacNally.

Some of the books in the library sadly reflect the political and religious difficulties of many of the people, and of the religious orders of seventeenth-century Ireland. Two scientific books which bear Marsh's motto originally belonged to the Jesuits in Dublin. Both have written across their title-pages the following note: 'Missionis Ibernicanae Soctis Jesu Dublinii' and one of these books also includes the signature 'Georg. Dillon S.J. emp. Lond'.

In a fine copy of a *Graduale Romanum* which was printed in Paris in 1668, an inscription in Latin says it was presented to Cashel Cathedral in 1688 by the archbishop of Cashel, John Brenan. Henry Cotton in his *Fasti ecclesiae Hibernicae* maintained that King James II had 'verbally' appointed a Catholic to this position.[58] It seems possible that Archbishop Marsh, who was appointed archbishop of Cashel after the battle of the Boyne, may well have taken this beautiful book to Dublin with him when he was appointed archbishop of Dublin in 1694. A book (Ignatius Galvam, *Discursus varii concionatoribus* ..., Lisbon, 1635) which the Dublin orientalist, Dudley Loftus, presented to Marsh bears the following annotation on the title-page: 'Ex libris P. Alexii Stafford Presbyteri fernensis'. According to Edward Seymour, Alex Stafford was a secular priest who had been appointed dean of Christ Church by King James II and was afterwards killed at the battle of Aughrim while officiating as a military chaplain.[59]

In a book written by Michael Ghislerius in Marsh's own collection the inscription says it belonged to the Jesuits in Waterford. It also contains the signature 'Gulielmus Vitus', who may have been a member of the Jesuit order in Waterford. But it must have come through London originally because another annotation on the upper endpapers has the signature of the London bookseller, Henry Featherstone.[60]

58 Henry Cotton, *Fasti ecclesiae Hibernicae, the succession of the prelates and members of the cathedral bodies in Ireland*, Dublin, Hodges & Smith, 1851, i, p. 16. See also Fr Cathaldus Giblin, 'The Stuart nomination of Irish bishops 1687–1765' in *Irish Ecclesiastical Record*, Jan. to June 1966, cv, fifth series, Dublin, Browne & Nolan, 1966, pp 35–6. **59** Edward Seymour, *Christ Church Cathedral, Dublin* ([London] s.n.) 1882, p. 42. See also Henry Cotton, op. cit., ii, p. 45 (footnote). A manuscript of Alexius Stafford's *Compendium logicae Conimbricensis*, which originally belonged to Dudley Loftus, is also in Marsh's Library. **60** H.R. Plomer, *A dictionary of the booksellers and printers who were at work in England, Scotland and Ireland from 1641 to 1667*, London, printed for the Bibliographical Society by Blades, East & Blades, 1907, p. 73.

Another interesting signature in Marsh's collection is that of the former provincial superior of the Irish Jesuits who afterwards became a member of the Church of Ireland, Andrew Sall. We have already mentioned the assistance which Andrew Sall gave to Marsh in the preparation of the Old Testament for printing and he may well have given his copy of J. Salianus, *Annalium epitome* (Cologne, 1639) to Marsh as a gift.

In a book by Jacobus Capreolus entitled *Sphaera* printed in Paris in 1623, also in Marsh's collection, the following inscription reads, 'Ex libris Laurence Moore praes: Clunfertensis in Hyberniâ anno domini (1682) 9 bris 10 [November]'. These books which I have mentioned were probably acquired by Marsh in Ireland but it would be particularly interesting to discover how the following five books came into the possession of Edward Stillingfleet, bishop of Worcester. The first is by Jacobus Gaulterius SJ, and is entitled *Tabula chronographica status ecclesiae catholicae a Christo nato ad annum* MDCXIV and it contains the following inscription, 'Ad usum fratris Boetii Egani'. This was, I think, Boetius Egan who was appointed Catholic bishop of Elphin in 1625.[61] (See also page 59 below.) It was printed in Lyon in 1616 and is bound in a fine brown calf with the armorial device and motto: 'sors mea dextra Dei'. These arms and device according to Davenport belonged to William Kerr, earl of Lothian (1605?–75).[62] The *DNB* says William Kerr was lieutenant-general of the Scots army in Ireland in 1641, and he may have acquired the book during this period. Some years later William Kerr got into financial difficulties and was forced to sell his estate.

The second book is by Andreas Vega OFM, *De justificatione doctrina universa* (Cologne, 1572). It is also bound with the device and motto of William Kerr on both covers and bears an inscription which says it belonged to 'Dominici O Ferail ordis praedicatorum'. The third book is *Lilia Cistercii* by Chrysostomus Henriquez and was printed in Douay in 1633. It has on the title-page a printed stamp with the words 'Ad usum Fratris Patricii Everardi Sacri Ordinis Cisterciensis Monachi, Hiberni Manapiensis 1638'. It may also have been specially bound for Fr Everard as his name has been stamped in gold on the cover but in a rather amateur fashion. It probably belonged to Fr Patrick Everard (*d.*1650), who was born in Waterford and became a

---

61 W.M. Brady, *The episcopal succession in England, Scotland and Ireland 1400–1875*, 3 vols, Rome, 1876–7, ii, pp 201–2, and see 'Miscellanea Vaticano-Hibernica. Elphin in 1631' in *Archivium Hibernicum*, Record Society of St Patrick's College, Maynooth, M.H. Gill, 1914, iii, p. 359.   **62** Cyril Davenport, *English heraldic book-stamps*, London, Archibald Constable, 1909, p. 261.

Cistercian monk.[63] He studied in Douay and returned to Ireland and was later appointed abbot of Dunbrody in Wexford. The fourth book is Cardinal Du Préau's (or Prateolus) *Elenchus haereticorum omnium*, which was printed in Cologne in 1605 and has the following note on the title-page: 'Ad usum pp Capucinorum in Hibernia'. Finally a copy of Cardinal Robert Bellarmine's *Apologia pro responsione sua ad librum Jacobi Magnae Britanniae regis*, printed in Cologne in 1610 has the following inscription: 'ad usum fris Antonii Gearnon [or Geaenon] pro conventu de Dundalke'. (Possibly Fr Anthony Gearnon OFM, who was vicar of St Anthony's College in Louvain and became chaplain to the queen mother and apostolic visitor in Armagh diocese.[64] He was a friend and supporter of Peter Walsh, (*d.*1688) and of the Irish Remonstrance and was subsequently exiled to France.)

Similarly there are three books in the Bishop Stearne collection which also belonged to the Irish Catholic clergy, the first being Thomas Bozius (Eugubinus), *De signis ecclesiae Dei* (Cologne, 1626) in which the following annotation appears: 'Ex libris fratris Patricii Barnewall pr Conventu Dublin 1678'. Fr Patrick Barnewall was Irish Franciscan procurator at London in 1671.[65] Fr Barnewall stayed for two months at the court in London and became acquainted with Peter Walsh, whom he tried to reconcile to his order and the church. He failed to persuade Walsh who subsequently denounced Barnewall to the royal council. In a copy of Johannes de Trittenheim's *De scriptoribus ecclesiasticis* printed by Johannes de Amerbach in Basle in 1494 the following annotation is inscribed on the title-page: 'Liber Johannis Waddingi presbiteri Wexfordensis'. It may have belonged to John Wadding of the diocese of Ferns.[66]

There is a fine copy of Colgan's *Acta sanctorum Hiberniae* (Louvain, 1645) in which the following annotation appears: 'Reverendissimo Domino Fri Boetio Egano Epo Elphinensi. Reverendissmus Do: Elphinesis hunc dedit Conventui de Killconnall anno do. 1649'.[67] It has been beautifully bound in

---

63 Revd Denis Murphy, ed., *Triumphalia chronologica monasterii sanctae crucis in Hibernia*, Dublin, pr. for the editor by Sealy, Bryers & Walker, A. Thom, 1891, p. 291.   64 Anselm Faulkner, 'Papers of Anthony Gearnon, OFM' in *Collectanea Hibernica*, General editor, Benignus Millett, Dublin, Clonmore & Reynolds, nos. 6 and 7, 1963–4, pp 212–24. (For further reading on Anthony Gearnon see above journal which also includes Benignus Millett's 'Calendar of Volume I [1625–68] of the collection Scritture riferite nei congressi, Irlanda, in Propaganda archives', pp 20–211.)   65 Cathaldus Giblin, 'Catalogue of material of Irish interest in the collection Nunziatura di Fiandra', Vatican archives, part 3, vols 81–101. In *Collectanea Hibernica*, 4, 1961, p. 53 and *Collectanea Hibernica*, 17, 1974–5, p. 51.   66 'Students of the Irish College, Salamanca 1595–1619' in *Archivium Hibernicum*, ii, 1913, pp 9–10.   67 Revd C.P. Meehan, *The rise and fall*

6 Title-page of Dr Cornelius Nary's *New Testament* (1719).

a fine reddish brown calf with blind tooling on the upper and lower covers.
From the type of crested roll used it could possibly have been bound by one
of the unidentified London binders.[68]

While the provenance of these books is sometimes curious and intriguing,
we think that the most interesting book in the library associated with those
difficult days was donated by the author himself, Dr Cornelius Nary, in

of the Irish Franciscan monasteries, 4th ed., Dublin, James Duffy, 1872. See page 361 for the following
reference to Bishop Egan: 'He passed the last two years of his life in the monastery of Kilconnell'.
68 See J.B. Oldham, *Shrewsbury school library bindings*, Oxford, At the University Press, 1943, p. 66,
D.IV.15 and Pl.LVI, D.IV.15 (1) and A.III. 10. Pl.XVI.

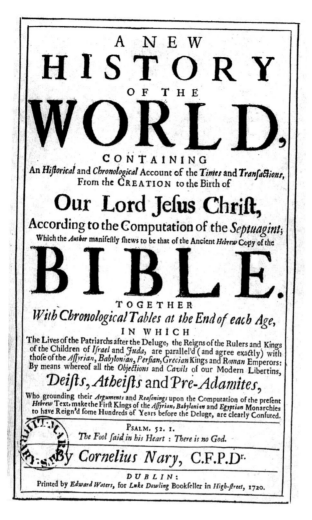

A NEW

HISTORY

OF THE

WORLD,

CONTAINING

An *Hiftorical* and *Chronological* Account of the *Times* and *Tranfactions*, From the CREATION to the Birth of

Our Lord Jefus Chrift,

According to the Computation of the *Septuagint;*

Which the *Author* manifeftly fhews to be that of the Ancient *Hebrew* Copy of the

BIBLE.

TOGETHER

With Chronological Tables at the End of each Age,

IN WHICH

The Lives of the Patriarchs after the Deluge, the Reigns of the Rulers and Kings of the Children of *Ifrael* and *Juda*, are parallel'd (and agree exactly) with thofe of the *Affyrian, Babylonian, Perfian, Grecian* Kings and *Roman* Emperors: By means whereof all the *Objections* and *Cavils* of our Modern Libertins,

Deifts, Atheifts and *Pre-Adamites,*

Who grounding their *Arguments* and *Reafonings* upon the Computation of the prefent *Hebrew* Text, make the Firft Kings of the *Affyrian, Babylonian* and *Egyptian* Monarchies to have Reign'd fome Hundreds of Years before the Deluge, are clearly Confuted.

PSALM. 52. I.

The Fool faid in his Heart : There is no God.

By Cornelius Nary, C.F.P.D[r].

DUBLIN:

Printed by *Edward Waters,* for *Luke Dowling* Bookfeller in *High-ftreet,* 1720.

7 Title-page of Cornelius Nary's *A new history of the world* (Dublin, 1720).

1720. Dr Nary was parish priest of St Michan's from 1700 to 1738.[69] The penal laws in the early part of the eighteenth century were being enforced against the Catholic population and Dr Nary was compelled to go 'on the run'. According to Bishop Donnelly, Dr Nary spent most of his time hiding

---

69 [Nicholas Donnelly], bishop of Canea, *Short histories of Dublin parishes*, Dublin, Catholic Truth Society of Ireland, 1912, pp 50–5. See also the following: John Meagher, 'Glimpses of eighteenth century priests' in *Repertorium Novum*, ii, no. 1, 1957–58, pp 129–47; John Kingston, 'Catholic families of the Pale' in *Repertorium Novum*, ii, no. 2, 1959–60, pp 254–5; Mary Purcell, 'Those were the days' in *The Bulletin*, Dublin diocesan press office, vol. 8, no. 8, Oct. 1974, p. 8; and Patrick Fagan, *Dublin's turbulent priest: Cornelius Nary 1658–1738*, Dublin, Royal Irish Academy, 1992, p. 79.

in Marsh's Library where he continued with his important literary activities and presumably writing his *A new history of the world*, a copy of which he presented to Marsh's. It was indeed an extraordinary ironic turn of events that Dr Nary should have been given shelter in the same library whose founder was himself responsible for writing some of the penal laws.

But not all the books in the library have such a tragic background. Marsh brought his own books with him from Oxford, and his own collection includes his school books which also contain the signature of his brother Onesiphorus. He may also have brought over with him three books which are marked Bodleian Library duplicates.

For the purchase of Hebrew books Marsh was in correspondence[70] with a Mr Aron Moses, and the Hebrew collection is one of the most valuable in the library. Marsh was a great admirer of the Dutch divine James Trigland (*d.*1705). Trigland like Marsh was an orientalist and became professor in Leiden. Two books written by James Trigland are in Marsh's own collection although curiously they do not bear his motto even though he specifically mentions these books in his correspondence.

The bishop of Clogher, John Stearne (*d.*1745), bequeathed his books to Marsh's Library in 1745 'as a small token of the great regard I have for the bountiful erector and endower of the library'.[71] There were about 3000 books in this bequest although it appears that he had already given many of his books to Marsh's. According to the *DNB,* Bishop Stearne bought many books at the sale held by the London bookseller, John Dunton, which was held in Dublin in 1698. A book in his collection entitled *Catalogue of discourses for and against popery in the time of King James II* (London, 1735), by Francis Peck, is an interleaved copy with extensive notes relating to books. It was, I think, annotated by Bishop Stearne himself.

Dr Elias Bouhéreau gave all his books to Marsh's Library when he was made the first librarian in 1701. Elias Bouhéreau was born in La Rochelle on 5 May 1643. He was the only surviving son of Elie Bouhéreau, a pastor and president of the Protestant consistory at La Rochelle. The Bouhéreaus were an important family and seem to have been fairly wealthy. Bouhéreau was sent to study at Saumur, one of the most renowned Protestant academies in France. Afterwards he took the degree of MD at the university of Orange. He married his cousin Marguerite Massiot on 4 November

70 Marsh's correspondence on microfilm in Marsh's Library.   **71** Newport J.D. White, op. cit., p. 9.

1668. They had seven children and at least two others who died before Bouhéreau left France.[72]

Dr Bouhéreau's library represents a typical scholar's library of the seventeenth century. Religious controversy, history, politics, science, medicine and many of the classical authors are well represented. Dr Jean-Paul Pittion in his article in *Long Room* said that Dr Bouhéreau's books 'constitute a unique source of information for the study of Calvinism in seventeenth century France'.[73]

One of the best-known Protestant writers on theology was the professor of theology at Saumur, Moïse Amyraut (*d.*1664). Dr Bouhéreau collected most of Amyraut's writings and many similar Protestant theological writers for his library. While a great many of Dr Bouhéreau's books are concerned with controversial continental theology there is also an interesting collection of medical books. Many of these are extensively annotated by Dr Bouhéreau and he also noted the prices which he paid for them. Some of the books have previous owners' signatures including Tanaquil Faber (or Taneguy le Fèvre), Madame Dacier's father, but these signatures and some of Bouhéreau's books are mainly of interest to French scholars who regularly correspond with or visit the library.

Dr Bouhéreau's books have possibly the most fascinating and romantic history of all the books in the library.[74] After the revocation of the edict of Nantes, life became impossible for the Protestants, and Dr Bouhéreau knew that his books would be regarded as heretical and liable to be burned by the common hangman. He was determined to save them. He went to Paris to see the English ambassador and arranged a pretended sale to him.[75] The ambassador got them out of France and brought them to England.

Bouhéreau also managed to escape with his family and arrived in England in January, 1686. (After his escape Bouhéreau was hanged in effigy by the authorities in La Rochelle.) He was first employed as secretary to Thomas Cox, envoy to the Swiss Cantons, and subsequently in Piedmont to

72 Details from Newport J.D. White, *Four good men* (No. 4, Elias Bouhéreau), Dublin, Hodges Figgis, 1927, pp 56–97. See also Muriel McCarthy, 'Elie Bouhéreau, first public librarian in Ireland' in *Proceedings of the Huguenot Society*, xxvii, no. 4, 2001, pp 543–60. **73** Jean-Paul Pittion, 'Notes for a Saumur bibliography' in *Long Room*, 2, Spring 1971, pp 9–22. **74** See Newport J.D. White, op. cit. (reprinted with some corrections, omissions and additions, from *PRIA*, xxvii, C4, 1908.) See also Newport J.D. White, 'Gleanings from the correspondence of a great Huguenot'. Reprinted from *Proceedings of the Huguenot Society of London*, 1910, ix, no. 2 (1910). **75** Newport J.D. White, *Four good men*, pp 79–81.

Henri de Massue de Ruvigny, deputy general of the Huguenots. Henri de Massue de Ruvigny was later made Lord Galway and one of the lords justices of Ireland, 1697–1701. Dr Bouhéreau accompanied Lord Galway to Ireland where he met Archbishop Marsh who was also one of the lords justices at this period.

In the correspondence between Dr Bouhéreau and John Ellis (1643?–1738) the under-secretary of state in England,[76] Bouhéreau mentions the public library and the proposals for his pension as librarian. Bouhéreau showed great anxiety concerning the granting of this pension and often refers to it in the letters as his 'petite affaire'. In one letter he said 'Le repos du reste de ma vie dépend du succés de cette affaire.'[77] It is also obvious from this correspondence that many important people were engaged to use their influence in England to secure this pension for Bouhéreau, including John Ellis himself, and Lord Galway, Sir Stephen Cox, the archbishop of Canterbury, and the secretary of state, James Vernon.

Although the library therefore is made up of four separate collections, they make a homogeneous collection because they were formed at the same time, during the latter half of the seventeenth century .The collectors were men of similar tastes and interests, and while this is reflected in their collections their own individual interests are also evident.

Stillingfleet was interested in history, antiquities, religious controversy and travel. Marsh was interested in science and mathematics but particularly in

---

76 This correspondence between Dr Elias Bouhéreau and John Ellis, the under-secretary of state in England, is in the British Library. The reference is in the *Index to the catalogue of additions to the manuscripts in the British Museum*, British Museum, 1880. Bouhéreau, Elie, M.D. secretary to Lord Galway, letters to J. Ellis 1697–1704, Fr. 28, 881–28, 894 passim. (Now on microfilm in Marsh's Library.) This correspondence is mainly a business correspondence. Bouhéreau notes the arrival and sending of 'paquets'. He seems to have been on very friendly terms with Ellis and sometimes writes about events in Ireland. In one letter he describes the effect of small pox on the lord lieutenant's wife, Lady Betty Berkeley (letter No 345, 31 Aug. 1700) and Lord Galway's attacks of gout (letter no. 259, July 1700 and letter no. 288). Bouhéreau was also very interested in the proposed changes in the calendar.   **77** Letter no. 181 dated 27 April 1700. Bouhéreau wrote almost all his letters in French. Some letters were written from Chapelizod, although he may not have lived there. (He began to live in the keeper's apartments in Marsh's Library on 16 Dec. 1703. From page 111, Bouhéreau's diary 1689–1719. Marsh pressmark MS Z2.2.2.) According to J.G. Simms in *Huguenot Portarlington*, p. 12, the duke of Ormond had set up the French linen weavers there. It seems likely that Bouhéreau may have acted as an interpreter for the refugees. For further references to Dr Bouhéreau's appointment as secretary to the lords justices see J.C. Sainty, 'The secretariat of the chief governors of Ireland, 1690–1800' in *PRIA* 77, C, no. 1, 1977, pp 13 and 19. See also MS Z1.1.16(2) in Marsh's Library, Copy of 'An establishment, or list containing all payments to be made for civill and military affairs in Ireland', Elias Bouhéreau's pension £200.00, on p. 6. (This copy was made by Dr Robert Travers.) See also Bodleian Library MS

oriental languages. Bishop Stearne had interests similar to those of Stillingfleet and Marsh. I have already mentioned Bouhéreau's special interests although the French books in the library are not found merely in Bouhéreau's collection. Stillingfleet also collected French books.

There is a small collection of manuscripts in the library which relate mainly to Irish history and ecclesiastical history. Marsh purchased all Dudley Loftus' manuscripts.[78] These included Irish historical and oriental manuscripts. There is also a charming collection of music manuscripts from the early part of the seventeenth century. Although Marsh did make some attempts to buy Bishop Stillingfleet's manuscripts, he considered that as they mostly related to English affairs they were not worth the amount of money which was being asked for them.[79]

When Narcissus Marsh lived in Oxford he formed part of a scholarly oriental circle which included such distinguished orientalists as Dr Edward Bernard and Dr Edward Pococke. Dr Pococke was the first Oxford professor of Arabic. Other friends included Dr Joseph Maynard, the rector of Lincoln College, and Dr Thomas Hyde, who was librarian of the Bodleian and Laudian professor of Arabic. Another friend was John James Buxtorf, professor of oriental languages in Basle, a member of one of the most distinguished families noted for their scholarly writings. Buxtorf gave Marsh a present of a Hebrew Bible and wrote on the lower endpapers in Latin, 'These few words to the most distinguished man ... in every branch of learning, particularly in oriental philology, most versed.' Dr Robert Huntington, the well-known orientalist who succeeded Marsh as provost of Trinity College, was also a friend and helped Marsh with the first translation of the Old Testament into the Irish language.

To get an idea of the richness of Archbishop Marsh's oriental collection it is important to examine Dr Edward Bernard's *Catalogi librorum manuscriptorum Angliae et Hiberniae* (Oxford, 1697) pt 2, pp 52–6. This catalogue includes Marsh's oriental manuscripts and shows the fine collection of over 500 manuscripts in Hebrew, Syriac, Arabic, Turkish, Armenian, Russian, Persian, Coptic and Greek and Latin which Marsh had. As one might expect

Rawl. D 359, described by C. McNeill in *Analecta Hibernica* ii (1931), p. 84. **78** Bodleian Library, MS Smith 45. Letter from Narcissus Marsh to Dr T. Smith 26 Nov. 1695. (Photostat in Marsh's Library.) **79** *Christian Examiner*, Nov. 1833, no. xxiv, p. 762. Letter from Marsh to Dr Smith, 19 Jan. 1706. There is also in Marsh's a photostat list of Stillingfleet's manuscripts, Rawl. D 878 in Bodleian Library.

there are manuscripts on subjects such as the liturgy, medicine, music, history, astronomy, poetry, law, grammar, mathematics and theology. According to Dr Colin Wakefield, some of these manuscripts, such as Qur'an fragments in Kufic script on vellum and a magnificent copy of Apollonius' *Conics*, are notable for their antiquity and beauty.[80]

Marsh left his great collection of oriental manuscripts to the Bodleian Library[81] and these included some manuscripts which had belonged to Dudley Loftus (*d.*1695). Marsh said in his will, 'My Oriental Mss with the boxes made for them I give to the Bodleian Library at Oxford.'

But Archbishop Marsh was not only interested in oriental manuscripts. In 1679, when he was appointed provost of Trinity College, he became interested in Irish manuscripts and later, when he was archbishop of Dublin, he wrote a letter to his friend Dr Arthur Charlett, master of University College, Oxford,[82] in which he gave a fascinating and detailed description of what he referred to as 'St Columbkille's Gospells'. Marsh said that he employed a limner to copy a part of the book in order to send a specimen to Dr Charlett. But the limner delayed so long that he himself was sending the specimen with some corrections and 'indeed have mended with my pen almost every letter after ye Limmer'. Marsh said that he was using a magnifying glass 'so yt yu will hardly every get a more exact draft yn this. When I say ye Copy is exact; I intend it as to ye magnitude of ye Letters.' In this letter he discusses the ligatures, the antiquity of the writing, the manner of it, verses and the divisions. Marsh also said that 'I cannot say, that they exactly correspond with your St Jerome's Epistles to Damascus'. He also transcribed an inscription in Latin and Irish signed by Ro. O'Flaherty. Marsh explained that when he was provost of Trinity College he had seen a silver cross on the cover of the book, 'But in ye time of ye late revolution yt ornamental silver cross was taken away; and 'tis well ye Book itself was preserv'd, wch now is bound up in a plain brown rough Lethern cover in 4to.' Dr William O'Sullivan believed that the manuscript which Marsh described was the book of Durrow.[83]

80 Colin Wakefield, 'Arabic manuscripts in the Bodleian Library' in G.A. Russell, ed., *The 'Arabick' interest of the natural philosophers in seventeenth-century England*, Leiden, 1994, p. 137.   81 Richard Mant, op. cit., letter from Marsh to Dr Smith, 4 May 1700, p. 111.But see also G.E.C. [i.e. George E. Cokayne] compiler, *Some notice of various families of the name of Marsh*, Exeter, W. Pollard, 1900 [*The Genealogist*, new series, vol. 16, Suppl.] p. 41, 'My Oriental MSS with the boxes made for them I give to the Bodleian Library at Oxford'.   82 Letter from Archbishop Marsh to Dr Charlett, 30 Nov. 1699. Seventy-two original letters and papers from Archbishop Marsh etc. to Dr Charlett, vol. 8, Bodleian Library, Ballard 8, fol. 6–7.   83 William O'Sullivan, 'The donor of the Book of Kells' in *Irish Historical Studies*, xi, no. 41,

There is no doubt that Marsh's oriental manuscripts in the Bodleian Library, together with his own printed books in Marsh's Library and his purchase of Bishop Edward Stillingfleet's collection, demonstrate that he was one of the most scholarly and important book collectors of the late seventeenth and early eighteenth century in these islands.

The Revd D.W. Macray in his *Annals of the Bodleian* says Marsh's donation is not mentioned in the records,[84] but it is mentioned as a deathbed legacy in Hearne's preface to Camden's *Elizabeth* (p. lxvi). Archbishop William King in his funeral sermon in St Patrick's Cathedral after Marsh's death said, 'His manuscripts, that are valued to several hundreds of pounds, he had promised long ago to Oxford, and they are left accordingly by his will.'[85]

Archbishop Marsh was just as expert and discerning in buying manuscripts as he was in buying books. He says in his diary in 1696 that he gave Dr Edward Bernard (*d*.1696) £220 to go to Holland and purchase on his behalf the choicest of Jacobus Golius' manuscripts which were being sold at Leiden.[86] This had a rather sad sequel. Dr Bernard died a short time later and Marsh wrote sadly to his friend Dr Smith, blaming himself for having agreed to Dr Bernard's journey and he added he 'would never have exposed ye precious life of so dear a friend to such manifest perills for all ye manuscripts in ye world'.[87] Edward Bernard was a fine scholar, and also an expert in oriental languages. He had supervised the catalogue of manuscripts in England and Ireland, which was published after his death in 1697.

The first meeting of the governors of Marsh's Library was held on 1 July 1708 and the first visitation on 14 October of that year.[88] Mr John Moland, the primate's secretary, was ordered to take an account of the meetings.[89] Marsh must have felt well satisfied. Some of the most important and influential men in Ireland were the governors and guardians. William King was already famous as a churchman (he had succeeded Marsh as archbishop of Dublin) and his celebrated book *The state of the Protestants of Ireland* stated vigorously the cause and sufferings of the Irish Protestants under King

March 1958, pp 5–7. **84** Revd W.D. Macray, *Annals of the Bodleian Library, Oxford, 1598–1867*, London, Oxford, Cambridge, Rivingtons, 1868, pp 132–3. **85** William King, *The remembrance of the righteous in a sermon preach'd at the funeral of ... Narcissus Marsh ... November 6th, 1713*, Dublin, Andrew Crooke, 1714. **86** Archbishop Marsh's diary, 16 Sept. 1696, p. 71, MS Z2.2.3b. **87** Microfilm of Marsh's correspondence in Marsh's Library. **88** Visitation book in Marsh's Library. **89** Sir Charles Simeon King, ed., *A great archbishop of Dublin*, 1906, p. 291. (Letter from T. Lindsay, bishop of Killaloe, to the bishop of Limerick mentioning the primate's secretary, Mr Moland.)

James. Another governor, the provost of Trinity, Peter Browne, wrote a reply to John Toland's book *Christianity not mysterious*, a book which had outraged the Protestant bishops, and to which we have already referred in Chapter 1.[90]

Initially the governors were concerned only with the rules and regulations, which were partly based on the rules of the Bodleian Library. In 1714 Dr Bouhéreau presented to the governors a catalogue of his own and Bishop Stillingfleet's collection. The only catalogue made by Bouhéreau remaining in the library is a superb shelf catalogue, and is a great tribute to the first librarian. It is in fact still in use today. Appropriately for the first librarian the first book catalogued is the Paris Polyglot Bible. Unfortunately there has been some confusion regarding Bouhéreau's catalogue. Dr G. T. Stokes in his article on Marsh's Library said Bouhéreau's catalogue fulfilled 'the double purpose of a dictionary of subjects and dictionary of authors'.[91] Dr Stokes was mistaken. This is a description of the catalogue compiled by Robert Dougatt, the librarian who succeeded Bouhéreau. William King, in a letter to Edward Southwell, said the catalogue was the work of his nephew Robert Dougatt. King said that Dougatt

> has contrived & made a catalogue, the most usefull in my opinion of any extant, in it may be found every Author and every Tretise [*sic*] contain'd in book(s) in the Library on any Subject, this was an immense labour & cost him years to bring it to perfection.[92]

Dougatt's catalogue is now bound in twelve volumes, and written in three different hands, and was probably completed by John Wynne, the third librarian of Marsh's Library.

The accounts of the early meetings represent them as fairly placid and uneventful. The library does not seem to have been entirely completed, because in 1718 Dr Bouhéreau complained to the governors that the windows in the first part of the library badly needed repairs, a rather extraordinary situation for a library so recently built.

Elias Bouhéreau continued as librarian of Marsh's with the assistance of his son John until his death in 1719. Bouhéreau was succeeded by Robert Dougatt, who was archdeacon of Dublin, and as already mentioned

90 G.Y. Goldberg, *Jonathan Swift and contemporary Cork*, Cork, Mercier Press, 1967, pp 67–8. See also A.R. Winnett, *Peter Browne*, London, S.P.C.K., 1974.   **91** G.T. Stokes, *Some worthies of the Irish church*, p. 119.   **92** Sir Charles Simeon King, ed., op. cit., letter from Archbishop King to Rt Hon. Edward Southwell, 9 Dec. 1727, pp 261–2.

Archbishop King's nephew. Archbishop King had a very high opinion of his nephew and said the reason he made Dougatt keeper, or librarian, of St Sepulchre's (as the library seems to have been called for many years) was 'because he understood the Oriental languages, and besides that was an universal Scholar, & so most fit of any I cou'd get'.[93]

One year after Dougatt's appointment he reported to the governors the repairs which he had been obliged to carry out at his own expense. These included enlarging the stairs, and carrying out repairs to the outside offices.[94] Robert Dougatt was librarian for eleven years and was succeeded in 1730 by the Revd John Wynne. John Wynne (*d.*1762) was quite an important man in Dublin at this time. He was a member of the Charitable Musical Society and a governor and trustee of Mercer's Hospital.[95] He was precentor of St Patrick's Cathedral while Jonathan Swift was dean, and during Swift's last illness he was appointed sub-dean and was influential in getting the choir of St Patrick's to sing in the first performance of 'Messiah'.

The first hint of trouble arises eight years later when John Wynne reported to the governors that 'a great number of books ... were very lately stolen out of the Library and that many other books were abused and rendered imperfect by having whole tracts, Maps, Pictures etc., tore out of them'. The governors ordered 'that if any person shall be detected, to have stolen, defaced, inter-lined or tore any book belonging to the said Library, he shall be prosecuted with the utmost rigor of Law without any Expectation of pardon'.[96]

Unfortunately the same complaint about the loss of books continues in Marsh's and the governors ordered the manuscripts to be deposited in the 'cages' for greater security.[97] These included 38 manuscripts which had

---

93 Ibid. Archbishop King's letter to Francis Annesley, M.P. 1 Dec. 1719, p. 53.   **94** Visitation book, information from account of the visitation held in 1720.   **95** Horatio Townsend, *An account of the visit of Handel to Dublin*, Dublin, James McGlashan, 1852, p. 46 and pp 56–7. John Wynne also seems to have allowed various meetings and disputations in Marsh's. See Louis Hyman, *The Jews of Ireland*, London/Jerusalem, 1972; on p. 39 the following appears: 'In the presence of the Rev. Dr Thomas Sheridan, friend and mentor of Swift and grandfather of Richard Brinsley Sheridan, the playwright, the Rev. John Alexander and other Hebrew scholars, Judah [Abraham Judah was lecturer in Hebrew in Trinity College in 1730] held a disputation in the public library of St. Sepulchre's in May 1733, with Christian Fandy, self-styled professor of Hebrew, who designed to publish a Hebrew grammar by subscription'. (Many years later when Revd Thomas Cradock was elected a governor of St Patrick's Hospital he acted as secretary to the hospital board. The minute books in St Patrick's Hospital give accounts of board meetings held in Marsh's Library as early as 1746/7. From the general board book, 29 Aug. 1746–Nov. 1796, and draft minute book, no. 5, 1797–1835, kept in St Patrick's Hospital. The board decided in 1828 to hold all future meetings in the Hospital.)   **96** Visitation book, information from account of meeting held in 1738.   **97** Ibid. Adjourned visitation meeting held in 1761.

belonged to Dudley Loftus. The governors recommended to the librarian to employ 'an honest Porter … to Watch and Search every Suspected Person that may happen to be Admitted into the Library'.[98] There is however no record of this 'honest porter' in the library. He seems to have been a pious hope with no real existence. And still the books continued to disappear.

In 1762 Thomas Cobbe was appointed librarian. Thomas Cobbe was an MP for Swords for many years.[99] He seems to have been a rather erratic librarian. Shortly after his appointment he furnished the library with a number of busts including one of Alexander Pope,[1] but it was fortunate for Marsh's that Thomas Cobbe stayed only four years. His first suggestion to the governors was that the chains which had been placed on the books many years earlier should be sold. This was agreed. These chains had at the request of Archbishop Marsh in about 1712 been put in use on the two lower shelves of all the bookcases in the library. Many visitors to the library today are curious to know how the books were chained, as the remains of the sockets can still be seen on the bookcases. Each book had a small metal clasp, attached to a chain on the end of which was a ring attached to a wooden rod. This rod was close to and parallel to the shelf to which the book belonged, and the chain was long enough to allow the book to rest on the reading-desk below.

When the chains were sold, Cobbe felt encouraged to make an even more unfortunate suggestion. At the next visitation he suggested that the beautiful seats in the Stillingfleet gallery should be sold 'as they only served to Collect Dust'. Alas, the governors agreed, and then declared the library to be in elegant order.

Thomas Cobbe was succeeded by William Blachford (prebendary of Tassaggart) who was librarian for seven years (1766–73). William Blachford is specifically mentioned by William Monck Mason in his *History of St Patrick's Cathedral* as having been a particularly good librarian.[2] More interesting, perhaps, was his beautiful daughter Mary Blachford, who before she married her cousin Henry Tighe MP was a great success socially, particularly at viceregal balls.[3] But Mary Tighe also wrote extraordinary poetry. One of her best-known pieces is an enormously long poem of about 400 nine-lined

98 Ibid. Visitation of 1747 and visitation of 1750.   99 John D'Alton, *The history of the county of Dublin*, Dublin, Hodges & Smith, 1838, p. 287.   1 Information supplied by Mr Alec Cobbe from his family's account books (1762). The bust of Alexander Pope cost £0.3s. 3d. and the bust of Shakespeare cost £0.18s. 0d.   2 W.M. Mason, op. cit., p. 14.   3 Details on Mary Blachford from *DNB* and Victoria Glendinning's article 'Mary, Mary quite contrary' published in the *Irish Times*, 7 March 1974.

8 Portrait of Mary Tighe, author of *Psyche*.

stanzas, entitled *Psyche*. It was described as a poem of 'suppressed eroticism'.
Mary announced, however, 'I have only pictured innocent love, such love as
the purest bosom might confess'. One verse might encourage readers to
decide for themselves, and judge its suppressed eroticism.

> Upon her purple couch was Psyche laid,
> Her radiant eyes a downy slumber sealed;
> In light transparent veil alone arrayed.
> Her bosom's opening charms were half revealed,
> And scarce the lucid folds her polished limbs concealed.

Success went to Mary's head and Tom Moore said, 'I regret very much to
find that she is becoming so *furieusement littéraire*; one used hardly to get a
peep at her blue stockings, but now I am afraid she shows them up to the
knee.' But Tom Moore was not the only person she irritated. Her family,
distressed by her writings, said when she became ill that her unhappiness
was caused by 'her own excessive love of admiration and desire to shine in
society, which quite withdrew her from hearth and home'. As she lay dying
her mother said, 'Oh my Mary, my Mary, the pride of literature has
destroyed you.'

William Blachford was succeeded in 1773 by William Cradock MA, prebendary of St Audoen's and archdeacon of Kilmore. William Cradock resigned three years later on being made dean of St Patrick's Cathedral and was succeeded by his brother, Thomas Cradock MA, prebendary of St Audoen's. Thus began the Cradocks' connection with Marsh's Library for almost one hundred years.

The most noticeable thing about this period in the library is the non-attendance of the governors at the annual visitations and the continuing complaint about the books being stolen. The governors in 1779 'Ordered that for the Future No Person whatever take down or read any Book but in the presence of the Librarian or the Librarian's assistant'. It is rather sad to see the number of times in the exquisite green vellum visitation book this entry appears: 'No business done as a sufficient number of Governors was not present.' Nevertheless some interesting governors did appear, including Lord Clare and Lord Norbury. Lord Norbury was at this time lord chief justice of the Common Pleas and on one occasion he took the chair and signed the visitation report.[4] Sometimes special meetings were held outside the library, usually to transact a particular piece of business, for example, the appointment of an assistant librarian. This did occur in 1798 when the meeting was held in the committee room of the house of lords, and later in the lord chancellor's chamber in the Four Courts. During these years the *Reports from the commissioners respecting the public records of Ireland, 1810–1815* were made. From the *Report by the commissioners* on Marsh's Library it appears that the library was being very well looked after.[5] It is useful perhaps to remember that many of the commissioners were also governors of Marsh's Library. In fact, when Cradock was asked by the commissioners if he could suggest any improvements for making the library more convenient to the public, he replied that he could not think of any, but if it should occur to him he would feel it his duty to inform the governors of the library.

There were some fascinating readers in Marsh's at this period, even if the library was not being particularly well run. Tom Moore was one.[6] He used to be locked into the library since he wished to work longer than the opening hours permitted, and he said, 'On these occasions I used to be

4 Visitation book. Lord Norbury's signature attached to account of the visitation held in 1806.
5 *Reports from the commissioners respecting the public records of Ireland, 1810–1815, ordered by the House of Commons, to be printed*, i, pp 323–4 and p. 444.   6 Newport J.D. White, *An account of Archbishop Marsh's Library, Dublin*, p. 19.

locked in there alone; and to the many solitary hours which I passed in hunting through the dusty tomes of this old library, I owe much of that odd and out-of-the-way sort of reading which may be found scattered through some of my earlier writings.' The novelist and dramatist Charles Robert Maturin (d.1824) also wrote in Marsh's. William Carleton mentions a visit to Marsh's Library in his *Autobiography*.[7] He tells us that 'Maturin had not only been a reader (in Marsh's) but wrote the greater portion of several of his novels on a small plain deal desk which he moved from place to place according as it suited his privacy or convenience.' Carleton also mentions an assistant librarian of Marsh's in his *Autobiography*. This was William Sisson, who Carleton says had suffered some dreadful accident and consequently had almost completely lost one of his legs; but his leg had been so well replaced that it now appeared as if he was only slightly lame. Carleton was deeply impressed with Marsh's Library and wrote that it was the first public library he had ever seen and he 'wondered at the time how such an incredible number of books could be read'. Carleton sadly noted how few people 'availed themselves of that noble institution'. But Carleton did observe one very important reader who was eventually to become one of the most remarkable men ever to be associated with Marsh's Library, Dr Robert Travers.

Thomas Cradock resigned in 1815 and was succeeded by his son, Thomas Russell Cradock MA. In 1814 the Royal Dublin Society offered the governors of Marsh's a site next to their own library for the purpose of constructing a suitable building.[8] This is indeed curious. There is no mention whatever in the visitation accounts of this proposal ever being discussed nor was there any proposal for moving, or any hint that anything was wrong. In fact in 1819 the governors reported, 'The Books appeared in perfect order and the Fabrick in staunch and sound Condition.'

One year later, in 1820, William Monck Mason published his *History of St Patrick's Cathedral*. In it he bitterly attacked the Cradock family, and he noted that not one of them was fitted to be a librarian of Marsh's Library.[9] He berated the governors for appointing such people as librarians and he

---

7 William Carleton, *The autobiography of William Carleton*, with a preface by Patrick Kavanagh, London, Macgibbon & Kee, 1968, p. 189. (It is interesting to note that in Thom's *Almanac and official directory*, 1859, under the entry for Marsh's Library, p. 662, it is stated that Goldsmith, Burke and Ledwich, as well as Moore and Maturin, read in Marsh's Library.) 8 H.F. Berry, *A history of the Royal Dublin Society*, London, Longmans Green, 1915, pp 177 and 287. 9 W.M. Mason, op. cit., p. 14.

quoted Marsh's own instructions for the qualities required of candidates. Monck Mason did take note that Marsh had not left sufficient funds to maintain the fabric, but he suggested that the governors could under the act governing the library make the librarian set aside part of his salary to repair the library. He noted that the library was rapidly falling into a state of utter ruin. This harsh criticism does not seem to have had any effect on the governors at the time, but two years later it was a very different story.

Despite Monck Mason's concern about money, a considerable sum had now accumulated in the library, and the governors (who included Lord Norbury) at the annual visitation appointed a special committee of the governors to inspect the library, purchase and repair books, and to 'report to the Board of Governors and Guardians the State of the Library as to the Fabric, the number and condition of the Books and Manuscripts therein and of the Duplicates which it may contain'.

Unless William Monck Mason was grossly exaggerating when he made his criticism of the library in 1820 the committee's report to the governors three years later is quite astonishing. They reported that 'The Books appeared in perfect Order, and the Fabric in staunch & sound Condition a considerable Sum having been laid out by the Librarian to repair the Injury done by the Storms of last Winter'.

In 1825 the annual visitation was adjourned three times and eventually it was held in the lord chancellor's house in St Stephen's Green. The governors may have known that the assistant librarian, William Sisson, intended to resign, and that the keeper, Thomas Russell Cradock, was proposing his son, Thomas Russell William Cradock, for the vacancy. Obviously they did not intend to hold the visitation until they could get a full attendance of the governors. William Monck Mason's harsh criticism which had specifically reminded the governors that at any future election the governors should remember the qualifications required for librarians in Marsh's, and that the qualifications should not be made subservient to the convenience of a private family, was not unrelated to the fact that the Cradocks lived in the library, and that they would probably be forced to leave if they held no office.[10]

The governors and guardians unanimously appointed Thomas Russell William Cradock as assistant librarian. But they were obviously unhappy

10 An act of parliament chap XIX of the 6th of Queen Anne, in the *Statutes at large passed in the parliaments held in Ireland*, p. 170, 'and hath likewise fitted and prepared the ground-rooms of the said house for the accommodation of the reverend Mr Elias Bohereau [*sic*], the present library-keeper, and

about their appointment. For the first time in the history of the library the governors added the following caution:

> That on the appointment of Every new Librarian or Assistant an Examination of the Books and State of the Books in the Library shall take place by persons appointed for the purpose by the Trustees and all deficiencies from the Catalogue noted and Returned to the Trustees.[11]

But the damage had already been done. The appointment of Thomas Russell William Cradock, who was still only a student in Trinity College, was one of the most unfortunate appointments ever made in Marsh's Library. Cradock junior was ignorant, stupid and careless. He eventually received a very undistinguished degree in Trinity College; his obvious lack of ability became clear very quickly, and his indifference almost ended Marsh's Library.

For the moment however everything seemed to have returned to normal and as usual the governors did not bother to attend the annual visitations until a special meeting was called for 15 April 1828. Even though the ink has faded in the beautiful green vellum-covered visitation book, the unusually large amount of space taken up by the account of this meeting makes its very appearance a dramatic one. Unusually too there were four governors present. The first thief had been caught, and he was a cheeky one. William Richard Underwood had not only stolen books from Marsh's and sold them elsewhere, but he himself actually had the audacity to present a book to the library; his name is written in the 'Donations book'.[12] From an examination of this presentation it is quite obvious even now that an earlier library stamp or pressmark has been erased. It is indeed quite conceivable that the book may even have belonged originally to Marsh's or some other Dublin library. The governors appear to have treated William Richard Underwood somewhat mildly (he was to 'be in future excluded from the Library'), but not so the librarians. The governors 'feel it is necessary to admonish the Librarian and the Assistant Librarian Hence forward to give more exact attention to the notice already in force relative to the Preservation of the Books'. They reiterated the notice of 1779 which said 'that no Person

his successors, keepers of the said library for ever'.   **11** Visitation book, adjourned meeting held on 22 Dec. 1825.   **12** Donations book, p. 11. Given by Mr William Underwood, 1826, Robertson's *Thesaurus linguae sanctae,* London 1680.

whatever shall for the future, take down or read any Book but in the presence of the Librarian or the Librarian's Assistant'. But they went even further; they also added, 'That no Person admitted to the Library be suffered to read any of the Books but at the publick Table, in the Librarian's Room.'[13] It makes depressing reading, but there was one bright note. The governors added their thanks to Mr Robert Travers, who 'has made laudable exertions for the Discovery of the said Thefts'. This is the first official mention by the governors of Robert Travers.

In March 1830 the governors requested the librarian to get estimates for repairing the roof and for new blinds for the library. Nothing seems to have happened as a result of these requests and the governors did not bother to attend the visitations. But at a special meeting held in March 1832 the librarian was ordered to procure estimates for binding the books and then the following suggestion was made by the governors: 'It is recommended that at the next Board the sale of the Duplicates be taken into consideration.' In May, a Mr Maguire, an auctioneer, was 'desired to print a Catalogue of the Duplicates now in the Library' and in the following October the librarian was instructed 'to communicate with Mr Maguire respecting the sale of the Duplicates at the same time as the sale of Mr Harrington's Library'. This was not a hasty decision. The fabric, in spite of earlier reports of its being in sound condition, was obviously in a bad way, particularly the roof which needed repairs. The governors do not seem to have approached the government, or made any kind of appeal, but instead took the easy way out by selling books. The Cradocks were indifferent. This one might expect, but who were the governors of Marsh's who took this fateful decision?

They were the archbishop of Dublin, Richard Whately, and the dean of St Patrick's, Richard Henry Dawson. Archbishop Whately (d. 1863) was an Englishman, who was to become one of the great bishops of the Church of Ireland.[14] He had, however, been only one year in Ireland, and may well have been ignorant of the importance of Marsh's Library. He was himself a fine writer on scholarly subjects and later made a great contribution to Irish education; he also contributed magnificently to the Irish Famine Relief Fund and voted for the Maynooth Grant. Richard Henry Dawson MA, the dean of St Patrick's, was according to Henry Cotton a liberal restorer of the cathedral, and a collector of valuable coins and medals and Irish relics of

---

13 Visitation book, meeting of the governors 15 April 1828.   14 *DNB* (Richard Whately).

antiquity.[15] He too, was interested in education. It does seem extraordinary that these two men could possibly have taken this unfortunate decision.

The auction of 'duplicates' belonging to Marsh's Library took place on Wednesday 8 May 1833; it was held by Charles Sharpe, Anglesea Street.[16] The duplicates were taken from all the collections in the library and, as many readers will have suspected, many of these so-called 'duplicates' were not duplicates at all.[17] The books sold included classical and oriental literature, grammars, lexicons, English and Irish history and ecclesiastical history, theology, liturgies, martyrologies, travel and some fine examples of early printings. One of the most important books sold was No. 268 in the catalogue, a Bordeaux *New Testament*. This book is a bit of a mystery. There is no record of its ever being in Marsh's, but it does confirm that books were added to the Marsh's books at the auction. Archdeacon Cotton bought the Bordeaux *New Testament* for £32.[18] Other well-known buyers included the Royal Irish Academy (fortunately they still have many of these books), the archbishop of Cashel, and the Revd Mr Todd. Another buyer was Robert Travers and a Mr Parnell who purchased *Nova legenda Anglie* printed by Wynkyn de Worde in 1516. Mr Parnell got this book for £2 10*s*. The total amount made at the auction when all expenses were paid appears to have been £185 16*s*. 1*d*. The governors immediately set about having the roof repaired and Mr William Sneynol was paid on 6 December 1833 the sum of £211 17*s*. 6*d*. for slating the roof etc., from which he had already deducted various amounts for keeping some old materials, and this included £20 for the materials from the old tower which he pulled down. The architect was a Mr Matthew Price.[19]

Once more Marsh's returned to its easy-going pattern. The governors attended intermittently. There was, however, one new interesting arrival. Maziere Brady as the new lord chief baron made his first appearance in

---

15 Henry Cotton, *Fasti ecclesiae Hibernicae*, ii, p. 107.   **16** *Bibliotheca Marsiana, Catalogue of books, the duplicate copies of the public library, Dublin … Sold by auction on Wednesday, May 8th 1833*, Dublin, Richard Davis Webb, MDCCCXXXIII.   **17** An example of this occurs in Blaise Pascal's *Les provinciales, or the mystery of Jesvitisme*, London, Richard Royston, 1658, 12° which was sold (no. 684 in the auction catalogue) from the Stillingfleet collection as a duplicate. This was presented back to Marsh's in 1905 by Edward Dowden. The only other copy in the library is in Archbishop Marsh's own collection and it is the 3rd edition printed by Richard Royston in 1679 in an 8° format, *Wing* P 642.   **18** Information on buyers and prices paid at the auction are taken from an annotated copy of the auction catalogue acquired by Miss M. Pollard for the library in 1968/69. This copy also contains manuscript notes made by Dr Robert Travers. There is also an auctioneer's (?) annotated copy in the British Library.   **19** Details from the accounts and receipts kept in the archives box in the library.

Marsh's at the governors' meeting in October 1841. It was also in October
1841 that the governors met to consider a proposal to allow the librarian, the
Revd Thomas Russell Cradock, to resign in favour of his son the assistant
librarian, the Revd Thomas Russell William Cradock, and to appoint Dr
Robert Travers as assistant librarian. The proposal was considered and approved
unanimously. The governors probably had great reservations about Cradock
junior, but they were already familiar with the qualifications of Dr Robert
Travers. He was a constant reader in the library and was attached to Trinity
College as a lecturer on medical jurisprudence. As we have seen he had, as
far back as 1828, been specially commended by the governors for his efforts
in catching a thief. From Dr Robert Travers' appointment in 1841 all the
visitation accounts and meetings in the library are written in his exquisite
handwriting. The dates and sometimes specially important words are written
in red ink, which provides a pleasing contrast to the slightly faded brown
ink, and the use of Roman numerals gives the vellum pages the appearance
of a medieval manuscript.

For the next few years the librarians and the governors were occupied
with the proceedings in the Rolls Court appealing for Marsh's exemption
from the poor rate.

Although Marsh's Library is the first public library in Ireland, it was never
a particularly popular library. Its very contents have limited its use to
scholars and readers interested in the more esoteric subjects, and its
unfortunate entrance through St Patrick's churchyard at this time was dreary
and depressing. The area itself was surrounded by tenements and populated
by a large and very poor population.[20] Unfortunately, too, St Patrick's
Cathedral was also in a deplorable state, but poverty and depression were not
confined to the 'Liberties'. In 1849 the worst of the Famine was over but
Ireland was still suffering from its effects and thousands were leaving the
country. A large amount of money was needed for public relief which may
have had something to do with the almost complete neglect of Marsh's
Library, which except for the RDS Library was still the only library in
Dublin open to the public.[21]

The select committee ordered by the house of commons to report on the
public libraries published its *Report* in 1849–50 and the evidence for Marsh's

---

20 T.P. O'Neill, 'A bad year in the Liberties' in *The Liberties of Dublin*, ed. Elgy Gillespie, Dublin, E. &
T. O'Brien, 1973, pp 76–83.   21 'The only free public library in the city until about 1820, when the
Royal Dublin Society first unreservedly opened its doors.' From Newport J.D. White's *An Account* ..., p. 6.

Library was given by the librarian, T.R.W. Cradock, Edward Edwards, assistant in the department of Printed Books in the British Museum, and E.R.P. Colles, a member of the Royal Dublin Society's library committee.[22]

Edward Edwards gave evidence which completely corroborated Monck Mason's remarks made nearly thirty years earlier. Edwards said the library had been mismanaged. One thousand two hundred books were missing from the foundation up to within twenty years earlier unrestricted admission had been allowed in the library, the books were unstamped and readers were permitted personally to go to the presses and take books down. But now everything was changed; the library was now under admirable management, although it was sorely cramped from lack of funds. Edwards then gave the surprising news that 915 people had visited Marsh's for the purposes of study during the past year. Edwards concluded with the report that Marsh's Library was attached to a manufacturing druggists' laboratory and was liable to be destroyed by a fire. This evidence was confirmed by the librarian who contributed the news that Marsh's Library was not even insured. Cradock did admit, however, that Dr Robert Travers, the assistant librarian, had suggested all the recent improvements in the library. These included reading at a table, and having all the books locked up. When E.R.P. Colles began his evidence, he recalled that one of the librarians in Marsh's had kept a piano in the library.

The governors in their usual way do not appear to have been in any hurry to do anything about this serious situation until 1853 when they requested the government to repair and insulate the library. From the repair accounts kept in the library[23] the librarian seems to have spent between 1842 and 1847 the sum of £498 1s. 7d. on repairs, although much of this was spent on improvements in his own quarters rather than on the fabric of the library; and it did not include the protection of the library against the danger of fire from the druggist's laboratory. In fact the earlier removal of the tower had been a bad idea in that it had given some protection to the library.

The government in replying to the governors' request seem to have suggested the removal of all the books in Marsh's Library to the proposed new Gallery of Painting, Sculpture and the Fine Arts. This suggestion was put to a special meeting of the governors in March 1856. The plans were approved and a special committee consisting of three of the governors (the

22 *Public libraries report, ordered by the House of Commons to be printed*, 9 February 1849, 2 vols, i, pp 15–16, 130–2, 160, 185–6.   23 Archives box, Marsh's Library.

lord chancellor, Maziere Brady, the Hon. Henry Pakenham, as dean of St Patrick's, and the provost of Trinity College, Richard McDonnell) was set up to confer with the trustees of the National Gallery to make all the arrangements for the removal of the books. There are no records of any discussions in the library and we have no way of knowing from the very brief accounts in the visitation book if any of the governors had reservations or protested at what was virtually the end of Marsh's Library. The governors seem to have given unanimous approval to this suggestion and made no effort whatsoever to preserve the library.[24] With some justification it could be said that the government was not prepared to help, although it was spending almost a lavish amount of money on the proposed new gallery.[25]

An entirely different view of this event is however given in the private correspondence of Dr Robert Travers to his friend Thomas Jones in Chetham's Library in Manchester.[26] From this curious correspondence it seems that not alone were the governors prepared to see the end of Marsh's Library but Travers thought it was part of a deliberate conspiracy. Robert Travers was indeed outraged that the library he had worked in for thirty years was about to disappear without any effort being made to save it, and in a letter to Thomas Jones dated 2 October 1854 he said:

> The subversion of the Library at St Patrick's might yet be prevented if the Trustees were faithful – but I apprehend the greatest danger is from themselves – some at least of them are not aware of the esoteric motives of the Scheme – it is really an act of hostility to the Church as well as one of spoliation'.

Travers then told Jones that he hoped to have dinner with Archbishop Whately and might get an opportunity to discuss the matter.

He does not appear to have been able to do this because on 3 November he wrote:

---

24 Visitation book, 1856.   **25** Thom's *Irish almanac and official directory*, Dublin, 1863, p. 852. The following amounts for the gallery are given: Dargan fund, £5000, from parliament £21,000 and for the purchase of paintings £2500.   **26** All the information concerning the proposed removal, and later information on the Cradock family in Marsh's is contained in Dr Robert Travers's correspondence to his friend, Thomas Jones, in Chetham's Library, Manchester, from 1848 to 1875, MS.A4.26. Xerox copies kept in Marsh's Library. Unfortunately Thomas Jones' replies to Robert Travers have not been traced. See also article by Muriel McCarthy on 'Dr Robert Travers and the Wilde libel case' in *Dublin Historical Record*, l, no. 2, Autumn 1997, pp 171–88.

> The Scheme for misappropriating the Library originates not in Hero-Worship, but in Rascal-Worship, which is, dextrously applied by the R. Catholic party to the extinguishment of an Institution which would always be an undeniable evidence of the generosity and public spirit of a prelate of the Established Church. Something to avert the catastrophe might yet be effected by disclosing to public view this esoteric motive of the projected removal, for which public convenience is falsely made the pretext – the more this is known the better.

Strong words, and a strange accusation. Since Catholic Emancipation many of the important legal positions in the state were available to Catholics, which meant that there were now governors in Marsh's who were Catholics. These were the chief justice of the Common Pleas, Henry Monahan, and the lord chief baron, David Pigot. But when the decision to accept the government's offer to remove the books to the National Gallery was made, neither of these men was at the meeting, and they were not appointed to the subcommittee to deal with the matter. Richard McDonnell, the provost of TCD, seems another unlikely person; he is remembered in Trinity more for the success of his financial administration than for anything else.[27] If there was a conspiracy, and Travers was convinced there was, then one very important name does crop up consistently in the library throughout this period, the lord chancellor, Maziere Brady.

Maziere Brady (d.1871) was the most regular attender of the meetings in the library at this time. As lord chancellor he was a very influential man, and he was connected with important societies and organisations, including the National Board of Education. He was vice-chancellor of the Queen's University and president of the Irish Art Union, but probably most significant of all he was chairman of the governors of the new National Gallery. F. Elrington Ball said that Brady 'was a protestant liberal of an advanced type' and he also said that Brady had become confidential adviser at Dublin Castle.[28]

Robert Travers never mentions any names in his accusations, and as far as we know he was on good terms with the governors, and with the most important governor of all, the archbishop of Dublin, Richard Whately. Whately may well have had an ambivalent attitude to the proposed removal.

---

27 Constantia Maxwell, *A history of Trinity College Dublin, 1591–1892*, Dublin, the University Press, 1946, p. 215. **28** F.E. Ball, *The judges in Ireland, 1221–1921*, 2 vols, New York, E.P. Dutton, 1927, ii, pp 284 and 434.

He may have been influenced by the deplorable condition of the building, and he was certainly aware of the ineptitude and stupidity of the librarian, Thomas Russell William Cradock. He also seems to have been indifferent to Marsh's as a public library and an institution in its own right. In 1834 he had considered, with the lord lieutenant, Lord Wellesley, using Marsh's Library and the Palace of St Sepulchre as an extension of the Divinity College in Trinity College. But because of opposition from the authorities in Trinity College, Whately changed his mind and decided on an independent establishment to be situated in another old archbishop's palace in Tallaght. This idea also met with strong opposition and the plan, to Whately's bitter disappointment, was dropped.[29]

But a stronger reason for his apathy may well have been that during the year of 1856 he had suffered a stroke which had affected the use of his leg and arm. We have seen that as a newly arrived archbishop in 1833 he had not objected apparently to the auction of the 'duplicates' but now, when the removal of the library was under consideration, he did at least give Travers the opportunity of stating his objections before the governors' meeting in October.

When the chief baron, David Pigot, came into the library for this visitation, Whately told Pigot that Travers objected to the removal. Curiously, Travers wrote that when asked for his reasons for objecting he 'thought it more prudent however to mention but one'. This was that there was not sufficient space allotted for the books in the new gallery. Travers wrote: 'the Chief Baron appearing much surprised said that if that were so it would put an end to the proposed removal'. Pigot then asked Travers how such a blunder could have been committed. Travers replied that those concerned in the plan knew nothing of the library. At this point the librarian, Cradock, whom Travers noted had not been asked for any opinion, contradicted Travers and said that a Mr Mulveany (as he improperly pronounced Mulvany) had measured the shelving. (Travers also noted that Cradock 'omitted to state that this did not occur till about twelve months after the Act had been hurried through Parliament'.)[30] George F. Mulvany's arrival to measure the

29 E.J. Whately, *Life and correspondence of Richard Whately, D.D.*, 2 vols, London, Longmans Green, 1866, i, pp 217 and 434. See also, 'The Kevin-street College' in *Dublin University Magazine*, no. xviii, June 1834, vol. III, pp 695–712.   **30** Letter from Robert Travers to Thomas Jones, 20 Oct. 1856. It would appear from Catherine de Courcy's book, *The foundation of the National Gallery of Ireland* (National Gallery of Ireland, 1985) that Lord Chief Baron David Pigot and his son John, together with Lord Talbot de Malahide, were particularly interested in moving the books in Marsh's Library to the new

shelving is particularly interesting. He was an artist and, like the lord chancellor, was connected with the National Gallery. Indeed he was the first director to be elected (in 1854).[31]

The librarian was apparently in full agreement with the proposed removal, in spite of the fact that after the removal the building would be sold leaving him with nowhere to live. But according to Travers, Cradock had deluded himself that he would be given a house in Merrion Square as a compensation. He had also attended the laying of the foundation stone of the new gallery, which Travers considered an act of treachery. At this stage the removal of the library appears to have been a foregone conclusion and the governors do not seem even to have discussed it any further.

In January 1862 a thief was caught pawning books which he had stolen from Marsh's Library and other libraries. He was George S. Mathews from Summerhill Parade, and this time the governors were not disposed to be so lenient. Mathews was prosecuted and sentenced to twelve months in prison with hard labour.[32]

The situation however was not as melancholy as it appeared to be. The Revd James Henthorn Todd and Archdeacon Cotton were interested in Marsh's and, more importantly, so was Benjamin Lee Guinness who did not approve of the plans for the removal.

He was at this time restoring St Patrick's Cathedral and was anxious to build a new road to it. Whether it was through Robert Travers' influence or not, and I think it must have been, Benjamin Lee Guinness wrote to the governors of the library on 21 February 1862 offering to build a new road across the passage to the library and to connect Kevin Street with the South Close of the cathedral.[33] Guinness suggested that this would improve the entrance to Marsh's Library, which had always been unpopular.[34] He concluded his letter somewhat tartly, when he suggested that if the governors agreed to his proposal they might be induced to leave the library where the founder had intended it and that the influential governors might exert

National Gallery. **31** *DNB* (George F. Mulvany). **32** A full account of this incident was written by Robert Travers in the Visitors' book, 1826–33, ff 56–7. **33** A copy of this important letter was written into the Visitation book by Robert Travers. **34** Newport J.D. White, *An Account* ..., p. 8, gives the following description of the original entrance: 'When Marsh built this house there was no direct access to it from the public street. The South Close did not extend beyond Chapter Lane, then Mitre Lane. The Dean and Chapter accordingly permitted the formation of a walled passage about nine feet wide, from the Close, opposite the transept, through the churchyard, to the corner of the library, on the west side of which the porch stood. There was also, later, a passage to the back of the library from Bride Street.'

themselves to apply for assistance for the library. Then with typical generosity
Guinness offered £1000 government stock in trust, the interest to apply for
the preservation and purchase of books, and the maintenance of the building.
He also intended to build a porch and to make some repairs to the building.

A special meeting of the governors was called by Archbishop Whately for
the following day.[35] The lord chancellor, Maziere Brady, and the chief justice
of the Common Pleas, James Henry Monahan, attended as well as the
provost of Trinity College, Richard McDonnell. The governors discussed
Mr Guinness' magnificent offer and approved the building of the new road
to the cathedral. The governors concluded, 'the other matters stated in Mr
Guinness's Letter be reserved for future consideration'. It would certainly
seem to give substance to Robert Travers' belief about a conspiracy against
the library, and indeed Travers did write to his friend Thomas Jones that 'the
Governors have neither accepted nor rejected this offer, there being still a
party desirous of subverting the establishment by transferring the books to
the new National Gallery'.[36]

It was nine months before the next visitation, although the archbishop
could call a meeting at any time. At the visitation in October the receipt for
the return of the documents relating to the Protestant consistory at La
Rochelle was produced. The return of these documents had been requested by
the La Rochelle consistory and Archbishop Whately agreed to their request.
Originally these documents had been brought to Marsh's Library by the first
librarian, Dr Bouhéreau, when he fled from France. Then the governors
discussed Jasper Robert Joly's offer of his library and this was refused.[37] The
refusal of this library was a pity as it contained a very fine collection of books,
many of which would have fitted in very well with the books in Marsh's.

Although some of the governors of Marsh's for reasons best known to
themselves appeared to be hesitating about accepting Benjamin Lee
Guinness' offer, this certainly does not apply to the dean of St Patrick's. He
must have been in a difficult position. Guinness was magnificently restoring
the cathedral and was about to do the same for Marsh's, and yet Marsh's
governors were hesitating. It was at this visitation that the governors
received and discussed the memorial from the dean and chapter of St
Patrick's against the proposed removal.[38] But still they made no decision.

35 Visitation book. Special meeting held on Saturday, 22 Feb. 1862.   36 Letter from Robert Travers to
Thomas Jones, 26 March 1862.   37 This fine collection is now in the National Library of Ireland.
38 Visitation book, 1862.

At the next visitation in the following October 1863 only the lord chancellor, Maziere Brady, turned up. Archbishop Whately was extremely ill and he did in fact die that day. The dean of St Patrick's may also have been ill; he too died a short time later. Whatever the reasons, still no reply was made to Mr Guinness.

The new year 1864 started well for the library. The new archbishop of Dublin was Richard Chenevix Trench (d.1886). He was a fine scholar and a prolific writer. The assistant librarian, Robert Travers, had been appointed professor of medical jurisprudence in Trinity College. Richard Chenevix Trench called a special meeting of the governors of the library for 28 July to consider Mr Guinness' offer. The new dean of St Patrick's, John West (d.1899), and the provost of Trinity College, Richard McDonnell, also attended. But strangely enough the lord chancellor did not. This meeting was adjourned for one week until 4 August. At the adjourned meeting the archbishop drew up a memorial which was sent to the lord lieutenant soliciting his influence in procuring an act of parliament 'to repeal so much of the National Gallery Ireland Act as relates to this Library'.

The following October the only governors to attend the visitation were the lord chancellor and the dean of St Patrick's. In January the lord lieutenant's reply was received saying he had no objection and he referred the governors to Mr Guinness' offer.[39] Another meeting was held on 3 January 1866 to consider Guinness' renewed offer (he had already transferred £1000 in government stock to the library) and his enquiry 'at what time it would be most expedient to commence the work'. The archbishop drafted an immediate reply telling Mr Guinness 'to commence the work of reparation whenever he pleases'. And so the work began after ten years of the most extraordinary behaviour on the part of some of the governors of the library which Robert Travers perhaps understandably saw as a plot. 'The job', he wrote, 'was contrived by some of the underlings of the late Government.'[40] (Although Travers saw the proposed removal of Marsh's Library to the new National Gallery as a Catholic plot to deny the generosity of a Protestant archbishop to provide a public library, an examination of Colonel Larcom's letterbooks in the archives of the National Gallery reveals a much more complicated plan.)[41]

39 Letter kept in archives box, Marsh's Library. 40 Letter from Robert Travers to Thomas Jones, 22 Feb. 1859. 41 See Colonel T.A. Larcom's letterbooks in the archives of the National Gallery, 2 vols. See also Catherine de Courcy, *The foundation of the National Gallery of Ireland*, Dublin, National Gallery of Ireland, 1985. The idea of incorporating the books in Marsh's into a new public library in the

By the end of 1866 most of the repairs had been completed.[42] Marsh's was separated from the manufacturing druggist's laboratory (Mr Leslie's Concerns); the handsome new entrance was built and the inscription was designed by Robert Travers. Travers wanted to include a reference to Guinness in the inscription, but he refused to allow it.[43] Marsh's Library was structurally safe at long last and was fortunately to remain so for a very long time indeed.

Everything returned to normal, and the governors as usual rarely attended the visitations. While the fabric at least was safe, the keeper was still Thomas Russell William Cradock. All the information about Cradock is contained in the private correspondence of Robert Travers to his friend Thomas Jones.

National Gallery, together with making the Royal Dublin Society library auxiliary to Marsh's, was supported by some of the most important state officials and heads of institutions. Two of these were governors of Marsh's: the lord chief baron, David Pigot, and the lord chancellor, Maziere Brady. Others included Lord Talbot de Malahide, president of the Irish Institution; Richard Griffith, chairman of the Board of Works; Sir John Young, chief secretary and privy councillor; George Roe, chairman of the Dargan committee; and Colonel Thomas Larcom, under-secretary. This group was obviously influenced by the dilapidated condition of the library which had been described in a letter to *Saunders Newsletter* on 9 August 1854 as 'at present buried in cobwebs and obscurity'. The chief baron and the lord chancellor as governors of the library were even more familiar with the condition of the building, its lack of funding and the ignorance and indifference of the librarian T.R.W. Cradock. It is clear from a letter written by another governor of the library, the primate Lord John Beresford, to Sir John Young that he too approved of the proposed removal of Marsh's although he also expressed concern that the resident librarian should be provided with accommodation. The chief baron David Pigot thought the building should be sold and the proceeds used to purchase a house for the librarian. Pigot was also dismissive of the governors of the library. He told Colonel Larcom that the governors of Marsh's consisted of four ecclesiastics and four lawyers 'and with the most profound respect for both professions, I think they ought not to be the exclusive directors of literature'. The individuals involved in the plan to move Marsh's to the National Gallery believed that this would add to the importance of the gallery. But they seemed unaware that Marsh's as a rare and early printed books collection was mainly used for reference by academics and scholars and would therefore have been unsuitable as the basis for a new public library. They also did not seem to realise that although it was a public library Marsh's was never a lending library. Neither did it receive public funding, except for £26 2s 8d for the deputy librarian. In spite of the efforts of Sir John Young, Maziere Brady and David Pigot to incorporate Marsh's Library into the new National Gallery it proved to be an impossible task. This was due to the conflicts between the various institutions who were also involved in the plans for the gallery regarding land, funding and the act of parliament. The scheme failed mainly because it became apparent that there was not sufficient space in the gallery for Marsh's collection. Even more important was Sir Benjamin Lee Guinness' offer to restore Marsh's Library which really put an end to the plan. However, the abandonment of the plan was too late to have any effect on the design of the gallery and the space for the library can still be seen as part of the building as originally designed.   **42** Description of repair work contained in a letter to the editor of the *Daily Express,* 27 March 1877. The letter was signed LL.D. Unfortunately there are no records of the repairs and improvements in the library, and the late earl of Iveagh said there are no records or correspondence in the family papers. It would appear that the whole west and north side of the library was refaced with cut stone.   **43** Letters from Robert Travers to Thomas Jones, 28 May 1864 and 10 April 1865.

These letters are of course entirely one-sided; Travers was utterly contemptuous of Cradock. But even if some of the incidents which Travers describes are exaggerated (and I don't think that they are) they give such an extraordinary account of what must have been one of the most incredible keepers appointed to the library that I think they should be recorded.

The Cradock family had been in Marsh's Library since 1773 when in that year William Cradock, prebendary of St Audoen's and archdeacon of Kilmore, was made keeper. William Cradock was a nephew of the archbishop of Dublin, John Cradock (d.1778). The Cradocks were almost all committed to the church for their professions although they were connected with important families.[44] The archbishop of Dublin's only son, John Francis Cradock, changed his name to Caradoc, and was created Baron Howden (d.1839). William Cradock was made dean of St Patrick's in 1775 (it was while he was dean that the beautiful deanery was burnt down, although both himself and the archbishop were specially commended for saving Jonathan Swift's portrait) and he resigned the librarianship of Marsh's in July 1776.[45] His brother Thomas Cradock, prebendary of St Audoen's, was elected keeper in 1776. Thomas Cradock resigned as keeper in 1815 and died in 1827. He was succeeded by his son Thomas Russell Cradock, curate assistant of St Audoen's and for 38 years incumbent of St Nicholas Within. Thomas Russell Cradock married Mary Bury, daughter of Major Bury (uncle to Charles William 2nd earl of Charleville) and niece of Richard, 4th Viscount Boyne. Thomas Russell Cradock's brother Frederick Cradock was librarian to the Royal Dublin Society for seven years. Thomas Russell Cradock was succeeded by his son, Thomas Russell William Cradock, some time curate assistant of St Nicholas Within. The *Irish Builder* said that St Nicholas Within was at this period almost a ruin and the services were held in the upper apartments of the schoolhouse in Nicholas Street.

Thomas Russell William Cradock (d.1872) believed that Marsh's Library belonged exclusively to the Cradock family. He considered that in return for showing people around the library no other duties were expected of him. The Cradocks had no conception of what was required for a library of this type and importance, and anybody who criticised them or made any kind of academic or literary enquiry was regarded as either a crank or a

---

44 Information on the Cradock family from the 'Genealogy of the Cradock family' contained in the *Irish Builder*, xxx, no. 691, 1 Oct. 1888, pp 251–2.   **45** Henry Cotton, *Fasti ecclesiae Hibernicae*, ii, pp 105–6 and W.M. Mason, op. cit., pp 449–50.

troublemaker. Although their continued appointment to this position was a disaster and, as we have seen, the governors were severely criticised as far back as 1820 by William Monck Mason for appointing them, the governors' position was in fact a difficult one. The Cradocks could claim long service in important positions in the church, and all the more important governors of Marsh's were themselves churchmen, but they were probably most influenced by the fact that if the Cradocks were not appointed they would be left entirely without accommodation. It could also be said with some truth in their defence that were it not for Marsh's clerical connections the library might not exist at all.

Thomas Russell William was the last of his family to hold the position of keeper in Marsh's Library. Throughout his period in the library the assistant librarian was Dr Robert Travers. Two more different men it is impossible to imagine. From Travers' correspondence it is clear that Cradock even made it difficult for Travers to gain access to the library. Cradock held the only key and he usually parted with it for as short a period as possible and then only grudgingly.[46] It is also clear from this correspondence what an ignorant man Cradock really was. From Cradock's replies to visitors it seems that he had never heard of the *Gentleman's Magazine*, Evelyn's or Pepys' *Diaries* and the beautiful decorated manuscripts he 'used hand out to every idle lounger that came into the Library'.[47] Travers said that these important manuscripts had suffered more in the last twenty years than in the previous 150 years. In a vain effort to prevent their further deterioration Travers had facsimiles made of Magna Carta and the warrants for the execution of Mary queen of Scots and Charles I. In this way he hoped to distract Cradock from showing the precious manuscripts needlessly to visitors. But Cradock refused to allow Travers to display them. Travers also said that the Cradocks used to remove books from one part of the library to another without making a corresponding change in the catalogue. But T.R.W. Cradock went even further. He erased the original pressmark both from the book and the catalogue and thereby completely baffled any investigator.[48]

While some of the stories which Travers tells are unfortunately quite alarming, they are sometimes amusing and even occasionally quite sad. The possibility does arise that T.R.W. Cradock may not have been altogether normal.

---

46 Letters from Robert Travers to Thomas Jones, 8 Sept. and 22 Sept. 1856.   **47** Ibid. 29 May 1857.
48 Ibid. 25 June 1856.

On one occasion when Robert Travers came into the library shortly after there had been a heavy shower of rain, he noticed that water was streaming into a crock which Cradock had placed under a leak in the roof. Travers said that Cradock was watching the flow of water like children admiring a swollen street kennel. Travers knew that this had happened before and asked Cradock why he had not had it repaired. Cradock replied, 'Sure it stopped.'[49] Cradock's behaviour was indeed sometimes very strange; Travers says he occasionally found Cradock standing in a vacant manner out on the lobby of the library, and he tried to persuade Cradock 'that it was not a becoming position, or one in which he should allow himself to be found'.[50]

When Archbishop Whately, the chief governor of Marsh's, died, Cradock refused to attend the funeral. Travers tried to persuade him that it was his duty to do so, but he still refused. Yet on the day of the funeral Cradock went into the streets to view the funeral from the footpath. He was of course seen by many of the other clergy who were attending the funeral and who spoke to Travers about it.[51] Sometime later Travers attempted to put Archbishop Whately's photograph in the reading room, but Cradock refused to allow it and said to Travers, 'There is already here, his bust in plaister.'[52]

When Cradock went on holiday, Travers was required to sleep in the library. On one occasion Travers used this extra time in the library to weed and clean the garden which had been neglected for thirty years and was now in a disgraceful condition. He even managed to plant some flowers. When Cradock returned and saw what had been done, he was furious and borrowed a goat which he let loose in the garden. When poor Travers protested, Cradock said, 'I hate a garden, I declare to God I hate the very sight of a garden.'[53]

Anything to do with literary activities Cradock found particularly annoying and he especially disliked literary people. On one occasion he said, 'What a foolish thing it is to be reading papers to those societies – I have the greatest contempt for people that read such papers, or listen to them.'[53a]

Saddest yet most hilarious of all was Cradock's attempt to get married. (Cradock had been married in 1844 to a Miss Caroline Crossley who died one year later.) He was now 54 years old, and he told Travers his intended bride was a Catholic and that her family objected. He also said there was a difference of rank as she was the daughter of a man in business, a builder, or

49 Ibid. 25 Aug. 1866. **50** Ibid. 6 Mar. 1857. **51** Ibid. 26 Oct. 1863. **52** Ibid. 22 Dec. 1866. **53** Ibid. 29 Oct. 1867. **53a** Ibid.

in the building trade. Travers discovered that she was the daughter of a labourer or whitewasher, that she did not even know the alphabet and that Cradock had to supply her with clothes. On the morning of the proposed marriage, Cradock's own family intervened and prevented it taking place.[54]

Poor Cradock was more to be pitied than laughed at. He was totally unfitted for the job which he had inherited. In spite of his truly dreadful ignorance and inability he did have some feeling for the library. In January 1872 when he was 67 years old he suffered a severe illness. Travers noted that although he was scarcely able to walk he insisted on coming up to the library.[55] Thomas Russell William Cradock died on 11 April 1872.[56] No further members of the Cradock family were keepers of Marsh's Library, but it was a position which they had held for a hundred years.

Travers added a note in a diary in the library:

> As a prudent precautionary measure rendered necessary by the character of the fever that so rapidly had proved fatal to Mr Cradock the Library was kept closed until the Annual Visitation had been held on 10th October, during which interval the cleansing and ventilation were effected.[57]

The library may have been closed to the public for six months, but there certainly was a good deal of activity there.

The keeper's job was now vacant for the first time in one hundred years. The obvious choice was Robert Travers, who had been assistant librarian for 31 years. He was also, as we have seen, professor of medical jurisprudence in Trinity College and was associated with several other medical institutions. His scholarship and learning were well-known in Dublin. He had contributed articles to the *Freeman's Journal*, the *Exhibition Expositor* and the *Daily Express*[58] on such varied subjects as Irish antiquities and Indian mythology.[59] In his own profession he had also contributed to leading medical journals. His love for the library was well-known, and he had already spent many years compiling a beautiful catalogue.

The archbishop of Dublin, Richard Chenevix Trench, called a meeting for 8 June 1872 to consider the nine applicants. With the exception of

---

54 Ibid. 5 Dec. 1859.   **55** Ibid. 22 Jan., and 30 Jan. 1872.   **56** Robert Travers wrote in the library diary (1871–86, MS Z1.2.1) that T.R.W. Cradock died of a very malignant fever.   **57** Ibid.   **58** *The Medical Press*, obituary notice, 4 April 1888, p. 364.   **59** Letters from Robert Travers to Thomas Jones, 26 Oct.

Robert Travers they were all clergymen. There was, unusually, a most impressive turn-out of the governors: the chief justice of the Common Pleas, James Henry Monahan, the chief justice of Ireland, James Whiteside, the chief baron, David Pigot, the archbishop, the dean of St Patrick's and the provost of Trinity College. The governors appointed as keeper the Revd William Maturin, vicar of Grangegorman and son of the novelist Charles Robert Maturin. It was a most extraordinary appointment. Maturin, although he was one of the best-known preachers of his day, also held extreme Tractarian views which many churchmen found very objectionable. But the archbishop was clearly determined to appoint Maturin.[60]

But why was the most obvious and best candidate Robert Travers not appointed? There could only be one reason. Eight years earlier Robert's daughter, Mary Josephine Travers, was involved in one of the most scandalous libel actions ever heard in Ireland. The *Irish Times* described it as 'a suit that shook society in Dublin like a thunderclap'.[61] Mary Josephine's action involved Sir William and Lady Wilde, and was heard on 12 December 1864 before Chief Justice Henry Monahan, who was of course a governor of the library. While ostensibly it was a libel action, it was really an action for assault by Sir William on Mary Josephine.

When Mary Josephine Travers was nineteen years old, her mother had taken her to Sir William Wilde for advice, since apparently Mary Josephine was threatened with deafness. Mary Josephine became a patient of Sir William's and, unfortunately for him, he became completely infatuated with her. He took her to exhibitions, gave her money and presents and she was a frequent visitor at his house. After some years Sir William got tired of Mary Josephine and tried to get rid of her. But Mary Josephine was not to be put off so easily. She began a campaign to annoy both Sir William and Lady Wilde. (Lady Wilde was equally well-known for her writings under the pen name of 'Speranza'.)

Mary Josephine wrote scurrilous apocryphal pieces to the papers, even going so far as to announce her death and dropping the notices in letter boxes.

1853 and 21 Nov. 1853.   **60** Newport J.D. White, *An account* ..., p. 17. See also Richard Chevenix Trench, *Letters and memorials* (ed. Maria Trench), 2 vols., London, 1888, ii, p. 147, 'I am not without hope that we shall be able to elect Maturin as Librarian of Marsh's Library'.   **61** *Irish Times*, 14 Dec. 1864. (On microfilm in the National Library of Ireland.) Terence de Vere White, *The parents of Oscar Wilde*, London, Hodder & Stoughton, 1967, p. 159 etc. See also T.G. Wilson, *Victorian doctor*, New York, L.B. Fischer, 1946. I have used the above books for the details of this famous case.

She hired newsboys to display offensive placards outside the Metropolitan Hall in Abbey Street shortly before Sir William was due to give a most important lecture. Finally after another outrageous episode Lady Wilde felt provoked into writing a letter of protest to Robert Travers. It was an arrogant letter in which Lady Wilde accused Mary Josephine of consorting with newsboys, having an intrigue with Sir William, and trying to extort money from them.

Sir William Wilde was at the height of his fame. He was one of the queen's physicians in Ireland. He had been knighted some months earlier at a splendid ceremony in Dublin Castle. There was therefore intense excitement in Dublin when the trial began. The applications for admission tickets to the court were so great in number that the police had to take special precautions against overcrowding. Some of the best-known barristers were engaged for both sides, including Isaac Butt for Mary Josephine. The evidence provided Dublin with the most sensational gossip and Mary Josephine's accounts of Sir William Wilde's ridiculous behaviour and her own equally silly, even ludicrous, attempts to annoy both Sir William and Lady Wilde provided column after column in the *Irish Times* and other newspapers.

The chief justice, Henry Monahan, in his summing up ridiculed Mary Josephine's evidence and her account of the supposed assault. But Mary Josephine did win the libel action. The jury however showed what they thought of Mary Josephine by awarding her one farthing's damages. The case almost ruined Sir William, although three years later he wrote one of his most popular books, *Lough Corrib*, and in 1873 the Royal Irish Academy awarded him the Cunningham medal. After his death in 1876 Lady Wilde went to live in London. Mary Josephine took an action against some of the newspapers for their comments on the case, which she lost. Her father, Dr Robert Travers, was not promoted to the keeper's job in Marsh's Library which he had so patiently waited for.

Apart from the scandal arising from the case, Travers himself did not come through unscathed. He was called briefly to give evidence that he had received Lady Wilde's letter and had replied to it. Travers had in fact thrown the letter in a press in his bedroom where Mary Josephine had found it, and it was Mary Josephine who had taken it to a solicitor. Travers' reply was not regarded as relevant to the case and was not read in court, although Lady Wilde when being cross-examined attempted to give the contents but was prevented. It was also clear from many of the barristers' questions in court that Travers was well-known and highly regarded both in medical and literary circles. But Lady Wilde arrogantly denied she knew anything of his literary activities, even though Travers had met Sir William Wilde and Wilde had asked Mary Josephine to ask her father to look at a manuscript he was working on.

This dreadful court case would have been a nightmare for any man, but for Robert Travers it must have been a shattering experience. In the series of letters which Travers wrote to his friend Thomas Jones in Chetham's Library in Manchester between the years 1848 and 1875, he conveys all the information about the difficulties in Marsh's Library in the nineteenth century, and he comments on politics, the trials of Mitchel and many others involved in the National Movement with which he had no sympathy whatsoever. But it is also in these letters that his wide scholarship is revealed and sometimes sad details of his personal life.

Robert Travers was born in Dublin in 1807. His father had been a member of the legal profession but had unfortunately gambled all his money and died when Travers was sixteen, leaving him penniless.[62] Since Travers had never been to school or had a tutor and was haphazardly educated at home, an offer of financial help from a relative encouraged him to prepare for the entrance examination to Trinity College. He courageously set to work entirely by himself and succeeded.

Travers entered Trinity College in 1823 and during his first year in college he became completely infatuated with a young English girl who capriciously rejected him.[63] Travers' excessive reaction to what was virtually a teenage romance seems to have remained with him for the rest of his life. At least he never forgot it. Nearly fifty years later he wrote sadly of the way he had been rejected. He became gloomy and anti-social and avoided communicating with people as much as possible, and this was the reason that he first came to Marsh's Library. He wrote to his friend that he 'took refuge in the seclusion of this library'.[64] But he did return to Trinity College and completed his studies in medicine.

From his letters Travers emerges as a rather cold, eccentric and introspective man, apparently unable to communicate with any of his family, and hardest of all probably was his lack of a sense of humour which might sometimes perhaps have helped him. Although Travers in his letters poured out his feelings about the preservation of the library, and particularly his contempt

---

62 Letter from Robert Travers to Thomas Jones, 11 Nov. 1865.   **63** Ibid.   **64** Ibid.

for the Cradocks, he only rarely spoke of his domestic affairs. At the time of Mary Josephine's court case, it appears that Mary Josephine was not on speaking terms with her mother, and it seems that Mrs Travers had left her husband and children. Travers' two sons had emigrated to Australia but his three daughters still lived with him. His house was not only uncomfortable but was also in a dilapidated condition.[65] For a man who spent most of his spare time either in Marsh's Library or some other library working on his literary researches, it is hardly surprising that his family reacted in the way that they did.

When Thomas Jones wrote to Travers sympathising with him on the death of his youngest son, Travers replied with a detailed account of his son's death. He explained that his son had run away from school and joined the army and had been sent to India, where he contracted dysentery and died. Travers' letter is unsympathetic to his unfortunate young son and is a little chilling to read.[66]

Later in a reference to his unhappy marriage he mentioned his earlier rejection and said, 'Unhappiest of all was entering into the married state which has not been productive of either quiet or domestic comfort which was all that I expected from it.'[67] It seems extraordinary that Travers, who was such a fervent Protestant, should have married a Catholic. Indeed Travers attended the service in the college chapel every day, but on Sundays he preferred to attend St Patrick's Cathedral which he knew would not be so crowded.[68] As he lived as far away as Williamstown in Blackrock, it was quite some distance to go to find a less crowded church – but it was of course beside Marsh's Library.

Travers also appeared to have been totally unaware of Mary Josephine's impending law action. Up to a short time before the trial began, Travers' letters are full of descriptions of how busy he was working on a friend's book. He was compiling an index and preparing Ledwich's *Anatomy* for printing.[69] But he was deeply distressed by the law action and was unable to write to Thomas Jones for nearly six months. When he eventually did write he hardly mentioned his personal difficulties or the libel action. It was a letter from a tired and very depressed man, but still a most dignified one. His only reference to the case was, 'I have had much of domestic and other annoyance and have perhaps yielded too much to its disheartening influence.'[70]

---

65 Ibid. 8 May 1875.   66 Ibid. 11 Feb. 1859.   67 Ibid. 11 Nov. 1865.   68 Ibid. 8 April 1864 and 25 Aug. 1866.   69 Ibid. 8 Oct. 1864.   70 Ibid. 2 March 1865.

Apart from the professorship of medical jurisprudence in Trinity College
and lecturing in other medical schools, Travers seems to have been completely uninterested in building up a private practice, which would have
brought him much more money. He did however do trojan work for the
poor in Dublin. He worked for the Sick Poor Institution in Meath Street
and it was while he was working there that he discovered Jenny Lind, the
great Swedish singer, had given £400 to the archbishop of Dublin for
distribution to the poor.[71] Travers applied for some money for his institution
but the archbishop informed him that Jenny Lind had expressly left the
money for distribution to the private poor whom nobody ever thought of,
and not for institutions. Travers thought her request was a noble one and
was not disappointed by this refusal.

He also worked in the South Dublin Cholera Hospital in Cork Street,
and although not required to live in the hospital he thought it better to do
so. He worked under the most uncomfortable and primitive conditions in
what was only a converted makeshift hospital. He was badly paid for his
work there, and furthermore could not earn money from medical students
which he would have received otherwise. His sympathy and concern for the
poor in Dublin and his descriptions of their terrible poverty and appalling
living conditions make his letters valuable and very moving.[72]

The law case in 1864 was not the only tragedy that year for Robert Travers.
He had been promoted professor of medical jurisprudence in Trinity College
but some months after his appointment he discovered that the authorities in
the college had paid his fees prematurely to his predecessor.[73] This meant that
for nearly four years Travers had to lecture to his students entirely without
payment. As a kind of compensation Travers applied to read for a law
degree, thinking that the board of the college might waive the fees in view
of his own predicament.[74] The board, while undoubtedly sympathetic to his
request, were unable to do so, and Travers gave up the idea of a law degree.[75]

It must have been a difficult time. While the scandal probably affected his
position, he was not ignored by everybody. Mr Benjamin Lee Guinness sent
Travers two tickets for the great re-opening service held in St Patrick's
Cathedral when the restoration work was complete. In view of the importance
of this occasion and the enormous demand for seats, Mr Guinness' kindness

---

71 Ibid. 28 Oct. 1848 and 2 Nov. 1848.   72 Ibid. 2 Oct., 3 Nov., 8 Dec. 1854 and undated letter no.
175a.   73 Ibid. 2 March and 9 March 1865.   74 Ibid. 13 June 1867.   75 Ibid. 20 Jan. 1868.

to Robert was a thoughtful gesture. Travers, as eccentric as ever, gave the
tickets away, but he did attend the rehearsals of the music for this great
service. Some time later at a dinner held in Trinity College for the British
Medical Association which Travers attended, the archbishop, Richard
Chenevix Trench, spoke to Travers at some length before they went in to
dinner. This incident seems to have pleased Travers considerably.[76]

These scandals were not only tragic for Robert Travers and his family;
they also had unfortunate consequences for the library itself. From the time
Travers had been made assistant librarian in 1841 he began collecting books
with the intention of leaving them to Marsh's Library.[77] The books were
purchased entirely from the £26 2s. 8d. per year which Travers received as
assistant librarian, for a period of over thirty years. (Strangely enough,
although Travers maintained that he had not been provided for by his father,
he seems to have acquired a very valuable library before he was thirty years
old. He never mentioned this library and it was sold by auction[78] in 1836.)
He had an interest in philology, archaeology, antiquities, church history, and
the classics and he also had an outstanding knowledge of books and bibliography. He had collected books which were intended to be a supplement to
the collections already in the library and these included Dublin printed and
reprinted books. Travers' knowledge of books was well-known. It seems
likely that he was responsible for the preparation of the sale catalogue[79] for
the auction of Marsh's 'duplicates' already mentioned. In 1842 he drew up
the catalogue[80] of the manuscripts in Lord Kingsborough's library, which
was sold that year, and he also wrote the preface to the sale catalogue and
added some notices to the printed books. Indeed, so sure was Travers that he

---

76 Ibid. 18 Sept. 1867.   **77** Ibid. 14 Oct., 19 Oct., 12 Nov., 14 Nov. 1872, and 19 Oct. 1875. In spite of
what Robert Travers wrote about not leaving his books to Marsh's, there are some books in the library,
particularly in the music section, which belonged to him. According to the donations book, Travers
donated only three books to Marsh's, and these were given before 1840. But from the date of Travers'
appointment as assistant librarian in 1841 not one entry was made in the donations book. He gave his
reasons for refusing donations in a letter to Thomas Jones on 3 Jan. 1856: 'We have few donations to
acknowledge, and all of them trifling – so far as I can I would discourage them unless the projected
spoliation could be averted and sufficient funds be obtained for the maintainance and extension of the
fabric – in which case I should be glad to see it gradually and judiciously augmented'. This curious and
unfortunate decision is a little hard to understand when we know the library was made secure in 1866
and that Travers was assistant librarian until 1888.   **78** *Catalogue of the library of Robert Travers, Esq. which
are to be sold by auction on Friday, the 18th March, 1836, and following days, by Charles Sharpe*, Dublin,
Richard Davis Webb [1836].   **79** In the catalogue of his own library, reference no. 149 on p. 36, he
wrote beside item no. 478, 'In addition to what I have said in Bibl. Mars'.   **80** Letter from Robert
Travers to Thomas Jones, 19 Jan. 1854.

would be appointed keeper that he had the rooms on the landing fitted with shelves for his books.[81] From the day of William Maturin's appointment Travers' disappointment was so great that he began sending the best books in his collection either to Chetham's Library itself or to his friends there,[82] and so Marsh's lost another great collection.

The new keeper, William Maturin, suffered from ill health and for this reason was obliged to live outside the city – in Howth.[83] He appears to have been exceptionally kind to Travers. He offered him the keeper's apartments, a second key to the library, and part of his salary, all of which Travers politely refused. The governors then decided to give the apartments to a tenant and this meant that Travers was obliged to give up possession of the three rooms on the landing which had been his for over twenty years.[84]

Travers wrote frequently of how determined he was to resign from the library but he found himself unable to do so. In fact he never did resign. In spite of family troubles and his own illnesses, particularly one very serious accident when he had been knocked down by a carriage in Nassau Street and suffered painful injuries,[85] he still managed to come up to the library. But there were compensations here for a man of his solitary habits and eccentricities. He did have the library almost entirely to himself, and just how few visitors there were he himself recorded when he wrote: 'From this date 14th October 1872 until 13th January 1873 there was but one visitor for the purpose of referring to any book in the Library, either for study or research'.[86] It is also clear that Travers did not encourage casual visitors and when Mr Beveridge the town clerk called in 1883 'enquiring whether Marsh's was adapted to the use of the working classes inhabiting the Coombe and its vicinity', Travers assured him 'that it was not, being even less fit for such purpose than Trinity College Library or the National Library'.[87]

The library was not always so deserted. Throughout the nineteenth century some interesting visitors and writers did come. Sir Walter Scott visited Marsh's in 1825[88] and later visitors included Thomas Davis, Emily Lawless, E.B. Pusey, J.K. Ingram, Richard H.M. Orpen, William Rowan Hamilton and Herbert F. Hore.[89] More interesting probably were three

81 Ibid., and 14 Oct. 1872.   82 Ibid. 14 Oct., 26 Oct., 12 Nov., 14 Nov. 1872 etc.   83 Ibid. 12 Nov. 1872.   84 Ibid. 16 Oct., 19 Oct., 9 Nov., 18 Nov. 1875.   85 Ibid. 7 Feb. 1866.   86 Visitors' book 1871–86, MS Z1.2.1.   87 Ibid. 13 July 1883.   88 D.J. O'Donoghue, *Sir Walter Scott's tour in Ireland in 1825*, Glasgow/Dublin, 1905, p. 32.   89 Visitors' book 1826–33, MS Z1.2.1. Thomas Davis, 17 May 1832, Emily Lawless, 9 Dec. 1889, E.B. Pusey, July 1841, J.K. Ingram, 7 Nov. 1838, Richard M. Orpen,

writers of this period. We have already mentioned Charles Robert Maturin who wrote his books in Marsh's, but so did that strange Spanish priest Dr Joaquín Lorenzo Villanueva who wrote his book *Ibernia Phoenicea* which was printed in Dublin in 1831 and which he presented to the library together with his other writings. Travers greatly admired Villanueva's scholarship, and he noted that although Villanueva's English was not good he spoke elegant Latin to Travers in their discussions.[90] The noted Shakespearean scholar Edward Dowden also worked in Marsh's, on a sixteenth-century manuscript containing a miscellany of prose and poetry in both Latin and English.[91] James Clarence Mangan, when he was employed as a copyist for the Ordnance Survey in about 1838, transcribed necessary documents in Marsh's. He also read in and visited the library frequently.[92]

Another reader in Marsh's was Bram (Abraham) Stoker (*b.*1847), the author of *Dracula*. He came to the library several times throughout 1866 while he was a student in Trinity College. His recommender was G.F. Shaw, a lay fellow in TCD. (It is interesting to note, in view of Stoker's subsequent career as manager to Henry Irving at the Lyceum Theatre in London, that G.F. Shaw was a friend of Irving and Ellen Terry.) At Marsh's Stoker read travel books, geographies, books on theology and popery, and the poetry of Spencer, Dryden, Chaucer and Ben Jonson. One of the books he consulted was Montesquieu's *Considérations sur les causes de la grandeur des Romains et de leur décadence* (1735). It is tempting to speculate that Stoker might have known that Charles Robert Maturin wrote his classic Gothic horror *Melmoth the wanderer* (1820) in Marsh's.

We have often been asked if women were allowed to visit or work in Marsh's. There was nothing in the rules to forbid them, and we know that Emily Lawless did visit. We think that because Jonathan Swift was a governor and lived beside the library he may have brought some of the women writers of his circle to see it. It would be rather surprising if Swift

March 1859, William Rowan Hamilton, 24 Jan. 1832, Herbert F. Hore, Jan. 1864. In the archives of the library there is also a note of recommendation by G.F. Shaw, TCD, to admit Bram Stoker to read in Marsh's in July 1866.   **90** Letter from Robert Travers to Thomas Jones, 22 Feb. 1853.   **91** Edward Dowden, 'An Elizabethan MS Collection: Henry Constable' in *The Modern Quarterly of Language and Literature*, now *Modern Language Quarterly*, i (1898) 3–4. Dowden also worked on another fascinating collection of early seventeenth-century poetry which included such writers as Nicholas Breton and Abraham Fraunce, and *Sir Philip Sydney's Ourania* by Nathaniel Baxter (London, 1606, STC 1598) (Original Marsh pressmark K4.4.27, now Z4.1.11).   **92** D.J. O'Donoghue, *The life and writings of James Clarence Mangan*, Edinburgh, Dublin, 1897, p. 91.

did not bring his great friend Stella to Marsh's, or encourage such distinguished literary figures as Mrs Delaney, Mrs Pilkington, Mrs Barber and Mrs
Constantia Grierson to visit the library and possibly carry out research for
some of their books.

Although our visitors books, which date from 1826, normally only record
the names of male readers and visitors, it is remarkable how often the words
'A stranger and two ladies', 'Stranger and a lady', 'Three ladies', or the male
visitor's name followed by 'and two ladies' appear. Fortunately the visitors
books do record the books that they examined and these include Bibles,
Clarendon's *History of the rebellion and civil wars in England*, Whitelaw, Walsh
and Warburton's *History of Dublin* (1818), and the writings of St Robert
Bellarmine. These ladies also examined some English translations of
seventeenth-century French novels, and some manuscripts.

While Frances Power Cobbe's name was, as usual, not given in the visitors
book, we know from her *Life* (London, 1894) that she did use Marsh's.
Frances Power Cobbe was one of the heroines of the Victorian women's
movement. She was born in Newbridge House in Co. Dublin in 1822 and
was the great granddaughter of Thomas Cobbe MP, who was keeper of
Marsh's Library from 1762 to 1766. She was a prolific writer and published
over thirty books. In her autobiography she said that she read in Archbishop
Marsh's old library in Dublin, where there were splendid old books. She also
used the books in Marsh's for the footnotes for her *Essay on the theory of
intuitive morals* (London, 1855). She was interested in astronomy, architecture,
and heraldry, and she studied theology and the works of Jeremy Taylor,
Ralph Cudworth, Aristotle and Montesquieu. These authors are well
represented in Marsh's and would have provided Frances Power Cobbe with
rich material for her research.

William Maturin was keeper in Marsh's for fifteen years and died in 1887.
This vacancy gave rise to a discussion in parliament and consequently the
Freeman's Journal sent a reporter up to see the library. The reporter described
how the bell for calling the porter was not working and that the door was
opened by the assistant librarian, 'a gentleman whose form is literally bowed
with the weight of years, Dr Robert Travers … who has been connected
with the institution for nearly half a century'.[93] Lord Plunket was now the
archbishop of Dublin and he called a meeting in 1887 to discuss the

---

93 *Freeman's Journal*, 7 Sept. 1887.

appointment. There was a particularly strong attendance of the governors
and the Travers–Wilde scandal nearly twenty-three years earlier was to be
remembered. The lord chief justice was now Michael Morris (Lord Killanin)
who had been counsel for the Wildes in the famous case. The governors
decided to advertise the position. There were 32 applicants. We do not know
if Travers applied; since Travers' great friend Thomas Jones died in 1875 and
Travers does not seem to have corresponded with anyone else, it is impossible
to say. But Travers was now over eighty years old and it does seem somewhat
unlikely that he did so.

A further meeting was held in September and the governors appointed
the Revd George Thomas Stokes DD, vicar of All Saints, Blackrock, and
professor of ecclesiastical history in Trinity College. He was also, like some
of the earlier keepers in Marsh's, prebendary of St Audoen's Church. The
annual visitation was held a few weeks later and it was the last annual
visitation attended by Robert Travers. We have already mentioned his
exquisite handwriting in these accounts of the annual visitations from the
date of his appointment in 1841. Another striking fact about his entries is
the absence of any mistakes. But now, for the first time, there is a mistake.
Under the act of parliament the annual visitation takes place on the second
Thursday in October; this last visitation which Travers attended, and which
he recorded, took place on a Friday. Preceding this account is a sad but still
beautifully written note by Travers which reads: 'By a mistake that he can
neither explain nor excuse, and of which he did not become conscious until
too late for attempting to correct it, the Assistant Librarian has convened for
tomorrow, the Meeting that should have been held on this day.' Professor
Stokes' appointment was confirmed, as also were the new rules for the future
management of the library.[94]

Two months later another meeting of the governors was held and for the
first time Travers did not attend. A note in the library says he was required
to attend in Trinity College that day. But was it really so? Was Travers now
finally too disheartened to make the journey up to Marsh's for this meeting?
Did he hope that the governors might perhaps have made him keeper, even
for a few short months? Professor G.T. Stokes was obviously worried about
him, and wrote offering him help and asking for Travers' view on the
management of the library and its new furniture. Travers gave a dignified

94 Visitation book, 1887.

and courteous refusal of Stokes' offer of help, and he went on to make suggestions for the re-opening date for the library.[95]

Robert Travers' life would appear to have been one of failure and of domestic unhappiness. His daughter was involved in a scandal, his sons emigrated and his wife deserted him, and he himself never became keeper in Marsh's Library. But Robert did achieve success. Only for his efforts and his influence with Sir Benjamin Lee Guinness, Marsh's Library would not exist at all. It was because of Robert Travers' devotion against opposition and indifference that this great library containing a magnificent collection of books still stands in the heart of the Liberties of Dublin. Visitors and scholars come from all over the world every year either to see or work in the library; and there they can also see Robert Travers' portrait hanging in the first gallery, close to the reading room where he himself had tried to place Archbishop Whately's photograph over one hundred years ago.

Robert Travers died on 28 March 1888. In his obituary notice in the *Medical Press* the writer paid tribute to Travers' great work during the cholera epidemic and then said that 'he was regarded as a phenomenon of erudition, and his extreme eccentricity of habits and costume gave strength to this impression'.[96]

Finally, as a small example which typifies Travers' love and devotion for Marsh's and its books and manuscripts, there is a quaint note which he himself wrote. Travers had been requested by the archbishop of Dublin to deliver a manuscript to the Royal Irish Academy for photographing. He brought the manuscript to the academy where it was photographed, but he added 'without leaving the custody of the assistant librarian'.[97]

Dr George T. Stokes was keeper of Marsh's for eleven years and was really the first librarian to publish anything substantial on the library.[98] He was a well-known historian and had already published extensively on ancient Irish church history. It was while Dr Stokes was keeper that a macabre discovery was made. A Mr Clover, an assistant librarian under Dr Stokes, found in one of the 'dark closets' a coffin which was apparently an Irish one, although covered with Egyptian hieroglyphics, containing a mummy. Some manuscripts

95 Letter from Robert Travers, 26 Oct. 1887, in archives box.   **96** *The Medical Press*, 4 April 1888, p. 364.   **97** Visitors' book 1871–86, note written by Robert Travers on 8 June 1872.   **98** G.T. Stokes, *Some worthies of the Irish church*, ed. with preface by H.J. Lawlor, London, Hodder & Stoughton, 1900, pp 65–141. See also N.J.D. White's *Some recollections of Trinity College, Dublin*, Dublin, Hodges Figgis, 1935. References to G.T. Stokes on pp 44–5.

were also found in the closet. (There is no information as to how this coffin came to Marsh's although there was some speculation that it might have been given by Provost Huntington of Trinity College who was an orientalist and friend of Marsh.) This coffin was given to the well-known Dublin doctor, Ninian Falkiner, on 17 November 1888.[99]

Dr G.T. Stokes died in 1896 and was succeeded by Newport John Davis White BD, regius professor of divinity in Trinity College and later chancellor of St Patrick's Cathedral. And so Marsh's again returned to its usual placid routine. Newport White began publishing sectional catalogues and biographies of Marsh and Elias Bouhéreau. These catalogues were a remarkable accomplishment.[1] Newport White's writings on St Patrick were well known in Ireland and Mario Esposito in an article in *Irish Historical Studies* said White's *Editio minor* 'is a masterly achievement'.[2] R.M. Gwynn also referred to White's 'notable service to Irish Church History by his editions of the Latin writings of St Patrick'.[3] White was regarded as a great stickler for decorum and R.M. Gwynn tells the following story of an incident which took place during a class in Trinity. One of White's students was reading aloud his sermon and referred to 'Paul'. He was gently reproved by White who said, 'Will you please say *Saint* Paul or, if you think that appellation savours of superstition you may say Mr Paul.' Newport White had a vigorous policy in regard to buying books for Marsh's. Even with the tiny pittance (never increased) allowed for book purchases he bought books mainly relating to Ireland and of Irish literary interest, and whenever possible for the purpose of replacing missing books. For this reason he will, we think, be remembered as one of the most scholarly and best librarians of Marsh's Library.

99 Entry in Visitors' book on 17 Nov. 1888. See also newspaper cutting in scrapbook in Marsh's, referring to annual visitation 1898. Another newspaper cutting (*Irish Times*?) describing this discovery has been inserted in a copy of *Bibliotheca Marsiana, catalogue of books, the duplicate copies of the public library, Dublin*, kept in the National Library of Ireland.   **1** Newport J.D. White, *A short catalogue of English books in Archbishop Marsh's Library Dublin, printed before mdcxli*, At the Oxford University Press, printed for the Bibliographical Society, 1905. *A catalogue of books in the French language printed on or before A.D. 1715, remaining in Archbishop Marsh's Library, Dublin*, Dublin, printed at the University Press, 1918. *An account of Archbishop Marsh's Library, Dublin*, by Newport J.D. White, *With a note on autographs*, by Newport B. White, Dublin, Hodges Figgis, 1926. *Four good men: Luke Challoner, Jeremy Taylor, Narcissus Marsh, Elias Bouhéreau*, Dublin, Hodges Figgis, 1927. *Catalogue of the manuscripts remaining in Marsh's Library, Dublin*, ed. N.J.D. White, compiled by J.R. Scott. Dublin, A. Thom, [1913].   **2** Mario Esposito, 'St Patrick's "Confessio" and the Book of Armagh' in *Irish Historical Studies*, ix, no. 33, March 1954, pp 7–8. **3** R.M. Gwynn, 'Newport John Davis White' in *Divinity, a Church of Ireland Quarterly Review*, v, no. 12, Sept. 1951, pp 3–6.

It was during Newport J.D. White's period as keeper that James Joyce visited Marsh's in October 1902. Joyce wrote his name and address in the visitors' book on 22 and 23 October. It seems that he consulted a book in the Bouhéreau collection entitled *Vaticinia, siue Prophetiae Abbatis Joachimi & Anselmi Episcopi Marsicani, cum adnotationibus Paschalini Regiselmi, Latine et Italice.* This book, which is unfortunately imperfect and mutilated, was printed in Venice in 1589. It contains interesting illustrations. Joyce remembered his visit to Marsh's in his great work *Ulysses* and said, 'Houses of decay, mine, his and all. You told the Clongowes gentry you had an uncle a judge and an uncle a general in the army. Come out of them, Stephen. Beauty is not there. Nor in the stagnant bay of Marsh's library where you read the fading prophecies of Joachim Abbas.'

In 1903 Marsh's leased a small portion of its ground to the Representative Church Body and unfortunately that year also suffered much damage during a dreadful storm.[4]

Mr T.P. Le Fanu returned to Marsh's some very interesting letters which had belonged to Dr La Touche and which had all been addressed to Dr Bouhéreau in the years 1662–85. Three years later Lord Iveagh presented letters addressed to Dr Bouhéreau which he had purchased from the representatives of Dr Robert Travers. Newport White said that when the Huguenot Archives were restored to La Rochelle in 1862, the Revd T.R.W. Cradock presented these letters to Dr Travers on the ground that they were not worth preserving![5] They are of course of interest particularly in regard to the intellectual life of seventeenth-century France and are also of some literary interest.

In great contrast to the scholarly activities in Marsh's, great changes and dramatic political events accompanied by violence were taking place in Ireland. During Easter Week 1916, when British troops were camped in St Patrick's Park and the IRA had taken over Jacobs' factory, Marsh's was almost directly in the firing line. On the Sunday morning of that fateful week a British soldier apparently by mistake machine-gunned the library. The bullets shattered the glass in the window and one of the doors in the reading room and bullets penetrated many books throughout the library.[6] It was also in St Patrick's Park that the surrender of Jacobs' garrison under Commandant MacDonagh took place,[7] an event that would have been

4 Visitation book. Special meetings were called in March and November to discuss the damage done by the great storm in February 1903, and the leasing of a small area of land. 5 Newport J.D. White, *Four good men ...*, pp 58–60. 6 Visitation book, 1916. 7 James Carty, compiler and editor, *Ireland from*

9 Illustration from Joachim, abbot of Fiore's *Vaticinia* (Venice, 1589).

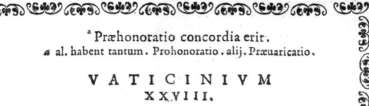

10 Illustration from Joachim, abbot of Fiore's *Vaticinia* (Venice, 1589).

clearly visible from the library. Unfortunately the shattered doors, windows and
books were not Marsh's only loss at this time. Many books and pamphlets were
being repaired or rebound in Messrs Thom's premises in Abbey Street and
all of these perished in the fire which destroyed that premises.[8] Marsh's
received the small sum of £16 compensation for loss and damage. The
balance was somewhat restored by the donation to the library in 1918 of the
Revd Godfrey Everth's collection of books.[9] Nicest of all was Miss Isabel
Travers' gift of her father's portrait in oils.[10] In 1935 the books from Cashel
Library which had been deposited in Marsh's, possibly intended to be a
permanent loan, were returned to the Representative Church Body. They
are now back in Cashel.

Newport J.D. White resigned in 1930–1 and was succeeded by his
nephew, the delightful Newport Benjamin White, whom so many visitors
and scholars still remember. Newport Benjamin White carried on many of the
fine ideas of his uncle and published on Marsh's as well as editing important
work for the Irish Manuscripts Commission.[11] It was while Newport
Benjamin was keeper that electricity was introduced into the library but
only in the librarian's residence and the caretaker's apartments.[12] On 4 July
1953 Newport Benjamin White used a telephone in the library for the first
time.[13] He died in 1956 and was succeeded by Robert Ormes Dougan MA.
Dougan was shortly afterwards appointed to a position in the Huntington
Library in California and so has the distinction of holding office for the
shortest period in Marsh's history.

In 1957 the governors appointed as assistant librarian the first woman to
hold office in Marsh's, Miss M. Pollard, rare books librarian in Trinity College.
Dr R.B. McDowell was appointed keeper in 1958; he had been assistant

the great famine to the treaty, 1851–1921, a documentary record, Dublin, C.J. Fallon, 1951, pp 186–7.
8 Visitation book, 1916. (The books destroyed in this fire included Lawrence Deios, *That the pope is that
antichrist …*, London, 1590, *STC* 6475.)   **9** Donations book, 1918 and Newport J.D. White, *An account
…*, p. 9.   **10** Donations book, 1923 and Newport J.D. White, *An account …*, p. 11.   **11** Newport B.
White, 'Manuscript and printed music in Marsh's Library' in *Music in Ireland*, ed. Aloys Fleischman,
Cork University Press, Oxford, B.H. Blackwell, 1952, pp 319–21. See also Irish Manuscripts
Commission, *Analecta Hibernica* index to nos. I–IV (and later indexes) compiled by Newport B. White,
Dublin, Stationery Office, 1934. See also I. MSS. Comm., *The 'Dignitas decani' of St Patrick's Cathedral,
Dublin*, ed. N.B. White, with an intro. by Aubrey Gwynn, Dublin, 1957.   **12** On 12 Jan. 1939. Diary
and memoranda for the years 1933–49, Marsh pressmark Z1.2.1(h), p. 48. Although electricity was
already in the librarian's room, it was not until 1967 that electricity was installed throughout the whole
library.   **13** Library diary from 27 May 1949 to June 1956, f. 34. The diaries for the years 1933–49 and
1949–56 were kept by Newport Benjamin White.

librarian from 1939 to 1944. Miss Pollard retired in 1967 and Dr McDowell retired in 1974.

In 1958 the deterioration of the roof of the library had reached an alarming state and so began the huge task of organising an appeal for its restoration. Money came from many organisations and many countries and the government was also generous, and within quite a short time the restoration work was completed. Marsh's Library is now used by scholars and historians from all over the world. It is also included in almost every guide and tourist book published in Ireland.

It would seem appropriate at the end of this history of the library to return to the very beginning when Narcissus Marsh so generously decided to provide for the people of this country a magnificent library with its superb collections of books and when Dr Elias Bouhéreau came to take up duty as its first librarian. Bouhéreau had to flee with his family from France because of his religious beliefs and, as we have seen, managed to bring his library with him. It is comforting to think that this French scholar found refuge and peace in this beautiful Irish library, and it is appropriate too that the first catalogue which he compiled with such meticulous care and scholarship can still be used by us to find the books where he and Narcissus Marsh placed them three hundred years ago.

Chapter 3

Incunabula and Other Early Printings

RINTING WITH movable type in Europe was invented by Johann Gutenberg in about 1450 in Mainz, Germany.[1] Although conflicting claims have been made for many other countries, notably France and Holland, it is generally accepted that Gutenberg was the first person to print with movable type. Gutenberg had apparently been experimenting for some time but needed more money to continue his work and arranged a loan from a wealthy Mainz merchant, Johann Fust. Gutenberg secured the loan on his printing equipment and later when he was unable to repay, his equipment was confiscated. Johann Fust then began printing with his son-in-law Peter Schoeffer, and together they produced the first book, the 42-line Bible called the Gutenberg Bible.

It was a wonderful achievement. The Gutenberg Bible was completed before August 1456 and was printed on six printing presses, and by men who were probably learning to print for the first time.[2] The type used in this first Bible was a gothic type called *lettre de forme*. Even more magnificent was the printing of the Mainz Psalter which Fust and Schoeffer published in 1457. It bore the first 'colophon' (paragraph at the end of the book which usually gave the name of the printer, place of printing, etc.). It was printed in red and black throughout and all of the ten copies which have survived have been printed on vellum.

The books printed between the beginning of printing and 1501 are called incunabula which comes from the Latin word 'cunae' meaning cradle.[3] The majority of incunabula are in Latin and are mostly of a religious or educational content. The incunabula in Marsh's Library represent the writings of the early church fathers, classical writers, medieval writers and writers on ecclesiastical law.

1 Alfred Fairbank, *A book of scripts*, rev. ed., London, Penguin Books, 1968, p. 15.   2 Eric Quayle, *The collector's book of books*, London, November Books, Studio Vista, 1971, p. 24.   3 Warren Chappell, *A short history of the printed word*, London, Andre Deutsch, 1972, p. 59.

11 Portraits of famous early printers in Mich. Maittaire's *Annales typographici* (The Hague, 1719–26).

There are approximately eighty incunabula in the library and apart from their interesting contents they also illustrate transitional stages in early printing.[4] When manuscripts were being produced in the universities and ecclesiastical establishments no book or document was approved unless it had some ornamented or illuminated initials or decorated capital letters. The early printers were influenced by these rules and tried to reproduce their books to look as much like manuscripts as possible.[5] It is for this reason that so many of these early printed books have beautifully decorated initials and capital letters or some other decorative features of manuscripts. In many cases the first page only is decorated, the rest of the book shows blank spaces in the text which had obviously been intended for decoration. But by 1500 the printers realised that hand decoration of printed books was unnecessary and they later developed their own methods of book decoration with splendid woodcut illustrations and decorative borders.

Printing spread rapidly throughout Europe in the fifteenth century. The type which the early printers used was similar to the German cursive handwriting of this period or the formal special handwriting which was already familiar to readers of manuscripts. This type was a development of the Carolingian miniscule and was called gothic. Three types of gothic were used, *lettre de forme*, *lettre de somme*, and *lettre bâtarde*. In England the gothic type was usually known as black letter.[6]

From the four main collections in the library we give some examples of these early printings and particularly some of the magnificent examples of the great continental scholar printers.

Germany

Printing was confined to Mainz for some years but due to internal disturbances and the sack of the city many of the Mainz printers fled and so helped spread their art to other German cities and eventually throughout Europe.[7]

---

4 T.K. Abbott, *Catalogue of fifteenth-century books in the Library of Trinity College, Dublin, and in Marsh's Library, Dublin, with a few from other collections*, Dublin, Hodges Figgis, London, Longmans Green, 1905. (Since Abbott's catalogue was published at least two books in Marsh's, and possibly three, have been dated later than 1500 and two books have been dated before 1500.)   **5** H.G. Aldis, *The printed book*, 2nd rev. ed. by John Carter & E.A. Crutchley, Cambridge, At the University Press, 1941, p. 16. See also D.B. Updike, *Printing types*, Belknap Press of Harvard University Press, 1966, i, p. 39.   **6** R.B. McKerrow, *An introduction to bibliography*, 2nd imp., Oxford, At the Clarendon Press, 1928, pp 288–9. **7** Warren Chappell, op. cit., p. 64.

By 1500 printing had developed in Bamberg and Strassburg; the latter city was to become one of the most important centres of printing in Germany.

Before 1470 Johann Mentelin (*d.*1478) had completed a large Bible in German and there is in the Stearne collection a fine example of Mentelin's printing.[8] This work is entitled *Pharetra auctoritates et dicta doctorum continens* and it was printed by Mentelin in about 1472 (*Abbott* 420). But Johann Mentelin is not the only Strassburg printer represented in the library. There are also books printed by Martin Flach, Georg Husner, Johann Pruss and Johannes Gruninger, all before 1500.

COLOGNE

Ulrich Zel (d.1507?) was printing in Cologne in 1465[9] and we have in the Stillingfleet collection Jacobus de Voragine's *Legenda aurea* printed by Ulrich Zel in 1483 (Abbott 591). The *Golden legend* was one of the most popular books ever printed and consists of a collection of religious legends which were translated into several languages. This edition was printed by Zel in a small gothic type that has been described as 'the finest type of the kind in use in the fifteenth century'.[10] Many writers believe that it was Ulrich Zel who taught Caxton how to print.[11] Other Cologne printers in the library are Johannes Koelhoff de Lubeck and Hermannus Bomgart de Kerwych. But the most prolific of all the German printers was the Nuremberg printer, Anton Koberger (*d.*1513). Koberger began printing in 1470 and became one of the first entrepreneurs of printing.[12] He developed such a large business that he eventually commissioned other printers to print for him. There are three books printed by Anton Koberger before 1500 in the library. One is in the Stillingfleet collection and the other two are in the Stearne collection.

Of the German printed books in the library, however, pride of place undoubtedly must be given to Bernhard von Breydenbach's *Sanctarum pere-grinationum in montem Syon atque in montem Synai opusculum*, printed in Mainz in 1486 (*Abbott* 167), in the Stillingfleet collection. Breydenbach, the dean of Mainz, went on a pilgrimage to the Holy Land and took with him on the pilgrimage the artist Erhard Reuwich. Together they produced the

8 S.H. Steinberg, *Five hundred years of printing*, 3rd ed. rev. by James Moran, London, Penguin Books, 1974, p. 47.   9 H.G. Aldis, op. cit., p. 9.   10 *A guide to the exhibition in the king's library*, London, British Museum, 1926, p. 23.   11 See G.D. Painter, *William Caxton*, London, Chatto & Windus, 1976, p. 56. Painter says '[Johann] Veldener was Caxton's teacher …'.   12 S.H. Steinberg, op. cit., p. 58.

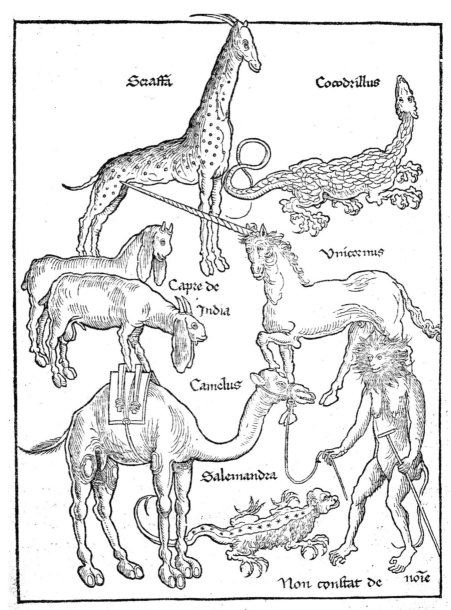

12   'Animals truely depicted as we saw them in the Holy Land.' Illustration from
     Bernhard von Breydenbach's *Sanctarum peregrinationum in montem Syon …*
     (Mainz, 1486).

first travel book with illustrations 'taken from life and not from the imagination'. This claim is a little hard to believe when we examine the illustration entitled 'Animals truly depicted as we saw them in the Holy Land'. The animals include 'Indian goats', a 'cocodrillus' and, most extra-ordinary of all, a 'unicorn'. Nevertheless it is a remarkable piece of early printing. There are also superb woodcuts showing the various cities which the travellers visited, and one of the finest illustrations in this book is a panorama of Venice which is nearly five feet long.

Switzerland

One of the most renowned printers in Basle was Johann Amerbach (d.1513). Amerbach was a scholar printer and was probably the first printer in Basle to use roman type instead of gothic type.[13] He printed with great care and accuracy and engaged many of the distinguished professors in Basle university to assist him in the work of editing the various editions of his printings. Johann Amerbach also worked in partnership with Johann Petri and Johann Froben. In the Stillingfleet collection there is a work by the fifteenth-century arch-bishop of Florence, St Antoninus, entitled *Summa theologica* which was printed by Amerbach, Petri and Froben. *Abbott's Catalogue* lists it as a fifteenth-century printing, but it has since been more correctly dated as being printed by them in 1511 (*Abbott* 55). It bears Amerbach and partners' full-page illustration of their beautiful device. This consists of a shield with the arms of Basle (said to be a chamois horn 'erased', is rather peculiar in shape and as is often the case has the notch on the wrong side). The creature is a basilisk or 'Amphisien Cockatrice'.[14] There are also two copies in the library of Johannes de Trittenheim's *De scriptoribus ecclesiasticis*, both printed by Amerbach in 1494 (*Abbott* 550 and 551).

Johann Froben (d.1527) like Amerbach engaged scholars to edit and correct for him. He encouraged Erasmus to edit and supervise his printings and employed Hans Holbein to design illustrations and title-pages for him.[15] This brilliant combination made Froben one of the most important printers in Europe and provided an immediate demand by scholars everywhere for his books. There are many books printed by Froben in the library but one of the best is probably Erasmus' *Omnia opera* which was printed by Johann

---

13 A. F. Johnson, *The first century of printing at Basle*, London, Ernest Benn, 1926, p. 7.   **14** H. W. Davies, *Devices of the early printers*, London, Grafton, 1935, p. 39.   **15** Warren Chappell, op. cit., p. 103.

Froben's son Hieronymus and son-in-law Nicolas Episeopius in Basle in 1540 and which is part of the Stillingfleet collection.

Italy

Italy was the second country to develop printing and the Italian printers were to become famous for their innovations in book production. They were the first to produce title-pages, pagination, pocket editions, music printings and, most important of all, the two kinds of type, roman and italic.[16]

The scholars of the Italian Renaissance developed a renewed interest both in the early classical authors, and in the search and rediscovery of the manuscripts of these authors whose works had been written in the beautiful Caroline hand.[17] It was this Caroline hand which the Renaissance scholars tried to copy and it became known as the humanistic or roman script. It was not identical with the earlier handwriting but was a more condensed hand.

In 1465 when the two Germans, Conrad Sweynheym and Arnold Pannartz, began printing at the monastery of Subiaco near Rome, they were obviously influenced by this fashionable handwriting and used a type which is regarded as a transitional roman type. The first roman fount used in Italy was that of Johannes and Wendelin de Spira in Venice in 1469, but the most perfect was that of Nicolas Jenson. Nicolas Jenson (*d.*1481) was a Frenchman whose arrival in Venice is surrounded by all kinds of colourful legends, but it has been established that he was originally a mint master in Tours before coming to Venice in 1468.

Jenson's famous roman type was an enormous success and was extensively copied but it has never been surpassed.[18] We have in the Stearne collection a fine copy of Jenson's printing in Venice in 1475 of St Augustine's *De civitate Dei* (*Abbott* 96). Jenson printed this edition in a small gothic text type, but the headline is printed in upper case roman and it is a very typical example of early printing. Other well-known Venetian printers in the collections include Bernardinus de Benalius, Christopher Pensi and Reynaldus de Novimagio.

There is in the Bouhéreau collection an edition of Eusebius, *De euangelica praeparatione, a Georgio Trapezuntio e graeco in latinum traductus,* which was printed by Bonetus Locatellus in Venice in 1500 (*Abbott* 236). This book was obviously of great interest to Dr Bouhéreau when he was writing his book,

---

16 S.H. Steinberg, op. cit., p. 65.   **17** Alfred Fairbank, op. cit., p. 14.   **18** R.B. McKerrow, op. cit., p. 292.

Traité d'Origène contre Celse; Eusebius was the 'father of church history' and is the main authority for information on Origen's life.[19]

After Nicolas Jenson the next most famous Venetian printer is Aldus Manutius. Aldus Manutius (*d*.1515) was born at Bassiano near Rome in about 1450. He studied in Rome and Ferrara and became deeply interested in the classics. In 1482 he came to La Mirandola where he stayed with the brilliant scholar Giovanni Pico. It was during this period that Aldus conceived the idea of printing the Greek classics and with the financial help of Pica's nephews he set up a printing press in Venice in 1490. After five years' preparation Aldus published his first book the *Erotemata* of Lascaris in 1495.[20] The type which Aldus commissioned for his printings of the Greek classics was based on the Greek cursive handwriting used for business letters and correspondence.[21] There are in the library examples of Aldus' first and largest Greek fount; his second and third Greek founts and his fourth and smallest fount can be seen in a commentary on Aristotle printed in Venice in 1503. Aldus also printed in a roman type which Francesco Griffo of Bologna designed for him. The edition of *Thesaurus cornucopiae et horti Adonidis*, edited by Aldus Pius Manutius and printed in Venice by Aldus in 1496 (*Abbott* 541), shows in the introductory matter to this work an example of one of the first of the Aldine romans cut by Francesco Griffo. The copy in the library is in the Stearne collection.

It was however Aldus Manutius' printings of the Latin classics in italic type which became known as the Aldine classics, that really made Aldus famous. The earlier printers tended to print the majority of their books in large folios, but Aldus who had a strong commercial instinct had different ideas. He realised that with the increased demand for printed books there was now a further demand for a more convenient type of book, a book which could be read more easily and carried about from place to place. In order to make the smaller book an economic proposition, as much type as possible had to be printed on each page. Aldus again commissioned Francesco Griffo of Bologna to design a new type for him.[22] Griffo's design was based on the chancery hand originally used by the papal secretaries in Rome, and like the earlier Greek type designed by Griffo it was a further development from cursive

19 *A dictionary of Christian biography and literature*, ed. Henry Wace and William C. Piercy, London, John Murray, 1911, p. 769.   **20** *A guide to the exhibition in the king's library*, p. 37.   **21** Ibid., p. 39.   **22** A.F. Johnson, *The Italian sixteenth century*, London, Ernest Benn, 1926, pp 6–7.

handwriting into type. An example of this first italic type designed by Griffo for Aldus can be seen in Joannes Baptista Egnatius' (pseudonym of G.B. Cipelli) *De Caesaribus libri III* and other works from the 'Augustan history'. This was printed by Aldus and his father-in-law in Venice in 1516 [1517] and is in the Stillingfleet collection.

Aldus has been severely criticised for his development of current handwriting into the new art of printing. D.B. Updike says that '[Aldus] appears to have been seduced by the amusing trickery of reproducing current handwriting by type; and that is the reason that in his italics, and still more in his Greek fonts, he was about nine times too clever.'[23] In spite of this modern criticism of Aldus, the development of italic type and the printings of the Greek and Latin classics was an extraordinary achievement and incidentally a huge commercial success. Many European printers copied and pirated Aldus' printings and the various editions of his books.

Like many of the other famous printers Aldus had his own device or printer's mark. The device used by Aldus was the dolphin and anchor together with the motto 'Festina Lente'. An example of Aldus' first device in its earliest state with the double border intact can be seen in an edition of *Poetae Christiani* printed in Venice by Aldus in 1502 and in the Stillingfleet collection.

Other well-known Venetian printers in Marsh's include Gabriel Giolito de' Ferrari and the Giunta (or Junta) family who printed both in Venice and in Florence in the sixteenth century. Gabriel Giolito was one of the most prolific and influential Italian printers and is regarded as the printer who had the greatest influence on his contemporaries. There are interesting examples of his work in the library. There are also books printed by Bernardo and Filippo Giunta in Florence and Lucantonio Giunta in Venice. Lucantonio Giunta died in 1538 and after his death the firm of Giunta continued to publish liturgies. The work of this family has been dismissed by S.H. Steinberg when he wrote, 'A firm like that of the Florentine, Lucantonio Giunta, is only remarkable for its shoddy mass-production.'[24] This harsh criticism is not borne out by one of the most superb service books in Marsh's Library. This is a *Pontificale Romanum* printed by the firm of Giunta in Venice in 1543. It has been magnificently printed in red and black throughout and includes a full-page woodcut of the Crucifixion. The title-page has a decorative border which shows at the top the twelve apostles, and at the sides pontifical implements and vestments.

23 D.B. Updike, op. cit., i, p. 131.   24 S.H. Steinberg, op. cit., p. 73.

13 Filippo Giunta's printer's device.

The Giunta family like many of the printers at this period also had a device – a particularly attractive one. W.H. Davies wrote, 'It would be difficult to find its equal for perfect balance and proportion. Two children each with a cornucopia support the Giunta arms above which is the Florentine lily in an elaborated form. The folded ribbon border is Florentine'. A fine example in the library of the first use of this device can be seen in Philostratus, *Icones Philostrati* (with other works), printed by Filippo Giunta in Florence in 1517. At a later date Bernardo Giunta used the more unusual device of a snake sloughing its skin, and this device can be seen in an edition of Agnolo Firenzuola's comedy, *La Trinutia*, printed by Bernardo Giunta in Florence in 1549.

While Aldus in Venice is chiefly associated with new developments in printing, important printing was also produced in other Italian cities, and this is also reflected in the books in the library printed in Italy. In Rome in 1520 the writing master Lodovico de' Arrighi da Vicenza, who was also a minor official and writer of apostolic briefs, designed a new italic.[25] This was based on the more formal chancery hand and is considered a more beautiful and graceful italic than that of Francesco Griffo. Antonio Blado (*d.* 1567?) who was one of Rome's most important printers began printing in 1516. Blado acquired Arrighi's larger italic fount and he also used two other italic founts. Blado's use of Arrighi's second fount with modifications can be seen in the Stillingfleet collection in Cardinal Joannes Hieronymus Albanus' *De Cardinalatu*, which Blado printed in 1541.[26] Examples of the third italic fount and the small Aldine fount used by Blado are also in the library .

Like Aldus in Venice, Blado also printed with a Greek type and printed many important books. In 1539 Blado was chosen by Pope Paul III and Cardinal Cervini to print the Greek manuscripts of the Vatican Library. A.F. Johnson said that before Blado began printing in Greek he consulted Aldus in Venice. The first book in this new Greek type was Eustathius' commentary on Homer printed in four volumes (1542–50) and there is a fine copy of this edition in the Stillingfleet collection. The Greek types were the property of Cardinal Cervini and were cut for him by Giovanni Onorio Magliese da Lecce.[27]

In 1549 Blado was given the title of Tipografo Camerale or printer to the Holy See, and in 1557 he had the dubious distinction of printing the first

25 A.F. Johnson, *The Italian sixteenth century*, p. 7.   26 Ibid., p. 11.   27 Ibid., p. 10.

Roman *Index librorum prohibitorum*. Blado also had his own device which was that of an eagle holding a cloth with the city below in the background. This device can be seen on the title-page of volume 4 of *Homer* and it also shows Blado's artistic use of 'piccoli ferri'.

The Italians also excelled in Hebrew printing and in the fifteenth and sixteenth centuries more books were printed in Hebrew in Italy than in the rest of Europe.[28]

The Soncino family of the village of Soncino near Cremona were famous for their printing. A work by Immanuel ben Solomon of Rome, *Sepher ham-Mahbaroth,* was printed in Brescia in 1491 by Gerson ben Moses of Soncino (not in *Abbott, Hain* 9137, *Proctor* 7021). Gerson went to Brescia in 1490 and printed there on his own. It is interesting that this book which belonged to Archbishop Marsh was over three hundred years ago regarded by him as a particularly valuable book; the archbishop inscribed the words 'Liber Rarissimus' on the title-page. It is possible that Archbishop Marsh may have known what a fine printer Gerson was, and probably found it quite difficult to get a copy of this book. Gerson was described by S.H. Steinberg in his book as 'the greatest Jewish printer the world has ever known'.[29] Unfortunately Gerson was driven out of business in Italy by the competition of a Venetian printer, Daniel Bomberg. Bomberg was a Christian business man who obtained from the senate a privilege for printing Hebrew books. A comparison of the works of these two printers can be seen by an examination of two Hebrew Bibles in the library printed by Bomberg in 1549 and 1572.

An Italian printer who printed both in Turin and in Genoa was Petrus Paulus Porrus. It was in Genoa that Porrus printed a *Polyglot Psalter* in 1516 which was edited by Agostino Giustiniano, bishop of Nebbio. The title-page of this Psalter has a magnificent oriental design of intersecting polygons, and the decorated initials are cut to match it. There are two copies of this superb book in the library.[30]

The archbishop's personal interest in oriental works and mathematics are reflected in an edition of Euclid's *Elementorum geometricorum libri tredecim,*

---

28 A.F. Johnson, 'Italian sixteenth-century books' in *The Library,* 5 ser., xiii, no. 3, Sept. 1958, p. 168.
29 S.H. Steinberg, op. cit., p. 114.   30 The first copy in the Bishop Stearne collection bears Marsh's Greek motto and an earlier pressmark which indicates it was in Marsh's own collection. It may have been moved at a later stage. See Robert Travers' complaint about the Cradocks' moving books. The second copy in Marsh's collection does not bear his Greek motto.

1594, and in *Alphabetum Arabicum*, 1592, both printed in the Typographia Medicea in Rome. Their beautiful Arabic letters were probably cut by the famous French type-cutter Robert Granjon.[31] Granjon was working in Rome in the 1580s and A.F. Johnson says that Granjon was employed both by the Typographia Vaticana and the Typographia Medicea principally in the cutting of oriental types.

The enterprise and ability of Italian printers were not confined to the types of printing already mentioned. The Italians printed more books of music during the sixteenth century than any other country;[32] the majority of these were printed in Venice by the Scoto and Gardano families. There are in the library some delightful books of madrigals printed by both of these families. They are beautifully printed, and are lavishly illustrated with 'printers' flowers', head and tail borders, and large woodcut initial letters.

Finally to complete this short account of some of the Italian printings in Marsh's we refer to two early printings from Milan. There is the first edition of Suidas' *Lexicon Graecum*, edited by Demetrius Chalcondylas and printed by Joannes Bissolas and Benedictus Mangius in 1499 (*Abbott* 529); and the second book is Cicero's *Epistolae ad familiares* printed in Milan by Pamplo Castaldi in 1472 (*Abbott* 602. Incorrect date and printer given; see *Gesamtkatalog* 6810). We have selected this latter book because not only is it the oldest printed book in the library, but it also illustrates so many of the characteristics of very early printing. It is a beautiful book and shows the transitional stage between manuscript and print. Only the first page is decorated like a manuscript in red, blue, green and gold. The rest of the book is undecorated, the line endings are uneven, there is no title-page or foliation, and the gatherings are unsigned. The type is one of the earliest roman faces and is printed on superb paper with lavishly wide margins.

France

At the invitation of two professors in the Sorbonne in Paris, three Germans, Ulrich Gering, Michael Friburger and Martin Kranz, set up a printing press at the Sorbonne in 1470.[33] Friburger and Kranz later returned to Germany but Gering continued working there. A book written by Johann Nider (or Nyder), *Preceptorium diuine legis*, was printed by Ulrich Gering in Paris in

---

31 A.F. Johnson, *The Italian sixteenth century*, p. 12.   32 A.F. Johnson, 'Italian sixteenth-century books', p. 170.   33 D.B. Updike, op. cit., i, pp 82–3.

14 Title-page of the *Polyglot Psalter* printed in Genoa by Petrus Paulus Porrus in 1516.

1482 (*Abbott* 382) and is part of the Stillingfleet collection (copy lacks title-page). Another early Paris printer, Georg Wolf, printed Magnus Aurelius Cassiodorus' *De regimine ecclie̅ primitiue hystoria tripartita, c.*1492–3 (*Abbott* 185. No date given. See Davies, *Devices of the early printers*, p.194). Like so many books in the library it also has another interesting feature. It bears an inscription by Sir Thomas Elyot to a friend. Sir Thomas Elyot (*d.*1546) was an English diplomat and writer; his book on the education of statesmen was the earliest English treatise on natural philosophy.

A book which would have appealed very much to Archbishop Marsh's taste, and which not very surprisingly he had in his collection, is Gulielmus de Occam's *Quotlibeta Guillermi holran*. It was printed in Paris in 1487 by Petrus Rubeus (*Abbott* 391). The type used by Rubeus for the printing of this work is the French *lettre bâtarde* and it is rubricated throughout in red and blue. It originally belonged to the English book collector Edward Gwynn. Other early Paris printers include Jean Higman, Philip Pigouchet and Francis Regnault.

Apart from these early well-known Paris printers, the books printed in France which are in the library represent the 'golden age' of the French scholar-printers both in Paris and Lyon. Curiously, France did not make a great contribution to the early stages of printing, but in the sixteenth century their great scholar printers virtually dominated it.

One of the best known of these early French scholar printers represented in Marsh's is Josse Bade. Bade usually used the Latinised version of his name Jodocus Badius Ascensius. Badius (*d.*1535) was born in Ghent and studied in Italy. Later he went to Lyon and learned to print at the printing house of Johann Trechsel.[34] Badius left Lyon in 1499 and went to Paris. He specialised in printing ancient and modern Latin writers and he called his firm the Praelum Ascensianum. Badius used as his device a printing press at work; an illustration on this device can be seen in a book by Joannes Major, *Historia Maioris Britanniae*, printed in 1521, in the Stillingfleet collection. Like so many of the books in the library it originally belonged to a famous owner, the author of the first English comedy *Ralph Roister Doister*, Nicholas Udall. When Badius died in 1535 the Praelum Ascensianum merged with that of another scholar printer, Henri Estienne (Henricus Stephanus). But Badius was not entirely forgotten. Michel Vascosan married Badius' daughter and

---

34 S.H. Steinberg, op. cit., p. 81.

was renowned for his printing of particularly fine books. A specimen of his printing can be seen in a book written by Paulus Aemilius. For this printing Vascosan used beautiful decorated initials which were probably designed by the French mathematician, Oronce Finé.

Probably the best-known artist associated with the scholar printers is Geofroy Tory. Geofroy Tory (*d.*1533) was born in Bruges and was a schoolmaster, lecturer in philosophy, bookseller and printer. He was astonishingly talented, so much so indeed that D.B. Updike described him as 'a divine jack-of-all-trades'.[35] Tory was the author of *Champ fleury*, a major work on letter design and the theory and proportion of roman letters; it also gave details of his private life. Tory's book was so influential that after its publication the majority of French books were printed in the roman type. A breviary printed by Geofroy Tory's successor, Oliver Mallard, in 1542 shows Tory's device of the 'pot casse'; this was a broken vessel on a clasped book and the motto 'Non plus'. This curious device is said to have been made in commemoration of the death of Tory's young daughter Agnes.[36]

The work of the scholar printers is best illustrated by the great French family, that of Estienne, or in the Latinised version of their name, Stephanus. The firm of Estienne was begun by Henri Estienne (*d.*1520) who became a printer in 1502 when he married the widow of Jean Higman. A superb *Quincuplex Psalterium*, in the Stearne collection, was printed by Henri Estienne in Paris in 1513. (There is an earlier edition of this work printed by Estienne in 1509 in the British Library.) In this work five versions of the Psalms are presented, three versions are placed side by side and the remaining two in an appendix printed in a double column. The printing is in red and black throughout and the use of ornaments to fill out broken lines, the floral arabesque and an entrelac unit in three varieties, make this printing a work of art.[37]

When Henri Estienne died, his widow married his foreman Simon de Colines as was the custom in the printing trade.[38] De Colines is believed to be the first French printer to print books entirely in italic type.[39] An example of Simon de Colines' printing in the Bouhéreau collection can be

35 D.B. Updike, op. cit., i, p. 188.   **36** H.W. Davies, *Devices of the early printers*, pp 682–3. See also Arundell Esdaile, *A student's manual of bibliography*, London, George Allen & Unwin, and the Library Association, 1931, p. 204.   **37** D.B. Updike, op. cit., i, p. 192. (Updike refers to the first edition of 1509. The edition in Marsh's is dated 1513.)   **38** A.F. Johnson, *French sixteenth century printing*, London, Ernest Benn, 1928, p. 7.   **39** D.B. Updike, op. cit., i, p. 191.

seen in a work by Horace which he printed in Paris in 1528. It also has de Colines' attractive device 'Tempus' on the title-page and is one of the very few books in the library to include a bookbinder's name, that of the French binder Jean Norvins. Simon de Colines carried on the business until Henri's son Robert Estienne took over in 1526.

Robert Estienne or Robertus Stephanus (*d*.1559) was the most distinguished member of his family. His printings included scholarly works, classical authors and Latin grammars, and he came to be known as the father of French lexicography.[40] There are two outstanding examples of Robert Estienne's work in the library. The first is his printing of the New Testament in Greek in 1550 which is in the Bouhéreau collection. The text for this New Testament was based on those of the Complutensian Polyglot and the editions of Erasmus with a few readings introduced from manuscripts, and it became known as the 'textus receptus'. The artist engraver, Claude Garamond (*d*.1561), cut the punches for the type used, a cursive based on the handwriting of Angelos Vergetios, a Greek copyist in the employment of Francis I. This type was called *grec du Roi* and the punches were cut in three sizes. A medium text type was first completed and used in 1544 for an edition of Eusebius, the smaller version was then finished, and in 1550 the large text type was used for the first time in this New Testament in which all three sizes appear.[41] The second great printing is one of Robert Estienne's finest achievements. Estienne was asked to provide a better dictionary than the current standard work.[42] He appealed to the scholars in Paris but they refused because of the enormous amount of work involved. Estienne did the work on his own and completed the dictionary in 1531. His splendid scholarly work has still not been surpassed. The copy of *Dictionarum seu Latinae linguae thesaurus* in the Stillingfleet collection is the improved second edition of 1543.

LYON

The first printer in Lyon was Guillaume Le Roy and he began printing in 1473.[43] Lyon was the great commercial centre and was free from many of the restrictions imposed in Paris by ecclesiastical censorship. An illustrated Bible printed in Lyon in 1522 which was given to Archbishop Marsh in

40 S.H. Steinberg, op. cit., p. 86.   **41** *A guide to the exhibition in the king's library*, p. 54.   **42** Elizabeth Armstrong, *Robert Estienne*, Cambridge, At the University Press, 1954, p. 84.   **43** *A guide to the exhibition in the king's library*, p. 46, and S.H. Steinberg, op. cit., pp 81 and 83.

1690 by Frances Guise contains portrait initials of saints and princes which are possibly the work of Guillaume Le Roy.

There are seven incunabula in the library which were printed in Lyon, four of which were printed by Johannes Trechsel. Two of the other three printings are editions of one of the most popular books of the fifteenth century, Werner Rolevinck's *Fasciculus temporum*. The first copy, which is in the Bouhéreau collection, was translated into French by Pierre Farget and it was printed in Lyon in 1483 (*Abbott* 461). The second copy, which is in the Stearne collection, is in Latin and was printed by Mathias Hus in Lyon and has no date of printing, but was probably printed in or about 1495 (*Abbott* 462). It contains a delightful illustration of the Ark, which is three storeys high with faces of animals and humans anxiously peering from every porthole. The final early Lyon printing is in the Stillingfleet collection and is Nicolaus de Lyra's *Postilla super Psalterium una cum Canticis*, printed in Lyon in 1497 (*Abbott* 352).

Jean de Tournes (*d*.1564) was born at Lyon and worked for Sebastian Gryphius until 1542. De Tournes is considered one of the greatest of the Lyon printers and he produced magnificent books.[44] His elegant use of arabesque woodcut borders and illustrations make many of his books works of art. These borders and an extraordinary Midas title-page border can be seen in Guillaume Paradin's *Memoriae nostrae libri quatuor* which de Tournes printed in Lyon in 1548. It is in the Bouhéreau collection. In the Stillingfleet collection there is a copy of Jean Froissart's *Premier (–quart) volume de l'histoire et cronique* printed by de Tournes between 1559 and 1561. It bears de Tournes' curious encircling snake device and motto on the title-page. De Tournes was also associated with the work of the great illustrator, Bernard Salomon.[45] Unfortunately we can only get a glimpse in Marsh's of the work of this great artist in copies of his illustrations which were used in Andreas Alciatus' *Emblemata* published in a very late edition for the heirs of Guillaume Rouille in Lyon in 1600. It is in the Stearne collection.

Sebastian Gryphius (*d*.1556) specialised in printing editions of the Latin classics in italic type but he also had the distinction of being the first printer of Rabelais' writings[46] and employed Rabelais as his editor.[47] Two interesting

---

44 A.F. Johnson, *French sixteenth century printing*, p. 20. See also T.M. MacRobert, 'Jean de Tournes' in *Motif*, 2, February 1959, pp 10–11.   45 T.M. MacRobert, *Printed books: a short introduction to fine typography*, London, Victoria and Albert Museum, HMSO, 1957, p. 4.   46 Warren Chappell, op. cit., p. 104.   47 S.H. Steinberg, op. cit., p. 92.

examples of Gryphius' printings in the library are Lazare de Baif's *De re nauali libellus ... ex Bayfii excerptus*, printed by Gryphius in 1540 (it is in Archbishop Marsh's collection) and St Cyprian's *Opera* printed by Gryphius in 1537. This second work was originally owned by Dr Bouhéreau and it is bound in a contemporary leather binding decorated with a small centre gilt ornament of a curious small sea monster on the upper and lower covers. Sebastian Gryphius had for his device the figure of a large griffin and like so many other printers' devices it was of course a pun on his own name.

Robert Granjon, a Parisian punch-cutter, supplied both Sebastian Gryphius and Jean de Tournes with italic founts. Granjon was also a printer and publisher and in 1557 he designed a new type for his own firm which was based on a very popular French gothic style contemporary handwriting. This new ingenious type was called *lettre de civilité*.[48] A small specimen of this type can be seen in the dedication of Pierre Heyn's *Le miroir du monde* which was printed in Antwerp in 1583 and is in the Stillingfleet collection.

While many of the books in the library's French collection were printed in the two most important centres of Paris and Lyon, there are also copies of books printed in other cities in France, notably in Rouen and La Rochelle. We end this short account of French printings with a book printed in Rouen and written by Nicolaus de Lyra. De Lyra (*d.*1340) was minister provincial of the Franciscan Order for the Paris Province. He wrote commentaries on the Old and New Testaments and his writings are believed to have influenced Martin Luther and Christian scholarship generally. It does seem however that de Lyra's influence on Luther was somewhat exaggerated, but it did not prevent Luther's enemies from inventing the couplet 'If Lyra had not harped profanation, Luther would never have danced the Reformation.'[49] Nicolaus de Lyra's book *Tractatus de differentia litterae Hebraicae a nostra translatione* is in the Stillingfleet collection and was printed by Martinus Morin in Rouen *c.*1495–7 (*Abbott* 354). It originally belonged to the English book-collector Edward Gwynn and was purchased by Edward Stillingfleet at Richard Smith's sale.

Belgium and the Netherlands

The first printing in Holland is a matter of great controversy mainly due to the existence of undated books known as 'Costeriana', which were printed

48 A.F. Johnson, *French sixteenth-century printing*, p. 23.   49 David Lass, 'A brief account of Nicholas De

partly from type and partly from blocks. But the first books printed in Holland by the Gutenberg method and with a printed date were printed by the Dutch printers Nicolaus Ketelaer and Gerard Leempt in Utrecht in 1473.[50] It is exciting to discover that a work in the Stearne collection entitled *Defensorium fidei contra Judeos hereticos et Sarracenos libros seu dyalogos septē continens* was printed by Ketelaer and Leempt in Utrecht in 1473 (*Abbott* 222), together with two similar pieces.

One of the most popular books of the middle ages was Boethius' *De consolatione philosophiae*, and there are numerous copies in the library. The most interesting edition belonged to Archbishop Marsh and it was printed in Deventer in 1490 by one of the most prolific of the Dutch printers, Jacobus de Breda (*Abbott* 148. Printer and place of printing not identified in *Abbott*. *Gesamtkatalog* 4546). A travel book written by Ludolphus de Suchen entitled *Libellus de itinere ad terram sanctam* was printed by the very fine Dutch printer Gerard Leeu at Gouda in about 1484 (*Abbott* 604. This book has no printer's name, place of printing or date. It was identified in 1960. *H.C.* 10309, *Campb.* 1622). It originally belonged to Edward Gwynn and is part of the Stillingfleet collection. Finally a rare work in the Stillingfleet collection, *Modus legendi in utroque jure*, was printed by Christian Snellaert in Delft in 1495 (*Abbott* 374).

These are of course the earliest Dutch printings in the library, but as in many other European countries printing in Holland is always associated with one particular family – that of the Elzevirs. As with Aldus in Italy the Elzevir press was a great commercial success because of their printings of small-sized editions of the classics and the enormous number of books which they produced. There are a large number of Elzevir printings in the collections in the library including some of their most popular printings. Unfortunately, however, the Elzevir classics because of their small size and popularity were also great favourites with thieves, and during the eighteenth century many of these volumes disappeared from the library.

Belgium in the fifteenth century had no separate existence, but in the area now regarded as modern Belgium printing began in the town of Alost in 1473.[51] Thierry Martens was the first printer there and once again it is exciting to know that there are two religious tracts in the Stearne collection

Lyra's *Tractatus de differentia nostrae …*' in *The Serif, Quarterly of the Kent State University Libraries*, 10, no. 2, Summer 1973, p. 20.   **50** Warren Chappell, op. cit., p. 72.   **51** Henry Cotton, *A typographical gazetteer*, 2nd ed., Oxford, At the University Press, 1831, p. 9.

printed by Thierry Martens in Alost in 1487. Another fine printer who worked with Martens in Alost before moving to Louvain was John of Westphalia. He printed in Louvain for over twenty years and one of his printings in the Stearne collection relates to Ireland. This is by the fourteenth-century archbishop of Armagh, Richard FitzRalph, and is entitled *Defensorium curatorum contra eos qui privilegiatos se dicunt*. FitzRalph in his book defended his views on evangelical poverty in the great controversy with the Franciscans. It was printed by John of Westphalia in about 1484 (*Abbott* 455). (It is bound together with a three-leaf letter from Pope Pius to Louis XI.)

It was the religious order of the Brothers of the Common Life who introduced printing into Brussels in 1475[52] and an example of their printing can be seen in a work by Henricus de Gorickem [Gorckham] entitled *Conclusiones super quattuor libros sententiarum*. It was printed by the Brothers in about 1480 (*Abbott* 266) in gothic type and rubricated throughout. It is now in Marsh's collection although it originally belonged to Bishop Stearne.

Christopher Plantin (*d.*1589) left France and settled in Antwerp and began printing in 1555. Between 1569 and 1572 he printed his great masterpiece the *Polyglot Bible*. Plantin employed Robert Granjon, the French punch cutter, to cut the Greek and Syriac type and there is a fine copy of this great work in the Stillingfleet collection. Plantin also printed liturgical books and there are examples of these in the library as well as a rare book written by Nicholas Harpsfield (see below, p. 164). After Plantin's death his Antwerp establishment was continued by his son-in-law Jan Moerentorf (Joannes Moretus) who carried on the business as the Plantin-Moretus Office. Another son-in-law, Franciscus Raphelengius, succeeded him as university printer in Leiden.[53] The business was again continued by Jan's son Balthasar (*d.*1641) who further increased the fame of this establishment by his employment of Peter Paul Rubens to design title-pages for their books. All the members of this famous family are represented in the library, not only by the works already mentioned but by some fine printings of botanical books.

The professor of physic at Leiden university, Rembert Dodoens (*d.*1585), wrote a book on purging and it included information on poisonous herbs, barks and roots. This is entitled *Purgantium aliarumque eo facientium, tum et radicum … ac deleteriarum herbarum historiae libri IIII*, and it was printed by

---

52 D.B. Updike, op. cit., i, p. 95.   53 Ibid., ii, p. 13.

Christopher Plantin in Antwerp in 1574. It originally belonged to Bishop Stearne.

Johann Moretus, Plantin's grandson, printed *Icones stirpium* in Antwerp in 1591 and it contains over 2000 very fine illustrations of plants. Another well-known writer on botanical subjects was Charles de l'Écluse (Clusius), (*d.*1609). His book *Rariorum plantarum historia* was also printed by Moretus in 1601, together with *Exoticorum libri X* which has Raphelengius' name as printer on the title-page and the date 1605. The last three works are in the Bouhéreau collection. Another copy of *Exoticorum libri X* dated 1609 in the Stillingfleet collection is bound together with another of Clusius' works, *Curae posteriores* …, dated Antwerp 1611. These books contain superb wood-cuts of animals and exotic fruits, and descriptions of rare plants.

It is hardly surprising that this great printing family used as their printer's mark a particularly fine device, that of a compass on a book and the motto 'Labore et Constantia'.

Spain

Printing in Spain began in Valencia in 1474. The first printer there was Lambert Palmart and he is believed to have been of Flemish origin.[54] There are no fifteenth-century Spanish printed books in the library, but in the Stillingfleet collection there is a copy of what is regarded as the finest of all Spanish printings, the first complete edition of the Polyglot Bible.

Cardinal Francisco Ximenes de Cisneros (*d.*1517) was archbishop of Toledo and the founder of the university of Alcalá. The cardinal was responsible for the idea and organisation of this Spanish Polyglot Bible. He employed as his printer Arnald Guillem de Brocar. De Brocar used roman types, gothic types and a superb Greek type which was copied from a beautiful early manuscript hand and is in great contrast to the cursive design adopted by Aldus in Venice. The completed Bible both in scholarship and workmanship is a magnificent and remarkable achievement. It became known as the *Complutensian Polyglot Bible* because it was printed in Alcalá de Henares (Complutum being the Latin name) between 1514 and 1517 and it cost the cardinal the huge sum of 50,000 gold ducats.[55]

Another book in the Stillingfleet collection printed at about this time in Alcalá is Petrus Martyr Anglerius' *Epistolae* printed by Miguel de Eguia in

54 A *guide to the exhibition in the king's library*, p. 42.   **55** S.H. Steinberg, op. cit., p. 98.

1530. De Eguia was de Brocar's successor and it is interesting to note that Henry Cotton in his *Typographical gazetteer* says that 'early Alcalá books are of considerable rarity'.

There are also some sixteenth- and seventeenth-century Spanish printings in the Stillingfleet collection, including one of the most important Indexes of forbidden books ever issued. This Index was issued by Antonio de Sotomayer, titular archbishop of Damascus and inquisitor general, and was printed in Madrid in 1640. Some of the greatest names in the philosophic and scientific world are condemned in it including Bodin, Erasmus, Grotius, Rabelais and Machiavelli. A book printed by Louis Sanchez in Madrid in 1611, also in the Stillingfleet collection, is of interest to students of the Spanish language; it was written by Sebastian de Cobarruvias Orozco and is entitled *Tesoro de la lengua Castellana, o Española*.

Archbishop Marsh also seems to have been interested in Spain and he collected the majority of the Spanish books in the library. They consist mainly of histories, dictionaries and books on agriculture and gardening. But one curious book in his collection does not bear the Greek motto which he invariably put on all his own books. It was written by Benito Remigio and is entitled *Práctica de exorcistas y ministros de la Iglesia* and was printed by Andres Garcia in Madrid in 1666. Other Spanish books in the library dating from the early part of the seventeenth century were printed in such cities as Granada in 1601, Valladolid 1603, Saragossa 1604, Pamplona 1605, Salamanca 1608, and Toledo 1618.

Denmark and Sweden

The German printer Johann Snell set up printing presses in Denmark and Sweden in about 1483.[56] There is a copy of the first book printed by Johann Snell in Stockholm in 1483 still extant in the university library in Uppsala.[57] The earliest surviving book printed in Copenhagen was not printed by Snell but by Gothefridus de Ghemen in 1493. The only Danish and Swedish printed books in Marsh's date from the seventeenth century and they are mainly in the Stillingfleet collection.

When King Christian IV of Denmark invited the Dutchman Joannes Meursius to become professor of history and politics in the university of Sora in 1625, Meursius began writing a history of Denmark. This work was

56 Ibid., p. 64.

entitled *Historiae Danicae* and was printed in Copenhagen in 1631 by Joachim Moltkenium. Joannes Meursius or Jan van Meurs (*d.*1639) was a prodigious writer;[58] his history of Denmark and many of his other writings are in the Stillingfleet collection.

The fashionable physician and professor of physic, Olaus Wormius (*d.*1654), also worked for King Christian IV and wrote on philosophy and Danish antiquities.[59] His book *De monumento Trygveldensi epistola ...* was printed in Copenhagen by Melchior Martzan in 1636 and is in the Stearne collection. Another Danish professor of physic and philosophy, Oliger Jacobaeus (*d.*1701), was employed by King Christian V to collect and arrange the famous antiquarian collection in Copenhagen.[60] His book on this collection entitled *Museum Regium, seu catalogus rerum ...* contains the weirdest illustrations of birds, fishes, animals and people. It was printed in Copenhagen in 1696 and is in the Stillingfleet collection.

A book which relates to Swedish political events and which originally belonged to the English book-collector Edward Gwynn is also in the Stillingfleet collection. It concerns Sigismund III, the Swedish prince who was elected king of Poland in 1587 and crowned king of Sweden in 1594.[61] Sigismund III (*d.*1632) was a Catholic which made him unpopular in Sweden where the majority of the people were Protestant. After various incidents Sigismund was forced to put his uncle Duke Charles who was a Protestant in charge of Swedish affairs.[62] This move worked for a short time only; further difficulties arose, Sigismund was dethroned, and eventually Duke Charles was made king of Sweden. The book is entitled *Exegesis historica ... commemorans causas, quibus amplissimi ordines regni Sueciae provocati, Sigismundum ... tertium ... Suecano exuerunt diademate ... ac Carolum IX ... coronarunt.* It was printed in Stockholm, ex Molybdographia Gutteruiciana, in 1620.

UPPSALA

Printing began in Uppsala in about 1510. That extraordinary genius Olaus (or Olof) Rudbeck (*d.*1702) lived and worked in Uppsala and set up his own printing press there in 1686.[63] Rudbeck was a professor of medicine

---

57 Henry Cotton, op. cit., p. 122.   **58** Alexander Chalmers, *The general biographical dictionary*, new ed. rev., London, 1815 (Joannes Meursius or Jan van Meurs).   **59** Ibid. (Olaus Wormius).   **60** Ibid. (Oliger Jacobaeus).   **61** *The Encyclopaedia Britannica*, ninth edition, Edinburgh, Adam & Charles Black, 1875–89 (Poland).   **62** Ibid. (Poland and Sweden).   **63** Alexander Chalmers, op. cit. (Olaus or Olof Rudbeck). And see Henry Cotton, op. cit., p. 317.

and discovered the lymphatic glands in the body. As well as writing books on botany he also wrote an astonishing book entitled *Atlantica*, 4 vols, which purported to prove the greatness of Sweden as the source of all learning and knowledge and the original earthly paradise of Adam and Eve. Rudbeck further maintained that Sweden was also the country where Atlantis had been discovered. There is an undated volume of this bizarre book in the Stillingfleet collection. It is believed to have been printed in 1675 which is the date of the first edition. We also have in the Stearne collection a copy of Rudbeck's *Tabulae* which contains illustrations of maps, coins, emblems and ancient buildings. The copperplate frontispiece represents Rudbeck explaining a globe of the world to several interested bystanders. This work was, according to Brunet, printed after 1675.[64] Rudbeck also edited Olaus Verelius' book, *Index linguae veteris Scytho-Scandicae sive Gothicae ex vetusti aevi monumentis … collectus*, printed in Uppsala in 1691. Another work written by Olaus Verelius on Scandinavian antiquities was printed in Uppsala in 1675. This is a particularly interesting book since it was printed partly in Runic type. Both this and the *Index* are in the Stillingfleet collection.

Russia

One of the most exciting events in recent years in Marsh's was the redis-covery by J.S.G. Simmons of six early Russian printed books in Archbishop Marsh's own collection.[65] Four of these books probably exist nowhere else outside Russia. Like almost all early printings the contents are entirely religious or educational. Three of the books were printed by the first Russian printer, Ivan Fedorov.

The first work is an *Apostol* (Liturgical Epistles) and is of the first issue of the first dated book printed in Russia; it was completed on 1 March 1564 by Ivan Fedorov and Petr Timofeev Mstislavets. Only one other copy of the *Apostol* has so far been found in Western Europe. The binding is contemporary Russian work with blind stamped calf over wooden boards, with the remains of bosses, studs and clasps. The second book is *Evangelie uchitel 'noe* (Liturgical Gospels) printed by Ivan Fedorov at Zabludov in Belorussia in 1569. This binding is also contemporary and shows the crucifix and symbols of the evangelists stamped in silver on the upper cover.

64 Jacques-Charles Brunet, *Manuel du libraire et de l'amateur de livres*, 4th ed., 5 vols, Paris, 1842–4, iv, p. 142.   65 J.S.G. Simmons, 'Early printed Cyrillic books in Archbishop Marsh's Library Dublin' in *The Irish Book*, ii, no. 2, Spring 1963, pp 37–42.

15 Illustration of the sacrament of baptism from *O Sakramentakh*, a devotional work on the sacraments printed at the Monastery of the Caves in Kiev in 1657.

The third book is a Psalter and New Testament printed at Ostrog in 1580 and is bound in plain vellum. Although some of the books are unfortunately imperfect, lacking title-pages and much else, and the leather bindings are also in a poor state, the standard of printing is remarkably high. The beautiful Cyrillic types used in these books are derived from the Cyrillic script similar to the letter form still used by Russians, Ukrainians, Bulgarians and Serbs. It is largely based on Greek uncial script of the ninth and tenth centuries. Simmons noted that this script in spite of its name was probably not in fact invented by St Cyril, the apostle of the Slavs, who it is thought is more likely to have been the inventor of the other ancient Slavonic letter-form, the Glagolitic alphabet. The *Apostol* is particularly striking, and is printed in red and black throughout. Some of the pages are decorated with beautiful woodcut ornaments which give a most pleasing and slightly exotic appearance to the pages.

The fourth book is a *Bukvar*, or elementary instruction book for children, and was printed at the Monastery Press at Kuteino near Orsha in Belorussia in 1653. Like the other books the reading matter provided is almost entirely religious, containing the ten commandments, Athanasian Creed, and morning and evening prayers. It also includes on the verso of the title-page a wood-cut of St Gregory the Theologian. The binding for this obviously much used prayer book is still in its original uncovered oak boards, bevelled internally and with a narrow leather spine.

The fifth book is a copy of Patriarch Nikon's *Pouchenie o morovom yazve* printed at Moscow in 1656. The text consists of a series of instructions against the dreadful plague which began in Moscow in 1654. The sixth book is the very rare *O sakramentakh*. This is a devotional work on the sacraments and it was printed in Kiev at the Monastery of the Caves on 26 November 1657. Again as with another rare printing (see below, p. 146) by some extraordinary coincidence there are two copies in the library. They contain superb woodcut illustrations and ornaments of the various sacraments, and these impressive illustrations were among the most notable features of the work of the Kiev press in the seventeenth century. They were bound together with the *Pouchenie* in a contemporary Western European leather binding and were presented to Archbishop Marsh by Frances Guise in 1690 when Marsh was bishop of Ferns and Leighlin.

North America

Printing began in the New World when the Spanish sent a printing press to Mexico City in 1539.[66] Strangely enough it was almost one hundred years before the first printing press was set up in a North American city, and it was an English printer Stephen Daye who first began to print there. Daye had been invited to America in 1638 and with his sons Stephen and Matthew he began printing in Cambridge, Massachusetts. The first book which they printed was the *Whole book of Psalms* in 1640. This became known as the *Bay Psalm Book*.[67]

It is not very surprising to discover that the majority of the books in the library which deal with America, and in particular the books on travel, were all printed in England. But there are two pamphlets on the subject of baptism which were printed in America and they were originally part of the Stillingfleet collection. The first pamphlet is entitled *Propositions concerning the subject of baptism* and was printed by S.G. (Samuel Green) in Cambridge, Massachusetts, for Hezekiah Usher at Boston in 1662. No author is given on the title-page but the *Wing catalogue* (*Wing* M 2292) attributes the authorship to Jonathan Mitchel.[68] Jonathan Mitchel (*d.*1668) emigrated from England to America and subsequently became a fellow of Harvard. He was a member of the synod of Boston which was held to discuss questions of church membership and discipline. According to the *DNB*, Mitchel, together with a fellow pastor, Richard Mather, was chiefly responsible for writing the second pamphlet, which again has no author on the title-page and is entitled *A defence of the answer and arguments of the synod*. This was also printed by Samuel Green but in partnership with M. Johnson in Cambridge, Massachusetts, for Hezekiah Usher of Boston in 1664 (*Wing* M 1271). Richard Mather (*d.*1669) was a Congregational divine and like Mitchel had emigrated from England to Massachusetts.[69] Mather later became a leader in the church councils of New England Congregationalism.

From the printing point of view it is interesting that it was Samuel Green who took over Stephen Daye's printing press in 1649 and it was also Green, together with Marmaduke Johnson, who was responsible for printing the first Indian Bible in 1663.[70] These early American printed pamphlets were probably sent to Bishop Stillingfleet from America as they originally formed

---

66 D.B. Updike, op. cit., ii, p. 60.   67 Warren Chappell, op. cit., p. 137.   68 *DNB* (Jonathan Mitchel).
69 Ibid. (Richard Mather).   70 Warren Chappell, op. cit., p. 137.

part of his collection; but they were later bound together with similar type pamphlets and are now kept in the second gallery in the 'cages'.

Ireland

The first book printed in Ireland was the *Book of Common Prayer*; it was printed in Dublin in 1551 by Humphrey Powell.[71] Since of course it was printed in English, it was not available to the majority of Irish people, who in the sixteenth century spoke Irish only. It was for this reason that Queen Elizabeth, who was anxious to promote the Protestant religion in Ireland, had a printing press with a fount of Irish type sent over to Ireland.

The Irish type designed for the purpose in 1571 was mainly a roman type, but with a few distinctively Irish letters. It was first used to print an Irish religious poem.[72] Edward Lynam (*d.*1950) noted that because this type was designed and cut in England it could possibly have been modelled on the Anglo-Saxon type used by the English printer John Day (*d.*1584). This early Irish type was again used by the third printer in Ireland, John Franckton, for his printing of William Ó Domhnuill's Irish translation of the New Testament, printed in Dublin in 1602/3,[73] and for the Book of Common Prayer also printed by Franckton in 1608.

There is a fine copy of the New Testament (*STC* 2958) in Archbishop Marsh's collection in the library which bears the archbishop's Greek motto, and also a copy of the Book of Common Prayer, *Leabhar na nurnaightheadh* (*STC* 16433), which unfortunately lacks its title-page although a facsimile has been pasted in.

The Anglo-Saxon type mentioned by E.W. Lynam as the model for the Irish type can be seen in Marsh's in a copy of John Day's printing of Aelfric's *A testimonie of antiquitie* which Day printed in 1566? (*STC* 159.5). This was in fact the first book for which a fount of Anglo-Saxon type was cast.

The development of Irish script into type had a history quite dissimilar to that of the Continent, where the development was influenced by the popular cursive handwriting and the examples of writing masters. Irish handwriting grew out of the early Roman alphabet and was a beautiful

71 E.R. McC. Dix, *Printing in Dublin prior to 1601*, 2nd ed., Dublin, Colm O'Lochlainn, 1932, Introduction, p. xi.   **72** E.W. Lynam, *The Irish character in print 1571–1923*, with introduction by Alf MacLochlainn, Irish University Press, 1969, p. 5.   **73** E.R. McC. Dix, Compiler, *Catalogue of early Dublin-printed books 1601–1700, in four parts with an historical introduction and biographical notes by C. Winston Dugan*, Dublin, 1898-1912, p. 11.

formal book-hand which had remained unchanged for almost one thousand years. The most popular handwriting in medieval Ireland was the round or half uncial and the pointed Irish. The pointed Irish was a more condensed hand and for economic reasons became more popular.

The second Irish type was designed by the exiled Irish Franciscan scholars in Belgium. These Irish scholars were naturally much more familiar with Irish handwriting and manuscripts, and their designs were really regarded as the first Irish type. The first book issued with this type was in Antwerp in 1611. In 1616 the printing press was moved to the new Franciscan College of St Anthony in Louvain. E.W. Lynam again noted that even though this Irish type was designed by Irish scholars it bore no resemblance to contemporary Irish handwriting, and he suggested that possibly it was because the type was cut in Belgium by a cutter who was obviously influenced by the current continental fashion for italic, and may well have taken italic as his guide.[74] This second Irish type can be seen in Marsh's in the unique *Suim riaghlacha S. Phroinsiais,* a summary of the rule of St Francis, in Gaelic (*STC* 11314.9, *A & R* 800a), which was printed in Louvain 1614–18?[75] A third Irish type was designed by a similar group of Irish scholars in Rome in about 1675 but there are no examples of this type in Marsh's.

When the Hon. Robert Boyle (*d.*1691), the Irish scientist, decided to reprint the Irish version of the New Testament which had originally been printed in 1602/3 a search was made for the first Irish type, but it had completely disappeared.[76] Boyle therefore had a new Irish type cut by Joseph Moxon which was apparently modelled on the type designed by the Franciscans in Louvain. This second New Testament in Irish was printed in London by Robert Everingham in 1681 (*Wing* B 2715) and the copy in Marsh's bears an inscription by Archbishop Marsh noting that it was a gift from Robert Boyle to him.

Narcissus Marsh at the time of the publication of the second New Testament in Irish was provost of Trinity College. We have already given details of the part which Marsh took in the preparation for printing of Bishop William Bedell's Irish translation of the Old Testament which was published in London in 1685.[77] There is a copy of this 1685 edition of the

74 E.W. Lynam, op. cit., p. 10.   **75** A.F. Allison and D.M. Rogers, *A catalogue of catholic books in English printed abroad or secretly in England 1558–1640,* Bognor Regis, Arundel Press, 1956, pt II, M–Z Biographical Studies, 3, no. 4, April 1956, p. 150.   **76** E.W. Lynam, op. cit., p. 8.   **77** *Christian Examiner, and Church of Ireland Magazine,* no. xxiv, vol. ii, November 1833, pp 761–72 (Letters from Archbishop

Old Testament (*Wing* B 2711) in Marsh's collection in the library. There are also in the library copies of twenty original letters from Robert Boyle to Marsh on the printing costs and other difficulties associated with the publication of the Old Testament.[78] The collection also includes copies of letters from Hugh Reily to Robert Boyle complaining about the mistakes contained in the transcripts sent over from Dublin.

Irish types then were designed in London, Louvain, and Rome. Between 1732 and 1742 a group of Irish exiles began to print in Paris with another new Irish type. Marsh's Library in recent years acquired one of their best-known publications, *The catechism* or *Christian doctrine* by Andrew Donlevy. Andrew Donlevy DD (*d*.1761) was the prefect in the Irish College in Paris and his Catechism was printed by a Frenchman, Jacques Guerin, in Paris in 1742.[79]

Many of the Irish types designed on the Continent were fairly successful; for political reasons very few Irish types were designed in Ireland. Indeed it was not until the nineteenth century that Irish designs appeared, some being the most perfect of such types ever designed.[80] These were created by George Petrie (*d*.1866) for the publications of the Irish Archaeological Society.

What is generally regarded as the most beautiful of the types designed by Petrie can be seen in *Leabhar Imuinn* by James Henthorn Todd. This was published by the University Press (M.H. Gill) in Dublin in 1855. The publications of the Irish Archaeological Society and similar publications are kept in Marsh's in a special room devoted to books of Irish interest.

Other examples of Irish types can be seen in Charles O'Conor's *Rerum Hibernicarum scriptores veteres*, 4 vols (J. Seeley, Buckinghamiae, 1814–26). The second volume of this notable work contains a special Irish type designed by Vincent Figgins.

The nineteenth-century Irish scholar Owen Connellan (*d*.1869) presented many of his books to Marsh's including his *Dissertation on Irish grammar*, Dublin, 1834, which includes a ferocious attack on H.J. Monck Mason's *Grammar*. The third edition of Monck Mason's *Grammar* which was printed in Dublin in 1842 was presented to Marsh's by the National Library of Ireland in 1943. Another earlier work by James Scurry entitled *An introduction to the Irish language*, printed in Waterford by John Bull in 1825 (2nd ed.), was also presented to Marsh's by the National Library. The secretary to the Gaelic

Marsh to Dr Thomas Smith, 19 Jan. 1706). **78** Copies of 20 original letters from Hon. Robert Boyle to Narcissus Marsh respecting the publication of the Old Testament in Irish, 1682–4. Marsh pressmark MS Z4.4.8. **79** E.W. Lynam, op. cit., p. 19. **80** Ibid., p. 29.

Society of Dublin, Patrick Lynch, wrote *An introduction to the knowledge of the Irish language* which was printed by Graisberry and Campbell in Dublin in 1815 and it is bound together with some pamphlets of Irish interest.

These are examples of printing with Irish types only, but there is also quite a large collection of books in the library printed by some of the earliest printers in Dublin who of course printed almost exclusively in English.

There are no examples of printing in Marsh's by the first printer in Dublin, Humphrey Powell. The second printer, William Kearney, is believed to have set the type for the New Testament which John Franckton printed in 1602/3 and which has already been mentioned.[81] John Franckton was the third printer in Dublin and his printing of Sir John Davies *Le primer report des cases … resolues en les courts del Roy* is also in the library. It was printed in Dublin in 1615 (*STC* 6361). Sir John Davies (*d.*1626) was attorney general and speaker of the Irish house of commons. Like most books of this period it was printed mainly in black letter but Franckton also used some roman type.

About three years after Franckton printed Davies' book he sold his patent rights as king's printer to Felix Kingston, Matthew Lownes and Bartholomew Downes who were all members of the Company of Stationers.[82] The Company of Stationers was an English company or guild which acted for the protection of its members, but it also engaged in trading activities and employed agents or factors to look after its interests in Dublin.[83] The Dublin Company when they began printing used Company of Stationers on the imprint of their books, but gradually they began to use the word Society instead of Company.[84]

One of the most important men at this period in Ireland was Archbishop James Ussher (*d.*1656). Ussher was a scholar and writer but his narrow religious views made him intolerant of any religion except his own.[85] In 1623 William Malone (*d.*1656), the Irish Jesuit, wrote a work on the

---

81 E.R. McC. Dix, 'History of early printing in Ireland' in *Reports and proceedings of the Belfast Natural History and Philosophical Society*. Session 1916–1917 (1918), Abstract, p. 9. See also E.R. McC. Dix, *The earliest Dublin printing, with list of books, proclamations, &c., printed in Dublin prior to 1601*, Dublin, O'Donoghue, 1901, p. 25. **82** E.R. McC. Dix, 'The earliest Dublin printers and the Company of Stationers of London' (A paper read before the Bibliographical Society, March 16, 1903), London, 1904, reprinted by Blades, East & Blades from the Society's *Transactions*, 1904, p. 4. **83** R.B. McKerrow, General editor, *A dictionary of printers and booksellers in England, Scotland and Ireland and of foreign printers of English books 1557–1640*, London, Bibliographical Society, 1910, p. 256. **84** E.R. McC. Dix, 'The earliest Dublin printers and the Company of Stationers of London', p. 6. **85** E.R. McC. Dix, *Catalogue of early Dublin-printed books 1601–1700*, p. 33.

antiquity of the Catholic Church.[86] Because of the penal laws, Malone's book could not be published in Ireland and for this reason it was probably printed in Douay. Archbishop Ussher replied to Malone in a book entitled *An answer to a challenge made by a jesuite* [W. Malone] *in Ireland* which was printed by the Society of Stationers in Dublin [a. London, Eliot's Court Press] in 1624 (*STC* 24542). A copy of this work was acquired for Marsh's in recent years. Another contributor to this controversy was George Synge. George Synge's (*d.*1653) *A rejoynder to the reply* … which was also printed by the Society of Stationers in Dublin in 1632 (*STC* 23604) is rather surprisingly not in Marsh's collection but in Bishop Stillingfleet's collection. George Synge later became bishop of Cloyne.

Another leading scholar and friend of Archbishop Ussher at this period was Sir James Ware (*d.*1666). Ware has been called the 'father of Irish antiquities' and he devoted a great deal of his time to the collection of material relating to Ireland.[87] A treatise written by him entitled *Archiepiscoporum Casseliensium & Tuamensium vitae* was printed by the Society of Stationers (ex officina Soc. Bibliopolarum) in Dublin in 1626 (*STC* 25064). Two years later Ware wrote *De praesulibus Lageniae, sive provinciae Dubliniensis. Liber unus*, which was also printed by the Society of Stationers (ex off. Soc. Bibliopolarum). Both these works are in the Stearne collection, but Archbishop Marsh and Bishop Stillingfleet were also interested in Ware's writings and indeed there are three copies in the library of *De praesulibus Hiberniae*, printed by John Crook in Dublin in 1665 (*Wing* W 845, *Dix* p. 127).

Another interesting book printed in Dublin in 1637 by the Society of Stationers was James Barry's *The case of tenures upon the commission of defective titles* (*STC* 1530). James Barry (*d.*1673) was recorder of Dublin and chief justice of the King's Bench.[88] He was created Baron Santry in 1660. *The case of tenures* … was written at the request of Lord Wentworth and it is in Archbishop Marsh's collection. (It is interesting that there are several books in Marsh's which bear Lord Santry's signature, and one book which contains Wentworth's signature.)

The Society of Stationers continued printing in Dublin for some years although they do not appear to have been very successful. In about 1630

---

86 This work by William Malone is not in Marsh's Library. Malone's reply to Ussher's attack entitled, *A reply to Mr James Ussher his answere* (n.p.), 1627, [Douai?] is in Archbishop Marsh's collection. See A.F. Allison & D.M. Rogers, op. cit., pt II, M–Z, no. (494) p. 91, (222) *STC* 17213.   **87** *DNB* (Sir James Ware).   **88** Ibid. (James Barry, Lord Santry).

they appointed an English bookseller, William Bladen (d.1663), as factor to the company in Dublin.

William Bladen was a successful businessman and printer and he eventually bought all the stock of the Dublin Company. From about 1641 his name alone appears on the title-page as printer.[89] Bladen became sheriff and later lord mayor of Dublin.[90] He appears to have been as adept politically as he was commercially; he managed to become state printer in Ireland under the Commonwealth, and continued under the Restoration. One can judge this from a book printed by him in the Stearne collection. It consists of *Ordinances, Assesments, Declarations for the speedy raising of moneys towards the supply of the army*. Some of the *Assesments* are the only copies in Ireland. The earliest is entitled *A declaration for the payment of custom and excize* issued by the Commissioners of the Commonwealth of England, for the affairs of Ireland, and it was printed by William Bladen in 1654. A copy of another book printed by Bladen in Dublin in 1654 is in the Stearne collection: it is the only copy in Ireland. It was one of the earliest pieces on land surveying and was written by Henry Osborne.[91] We refer to this book under a different heading in a later section of this work (see p. 194).

William Bladen was succeeded by John Crooke[92] who was in turn succeeded by Benjamin Tooke.[93] Both John Crooke and Benjamin Tooke were made king's printers and they are both represented in the library. Many of their successors' printings are also included in the library and some of these books were printed by such well-known eighteenth-century printers as Stephen Powell, Joseph Ray, John Brocas, Aaron Rhames, George Grierson and the 'Prince of Dublin Printers' George Faulkner.

George Faulkner (d.1775) became famous and rich because of his printings of Jonathan Swift's writings. Faulkner's printings of the *Works* of Swift from 1735 to 1768 are in the library.[94] Unfortunately volume three

89 E.R. McC. Dix, 'The earliest Dublin printers and the Company of Stationers of London', p. 5. **90** J.W. Hammond, 'The king's printers in Ireland 1551–1919' (part II), in *Dublin Historical Record*, xi, March–May, 1950, no. 2, p. 61. See also H.R. Plomer, *A dictionary of the booksellers and printers who were at work in England, Scotland & Ireland from 1641 to 1667*, London, printed for the Bibliographical Society by Blades, East & Blades, 1907, pp 25–6. **91** K.T. Hoppen, *The common scientist in the seventeenth century*, London, Routledge & Kegan Paul, 1970, pp 13, 113–14. **92** H.R. Plomer, *A dictionary of the booksellers and printers ... 1641–1667*, p. 57. **93** H.R. Plomer, and others, *A dictionary of printers and booksellers who were at work in England, Scotland and Ireland from 1668 to 1725*, ed. Arundell Esdaile, printed for the Bibliographical Society, At the Oxford University Press, 1922, p. 293. **94** R.E. Ward, *Prince of Dublin printers: the letters of George Faulkner*, University Press of Kentucky, 1972, p. 11. **95** Dr J.G. Simms

which contains *Gulliver's travels* is missing from this nineteen-volume set.[95] (For those interested in consulting *Teerink*[96] I am including the dates of the volumes.) Faulkner was also responsible for producing the *Dublin Journal* and there are five bound volumes of *Faulkner's Journal* for the years 1740–51 (various numbers) in the library. In 1794 Faulkner produced his remarkable *Universal history* in seven folio volumes. This contains fascinating illustrations and happily there is a very fine copy of this work in the library. George Faulkner and many contemporary Dublin booksellers presented copies of their printings to Marsh's although the books mentioned above do not appear in the donations book.

There are few Irish books in Marsh's printed outside Dublin but one Waterford book is, we think, worth noting. This has been attributed to Patrick Comerford OSA, bishop of Waterford and Lismore (*d.*1652) and is entitled *The inquisition of a sermon by R. Daborne 1617. By the R.F.P.C.* It was printed in Waterford by Tho. Burke in 1644 (*Wing* C 5533D). It bears an interesting device on the title-page with the initials I.F. These probably belong to John Fowler of Bristol. E. R. McC. Dix stated that printing began in Waterford when the Confederate Catholics procured a printing press and employed Thomas Burke to print for them in 1643.[97] The attribution of this work to Bishop Patrick Comerford is a matter of controversy and, judging from correspondence in the library, it could also have been written by another Patrick Comerford, who was an Augustinian friar in Waterford but who had no connection with the bishop.

Finally there are two pieces relating to printing in Dublin which are kept in the manuscript section in the library. The first is a petition which relates to the printing of the New Testament in English and is entitled *State of the case of Thomas Somervell, merchant* (1698?).[98] It seems that Thos. Somervell, who was a publisher, intended to print an authorised version of the New Testament in 1698 but because of a dispute between the printers this edition, even though it was in fact already printed, was suppressed. The

donated a copy of volume 3 to complete this set.   **96** Herman Teerink, *A bibliography of the writings of Jonathan Swift*, 2nd ed. rev., Philadelphia, University of Pennsylvania Press, 1963. (Swift's *Works*, 19 vols, Dublin, printed by George Faulkner, 1735–68, 8°. Vols 1–4 printed in 1735, vols 5–6 in 1738, vols 7–11 in 1763, vols 12–13 in 1765, vols 14–16 in 1767, and vols 17–19 in 1768.)   **97** E.R. McC. Dix, 'Printing in the city of Waterford in the seventeenth century' in *PRIA* xxxii, section C, no. 21, January 1916, p. 333.   **98** See E.R. McC. Dix, 'The first printing of the New Testament in English at Dublin' in *PRIA* xxix, section C, no. 6, July 1911. Marsh's Library MS Z3.1.1 (lxxxviii).

second piece, which is in manuscript and print, is entitled, *The opinion of Rochfort and Brodrick (Attorney and Solicitor General) as to the right of Thornton the king's stationer, in 1698. With the Judge's Report*, 1712.[99]

England

William Caxton (*d*.1491) was the first person to begin printing in England. Caxton was born in England but he lived and worked on the Continent for almost thirty years and became governor to the English merchants in Bruges.[1]

It was during a business visit to Cologne that Caxton apparently learned to print. He returned to Bruges and began printing, probably with the help of a well-known professional calligrapher, Colard Mansion, the first book in English – the *Recuyell of the histories of Troye* – in 1475.[2] One year later Caxton returned to England and began printing at Westminster, producing in 1477 *The dictes or sayengis of the philosophres*, the first book printed in England which bore a date and place of printing.[3]

The early printers on the Continent printed their books in Latin, the international language of scholars. They printed Bibles and devotional works which were at that time guaranteed best-sellers. Caxton printed similar type books, but he also printed popular English literature and acted as editor and translator for many of his productions.

The English printers however did not achieve anything like the standard developed by the continental scholar printers. In the first place, the population of Elizabethan England was very small – about two million – and the average wage about five shillings. The cheapest book cost one shilling and although the exceptional literary renaissance of the Elizabethan age increased the output of the printing presses, nevertheless there was the inevitable limitation of scale.[4]

The first major piece of censorship began with the proclamation of 1538. This proclamation required all books dealing with certain subjects to be examined and approved before being printed.[5] It was the beginning of

---

99 With the Judge's Report, 1712. Marsh's Library MS Z1.1.13 (3).　1 *A guide to the exhibition in the king's library*, p. 56. See also William Blades, *The biography and typography of William Caxton*, London, Frederick Muller, 1971.　2 E.G. Duff, 'The introduction of printing into England and the early work of the press' in *CHEL,* ii, p. 311.　3 *A guide to the exhibition in the king's library*, p. 60.　4 R.B. McKerrow, *An introduction to bibliography,* pp 133–5. See also H.G. Aldis, 'The book-trade, 1557–1625' in *CHEL,* iv, pp 406–8.　5 R.B. McKerrow, General editor, *A dictionary of printers and booksellers … 1557–1640,* Introduction, p. x.

nearly two centuries of restrictive laws against books, booksellers, authors and printers. The political and religious conflicts resulted in spying for secret presses and heretical books; printers became discouraged, and with the exception of some of the royal printers, very few fine printings were produced.

In 1557 the Stationers' Company was granted a charter which was intended to help the printing trade.[6] Unfortunately, however, the Stationers' Company with their increased power confined printing to their own members and successfully operated a 'closed shop'. Again in 1637 the Stationers' Company were granted further increased powers which in effect enabled the company to carry out censorship on behalf of the government. For this and many other reasons, English booksellers found it easier and more profitable to import books from the Continent than to have them printed in England.

With the dramatic political events of the civil war and particularly the setting up of the Long Parliament a change took place. The new rulers were anxious to create a liberal atmosphere and appointed a committee for religion, which was initially sympathetic to the printers' complaints, and there was a slight improvement.[7] In 1644 John Milton, who had himself been attacked by the Stationers' Company for publishing books without a licence, wrote *Areopagitica*, in pamphlet form, one of the finest appeals for the freedom of the press that has ever been written. But the execution of Charles I, and the bitter reaction and criticism which followed, alarmed the authorities, and in 1649 laws of even greater severity were enacted.

The Restoration rather surprisingly brought only a slight improvement to the book trade.[8] The outbreak of the plague in 1665 and the terrible fire of London in 1666 devastated the area where the majority of printers and booksellers lived, and came as another heavy blow.[9] Fortunately the expiration of the licensing act in 1695 brought an improvement and the book trade began to recover. But it did not last for long. The introduction of a duty on imported paper badly affected the English printers,[10] but it did have one unforeseen advantage for both Ireland and Holland. It enabled the Dutch and Irish printers to print English books and export them to England, an opportunity which they took full advantage of.[11]

---

6 H.G. Aldis, 'The book-trade 1557–1625', p. 378.   7 H.R. Plomer, *A dictionary of booksellers …* *1641–1667*, Introduction, p. xii.   8 Ibid., Introduction, p. xx.   9 Ibid., Introduction, p. xxiii.   10 H.R. Plomer and others, *A dictionary of printers and booksellers … 1668–1725*, ed. Arundell Esdaile, Introduction, p. vii.   11 Ibid., Introduction, p. viii.

Early English printers and their books

There are in Marsh's Library approximately 1,260 English books printed before 1640. There are no books printed by Caxton in the library, but most of the printers who succeeded Caxton are well represented, including his manager or foreman, Wynkyn de Worde. De Worde (*d.*1534) was a Frenchman from the duchy of Lorraine and he may have come to England with Caxton in 1476. De Worde was not the best but he was the most prolific printer of his day,[12] and he is believed to have introduced title-pages and italic type into England.[13] He used as many as fifteen different devices on his books but he generally always retained Caxton's initials on them, probably as a small tribute to the first English printer.[14] (There is one book in Marsh's printed by Wynkyn de Worde with Caxton's device only.)

There are six books printed by de Worde in the library; and a fragment of his printing in the binding of *Three kynges of Coleyne* which was printed in Paris in 1511. One of the books printed by de Worde (the earliest piece of English printing in the library)[15] is William Caxton's *Here begynneth a shorte & a breue/table … (The descrypcyon of Englonde)*, 2pts., 1502 (*STC* 9997). Another de Worde printing is *Noua legēda anglie* which he printed in 1516 (*STC* 4601). This work has always been attributed to John Capgrave but Mr Peter Lucas[16] strongly argues that it has been erroneously attributed to Capgrave mainly through the errors of Leland and Bale. It was bound specially for its previous owner Sir Christopher Hatton and it bears Sir Christopher's arms stamped in gold on both covers. Both of these printings are in the Stillingfleet collection.

The six books in the library which were printed by Wynkyn de Worde are in black letter type, the name by which gothic type is known in England. De Worde's black letter types are a more pointed type than the gothic types used by the continental printers and are a development of the various types which Caxton used. Similar pointed gothic types were used by Richard Pynson, Thomas Berthelet and many of the earliest English

---

12 *A guide to the exhibition in the king's library*, p. 64.   **13** D.B. Updike, op. cit., ii, p. 90.   **14** *A guide to the exhibition in the king's library*, p. 64.   **15** There were at least two earlier printed books but they are listed in the library in the 'Missing books' catalogue. They appear to have been missing since the early part of the eighteenth century. The first was by Henry Parker and it was entitled *Dives and pauper* and was probably printed by Wynkyn de Worde in 1496. The second book was a *Sarum Missal* which was printed in Venice in 1494. They originally belonged to the Stillingfleet collection.   **16** P.J. Lucas, 'John Capgrave and the *Nova legenda Anglie*: a survey' in *The Library*, 5 ser., xxv, no. 1, March 1970, pp 1–10.

printers. These pointed English gothic types, according to D.B. Updike, became the characteristic of English printing and were used in England until the seventeenth century and even continued for certain types of books into the eighteenth century.[17]

Normally speaking three types of gothic were used and they are generally known by their French names: *lettre de forme* (formal) for important liturgical books, *lettre de somme* (less formal) for serious and classical books, and *lettre bâtarde* (cursive), which was used for vernacular literature and which was specially popular in France.

From the library's point of view many of these early English printings have another exciting aspect. From previous owners' signatures it is sometimes possible to trace their provenance, and from auction records the prices which were paid for them.

The most important English printer after Wynkyn de Worde is probably Richard Pynson. Richard Pynson (d.1530) was a native of Normandy and he began printing in London in 1492. His entire output was only half that of de Worde's but he has always been regarded as a far better printer and was appointed printer to Henry VIII in 1510. Like Wynkyn de Worde, Richard Pynson also used black letter type but Pynson has been credited with introducing roman type into England.[18] There are four books printed by Richard Pynson in Marsh's Library and they are good illustrations of his printing and the different types which he used.

The earliest of his books is believed to be the first book printed in roman type in England. This work is Peter Gryphus' *Oratio quam erat habiturus Petrus Gryphus ... ad Hēricū vij Anglię regē: ni paratā expositionē immatura regis mors preuenisset* and it was printed by Pynson in 1509 (*STC* 12413). Peter Gryphus was the papal nuncio and he was prevented from delivering his speech by the death of the king. What is remarkable about this book is that there are only three copies known to exist and by some extraordinary coincidence two of the three copies are in Marsh's Library. The third copy is in the British Library. One of the copies in Marsh's was purchased at the sale of Richard Smith's books in 1682. It was purchased by 'Mr Patrick' for Bishop Stillingfleet. 'Mr Patrick' paid the sum of 4*s*. 2*d*. but the price included other books as well.[19]

---

17 D.B. Updike, op. cit., ii, p. 88.   **18** *A guide to the exhibition in the king's library*, p. 71.   **19** E.G. Duff, 'Notes on a visit to Archbishop Marsh's Library' (July 1903), reprinted from vol. vi of the *Publications of the Edinburgh Bibliographical Society*, Edinburgh, MCMVI, p. 139.

There is a fine copy in the Stillingfleet collection of Robert Fabyan's *Prima pars cronecarum* which Pynson printed in 1516 (*STC* 10659) but it is unfortunately lacking its title-page. Fabyan's *Chronicle* is a valuable source book for the history of the English navy; it includes accounts of early naval engagements, and fine descriptions of sea battles fought by English fleets. A rare book on surveying printed by Richard Pynson, in the Stearne collection, is John Fitzherbert's *Here begynneth a ryght frutefull mater* ... which Pynson printed in 1523 (*STC* 11005) and like Robert Fabyan's *Chronicle* it is also printed in black letter.

Finally there is, in the Stillingfleet collection, the most important Pynson printing, the *Psalterium cum hymnis*, printed by him in 1524 (*STC* 16262) and of which there is only one other copy known. This Psalter is printed in red and black throughout and the type is a most handsome *lettre de forme*. It has many unique features. It is still in its original blind stamped calf binding decorated with the Tudor rose and vine leaves, and pasted inside the upper cover is an indulgence issued by Cardinals Wolsey and Campeggio in order to obtain money for building at Hereford Cathedral. The indulgence was printed earlier than the Psalter, by Richard Faques in about 1518 (*STC* 14077.42).

Another fine purchase by 'Mr Patrick' for Bishop Stillingfleet was Julian Notary's printing of the so-called Nicodemus gospel *Here begynneth the treatys of Nycodemus gospell*. 'Mr Patrick' paid 4*s*. 8*d*. for this copy but again the price included some other books.[20] Julian Notary (*d*.1520) had a considerable reputation as a printer although like Richard Pynson his output was small – fewer than fifty books.[21] Notary printed Nicodemus' *Gospel* in 1507 (*STC* 18565).[22] It consists of a tract of twenty-two leaves with illustrations, three being engraved on metal in the 'maniere criblee'. The *Short Title Catalogue* and *Ramage* give Marsh's as having the only known copy of this edition. The second book in the library printed by Julian Notary is Gulielmus Parisiensis' *Postilla siue expositio epystolarum & euangeliorum dominicalium* which Notary printed in 1509 (*STC* 12513) and which bears Notary's device consisting of his initials, and flowers, birds, trees, and two fabulous beasts. The title-page contains the signature of the previous owner Margaret Ussher and the book is in the Stearne collection. It seems highly

20 Ibid. **21** E.G. Duff, 'The introduction of printing into England and the early work of the press' in *CHEL*, ii, p. 326. See also Hugh Shields, 'Bishop Turpin and the source of *Nycodemus gospell*' in *English Studies*, 53, 6 December 1972, pp 6. **22** Colin Clair, *A history of printing in Britain*, London, Cassell, 1965, p. 42.

probable that Margaret Ussher was a relative of Bishop Stearne because Bishop Stearne's father, John Stearne (*d*.1669), was a grandnephew of Archbishop James Ussher. Judging from the books in the Stearne collection which bear Margaret Ussher's signature she appears to have been a woman of considerable learning.

Richard Faques (or Fawkes) was probably the son of William Faques who had been appointed the first king's printer. Richard Faques' printing of *Here after folowith the boke callyd the Myrroure of oure lady* (sometimes attributed to T. Gascoigne), which Faques printed in 1530 (*STC* 17542), is in the Stillingfleet collection and it shows Faques' device of two unicorns and a shield. While the book itself is in excellent condition it unfortunately lacks the title-page and the last part. It originally belonged to the English book-collector Humphrey Dyson who paid five shillings for it,[23] afterwards to Richard Smith, and then to Bishop Stillingfleet. A book in the library printed in Paris by J. Petit in about 1515 was, according to G.D. Hobson, bound by Richard Faques.[24] It is in a calf binding with a blind stamped design of St George and the dragon on the upper cover and St Michael and the dragon on the lower cover.

Thomas Berthelet (*d*.1555), like so many of the early London printers, was of French descent. Colin Clair noted that until 1535 two thirds of those connected with the book trade were aliens and in some instances this led to ill feeling against them. Indeed Richard Pynson had been forced to appeal to the Court of the Star Chamber because of the animosity and opposition shown towards him. Feelings ran so high that at one stage they led to actual violence.[25]

Thomas Berthelet succeeded Richard Pynson as king's printer and he used both roman and black letter types for his printings. A book printed by Berthelet in about 1533 entitled *Kotser codicis R. Wakfeldi …* (*STC* 24943) is a good example of Berthelet's roman type and it also has an interesting provenance. Robert Wakefield (d.1537) was an oriental scholar and taught in Oxford University. This copy of Wakefield's book was presented to Archbishop Marsh in 1690 by Frances Guise, the widow of another well-known Oxford orientalist, William Guise (*d*.1683).

One of the most important books relating to Henry VIII's divorce, entitled *Grauissimae … totius Italiæ, et Galliæ Academiarū censuræ*, was printed

---

23 E.G. Duff, 'Notes on a visit to Archbishop Marsh's Library', p. 137.   **24** Information received from G.D. Hobson, 10 January 1945.   **25** Colin Clair, op. cit., p. 105.

by Thomas Berthelet in 1530 (*STC* 14286) and there is a copy in the Stillingfleet collection; it is in its original binding. (A manuscript copy of this work in the library bears the signature of Hugh Latymer 1535. Latimer was the bishop of Oxford and he was, together with other Protestant bishops, burnt as a heretic in 1555.)

Another well-known book in the Stillingfleet collection, which Berthelet printed in 1543, is *A necessary doctrine and erudition for any christen man …* (*STC* 5169). This book became known as 'King's book' and it was a revision, with a preface written by Henry VIII, of *The institution of a christen man* which in the form in which it had been originally printed in 1537 was known as 'Bishop's book'. It contained a small collection of articles of religious beliefs collected by the bishops and issued with the king's authority. In 1531 Berthelet printed the legal and controversial writer, Christopher Saint German's *Here after foloweth a lytell treatise called the newe addicions*. Berthelet had in fact already printed two editions of this work in 1531 but this third edition (*STC* 21564) is without the abbreviated 'Fo' before the folio numbers. The copy in the library is in the Stillingfleet collection and it originally belonged to Humphrey Dyson who paid one shilling for it.[26] Thomas Berthelet was renowned for his fine bindings and he had many superb books specially bound for the king. But recent scholarship seems to suggest that Berthelet himself was not the actual binder of the bindings attributed to him.[27]

John Byddell (*d.*1545), the printer and bookseller, had been an assistant to Wynkyn de Worde and was noted for his printing of books on theology.[28] Byddell printed the book by the Protestant controversial writer George Joye, *A compendyouse somme of the very christen relygyon*, in 1535 (*STC* 14821). This edition of Joye's book in Marsh's is the only known copy and the work itself is apparently a translation of *Summa totius sacrae scripturae* which was originally printed in Antwerp by John Grapheus in 1533.

Richard Grafton (*d.*1573) succeeded Berthelet as king's printer and was already a wealthy merchant before he became interested in printing. Earlier with Edward Whitchurch he had printed the *Great Bible*; he was noted for his liturgical printings of which there are two very interesting examples in the library. Grafton was on many occasions in trouble with the authorities

26 E.G. Duff, 'Notes on a visit to Archbishop Marsh's Library', p. 138.   **27** H.M. Nixon, 'Early English gold-tooled bookbindings' in *Estratto dal volume III di Studi di bibliografia e di storia in onore di Tammaro de Marinis*, Verona, 1964, p. 286.   **28** Colin Clair, op. cit., p. 59.

for printing seditious books and eventually found himself in prison because of one particular indiscretion.[29] Grafton did not confine himself to religious material, as can be seen from his printing in 1550 of Edward Halle's *The vnion of the two noble and illustrate famelies of Lancastre & Yorke* (*STC* 12723) which is in the Stillingfleet collection. It is extensively illustrated with heraldic and pictorial capitals. Halle's book gives colourful accounts of the early years of Henry VIII, Cardinal Wolsey's administration and the social events of those turbulent years. Shakespeare is believed to have used Halle's work for the historical events in his plays.[30] Richard Grafton like so many other printers used a rather amusing punning device as a printer's mark. It consisted of an illustration of a tree bearing grafts inserted in a tun or barrel and the device included his motto.

Richard Tottell (*d.*1593) was Richard Grafton's brother-in-law and was a printer for nearly forty years. He specialised in printing law books for which he had been granted a monopoly,[31] and there are in the Stillingfleet and Stearne collections such well-known popular law books printed by Richard Tottell as *La vieux natura breuium,* 1584 (*STC* 18402) and Sir Thomas Littleton's *Les tenures* which he printed in 1591 (*STC* 15749). But these law books were already so popular that they had been printed over one hundred years earlier by other English printers. In fact Tottell first began printing editions of *Les tenures* in 1554 and the edition in the library is almost the last edition which he printed.

There is also in the Stearne collection Edmund Plowden's *Les commentaries, ou reportes … de diuers cases … Ouesque vn table per W. Fletewoode.* It was printed by Tottell in 1578 (*STC* 20041 and it includes 20046.3; his first printing of it was seven years earlier). Apart from these important law books there is also in the Stearne collection a book which has an interesting association with Ireland. This is Gerard Legh's *The accedens of armory* printed by Tottell in 1568 (*STC* 15389). It is the second edition of this work and it contains manuscript notes and achievements signed by John Hooker (alias Vowell). John Hooker (*d.*1601) was an English antiquary who became solicitor to Sir Peter Carew and was sent over to Ireland.[32] He was elected to the Irish parliament as a member for Athenry. Hooker while he was in Ireland made a particularly intemperate speech in support of the royal prerogative and he had to be

29 Ibid., p. 65.   **30** *DNB* (Edward Hall or Halle).   **31** Colin Clair, op. cit., p. 73.   **32** *DNB* (John Hooker alias Vowell).

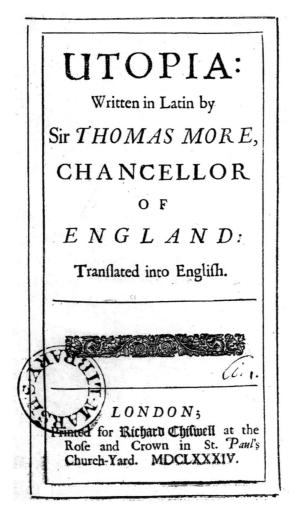

16 Title-page of Sir Thomas More's famous book *Utopia* (London, 1684), translated into English by Bishop Gilbert Burnet.

escorted to his house because of the threat of violence. Another important book in the Stillingfleet collection is an edition of Sir Thomas More's *Workes* which was printed in London in 1557 (*STC* 18076). According to the *STC*, the first quire of this work was printed by J. Cawood and the rest by Richard Tottell.

Henry Denham (*d.*1591) was apprenticed to Richard Tottell and is considered to be one of the better English printers of this period. In 1580 he printed *Psalmi Dauidis ex Hebraeo in Latinum conuersi ... ab I. Tremellio et F. Iunio* (*STC* 2360) for which he used both an italic and a roman type. The title-page of this book also contains the name of another English printer,

William Seres, who had earlier given to Denham his patent for printing books of private prayer in Latin and English. Denham printed in 1569 *A setting open of the subtyle sophistrie of T. Watson* (*STC* 6093) by the controversial Puritan writer Robert Crowley (*d.*1588) and it is part of the Stearne collection in the library.

Henry Denham gained quite a reputation for his ingenious use of a printer's ornament as a border for the title-pages of his printings.[33] By this means Denham gave title-pages a most attractive lace border and the title-page of Watson's book is no exception. Unfortunately, however, the paper seems to have been incorrectly placed for printing and the title-page has a most curious lopsided appearance. The book also shows Denham's device of a star surrounded by his motto in Latin. Another interesting work in the Stillingfleet collection is *An answer to the two first ... treatises of a certeine factious libell*, 1584 (*STC* 5815) by Richard Cosin (*d.*1597) which shows many of Denham's initial ornaments.

The edition of *An aluearie or quadruple dictionarie* by John Baret (*d.*1580?) was printed by Denham in 1580 (*STC* 1411) and it includes Greek definitions.[34] (Denham had printed an earlier edition in 1573 which did not include these Greek definitions.) The copy in the Stearne collection is unfortunately imperfect.

Henry Bynneman (*d.*1583) worked in partnership with Henry Denham for some years. Bynneman was regarded as a very good printer and there are in the library books which illustrate examples of his roman, italic, and handsome black letter types. There are two copies of *An answere to a certen libel intituled, An admonition* by Archbishop John Whitgift (*d.*1604). The first edition was printed by Bynneman in 1572 (*STC* 25427) and an imperfect copy was acquired for the library in recent years. The second edition in 1572 (1573) (*STC* 25428) is in the Stillingfleet collection but unfortunately it also is slightly imperfect. But it does have an interesting provenance. The title-page bears the signature of the curious Cambridge physician Myles Blomfielde. Blomfielde (*d.*1601) was, according to the *DNB*, a collector of old and curious books. He also left a manuscript in the Cambridge University Library which has been described as 'hardly the production of a sane mind'.

There are also in the Stillingfleet collection three pieces by the Cambridge poet Gabriel Harvey (*d.*1630) which are contained in a book

33 Colin Clair, op. cit., p. 86.   34 Ibid., p. 87.

printed by Bynneman in 1577–78. On the lower endpapers of this book a fascinating seventeenth-century annotation appears. This annotation gives details of money spent by a student on a visit to Cambridge.[35] Henry Bynneman also printed Arthur Hall's controversial *A letter sent by F.A. touchyng a quarell betweene A. Hall and M. Mallerie* in [1576?] (*STC* 12629). Arthur Hall, the author of this book, was a member of parliament for Grantham. Hall was a notoriously quarrelsome character.[36] Shortly after his second election to parliament he was accused of making 'sundry lewd speeches' and he was forced to apologise. One year later Hall was in even more serious trouble. While he was playing cards with Melchisedech Mallory he accused Mallory of cheating. A violent quarrel developed which excited widespread controversy on both sides. Hall in an attempt to justify his actions wrote a long account of the quarrel which Henry Bynneman printed. Hall's book was condemned by parliament as a slanderous libel and he was committed to the Tower for six months. This book is in the Stillingfleet collection and originally belonged to the English book-collector, Humphrey Dyson. (According to the *STC*, approximately 80 copies were printed, of which there are only four copies in existence: one in Marsh's, one in the British Library, one in Armagh Public Library, and an imperfect copy in Harvard University.)

During the persecution of the Protestants in France in the sixteenth century many of the Huguenots were forced to leave. Thomas Vautrollier (*d.*1587), a Huguenot from Troyes, fled with his wife Jacqueline to London and began printing there in 1568. Vautrollier became so successful in his new country that he succeeded in extending his business to Edinburgh.[37] Vautrollier printed many of the writings of the French Reformers, notably the writings of such well-known people as Theodore de Bèze and Pierre de la Ramée. But Vautrollier did not confine himself to printing the works of the French Reformers only; he also printed English writers although many of these also had strong Calvinist views, including such writers as William

---

35 This annotation was printed in *Notes & Queries*, vol. 150, no. 23, 5 June 1926, p. 405. It reads as follows: 'When I commenced my Journey to Cambridge stood me in £0–11s.–10d. viz 7s. for the Coach-hire and my other expenses on the way £0–4s.–4d. It. To the House £4.0s.0d. (Whereof I received £1.0s.0d. back againe at my coming away). It. To the Lecturer for subscription £0–1s.–0d. It. To the Stewards of the yeare £0–13s.–4d. It. for the Proctours booke 7s.6d. It. To his men £0–1s.–0d. It. To the Beadle £0–5s.–4d. It. To the Proctour £2–16s.–0d. It. To the Register £0–0s.–6d. My Commons & Sizemas whilest I was there stood me in 0–8s.–9d. My Horse-hire backe 8s. Expenses on the way 2s. Hose and shoes 7s.6d. **36** *DNB* (Arthur Hall). **37** Colin Clair, op. cit., p. 89.

Whitaker. Whitaker (*d.*1595) became master of St John's College, Cambridge, and in 1583 he wrote *Ad N. Sanderi demonstrationes quadraginta … responsio* (*STC* 25357). The copy in the library originally belonged to Dr Bouhéreau. Many of the types which Vautrollier used for his printings are particularly attractive and were apparently designed by the French designers, Robert Granjon and Claude Garamond.[38]

A rare medical book in the Stillingfleet collection written by Philip Barrow or Barrough (*fl.*1590), entitled *The methode of phisicke*, was printed by Vautrollier in 1583 (*STC* 1508). This book became so popular that ten editions were printed before 1652. Barrow dealt with almost every known disease and suggested a cure for them which probably accounts for the book's great popularity. The following is the cure given by Barrow to enable readers to survive 'a headache caused by dronkennesse': 'You must have a special regard and procure that the patient does sleepe, and rest, and when thou hast washed him, let him eat meates of good iuce, but not over hote.'

After Vautrollier's death in 1587 his business was continued by his widow Jacqueline and his apprentice, Richard Field, whom she married. A book printed some months after Vautrollier's death, entitled *Certaine aduertisements out of Ireland, concerning the losses to the Spanish nauie,* 1588 (*STC* 14257 pt. 2 of 15412), has on the title-page 'Imprinted at London by I. Vautrollier for Richard Field'. This book is particularly interesting as it deals with the dispersal and fate of the Spanish ships after their defeat by the English fleet in 1588. Vautrollier's device of an anchor held by a hand issuing from clouds, surrounded by laurel branches, and the motto 'Anchora Spei' enclosed in an oval frame can be seen on the title-page.

Reginald Wolfe (*d.*1573) was a native of Gelderland and came to England in about 1530. Wolfe produced the first book printed in Greek in England and became royal printer for books in Latin, Greek and Hebrew.[39] His printing of St John Chrysostom's *De prouidentia Dei, ac fato, orationes sex. J. Checo interprete* in 1545 (*STC* 14630) is in the Stillingfleet collection. It has the previous owner's signature, Samuel Lynford, on the title-page. There are at least 31 books in the Stillingfleet collection which bear Lynford's name. Although it is not certain, he may have been the father of Thomas Lynford, archdeacon of Barnstable, who died in 1724.

---

38 Ibid., p. 91.   **39** *A guide to the exhibition in the king's library*, p. 82.

Other printings by Wolfe in the library include *Naeniae in mortem T. Viati equitis incomparabilis* [Sir T. Wyatt] (*STC* 15446) by the English antiquary John Leland. It was printed by Reginald Wolfe in 1542 and has on the verso of the title-page a portrait of Wyatt which has been attributed to Holbein.[40] Leland's elegy has been bound together with his *Genethliacon illustrissimi Eäduerdi principis Cambriae* (*STC* 15443), a poem written by Leland on the birth of Edward, prince of Wales, and dedicated to Henry VIII. It was printed by Wolfe in 1543 and is in the Stillingfleet collection. It also contains an illustration of Wolfe's charming device of two small children knocking down apples from an apple tree, and the motto 'Charitas'.

To complete this short account of some of the earliest English printers in Marsh's we must refer to John Day (*d.*1584), the printer who is regarded as having produced the most outstanding typographical work of this early period. He began printing in about 1546 and the earliest example we have of his printings is a book in the Bishop Stearne collection; it is entitled *A simple, and religious consultation* and was written by Herman V., archbishop of Cologne, and printed by Day in 1547 (*STC* 13213). Although it has been generally accepted that Day was the printer of this book, Colin Clair has pointed out that many of the books printed by John Day and William Seres between 1546 and 1549 have all the appearance of books printed in the Low Countries – in particular by Steven Mierdman in Antwerp.[41]

In Archbishop Marsh's collection there is a pamphlet originally owned by Michael Jephson, which was printed by John Day in 1564. This is entitled *A godly and necessarye admonition of the decrees and canons of the counsel of Trent* (*STC* 24265). Day was a zealous Protestant and during the reign of Queen Mary he was imprisoned many times and may possibly have had to flee to the Continent. Another book printed by Day in 1570 is Roger Ascham's *The scholemaster* (*STC* 832). Ascham (*d.*1568) was private tutor to Queen Elizabeth and his book is regarded as a classic in the history of education. The copy in the library is in the Stillingfleet collection but is unfortunately lacking its title-page. We have already mentioned one of the books printed by Day: Aelfric's *Homily*, published as *A testimonie of antiquitie* in 1566? (*STC* 159.5). This book is consistently referred to as an outstanding typographical achievement and it is therefore very exciting that there is a copy in the Bishop Stearne collection in the library. Day printed the book under the direction of Archbishop Parker. It was in this book that Day's new Anglo-

40 *DNB* (Sir Thomas Wyatt).   **41** Colin Clair, op. cit., p. 75.

Saxon fount was first used.[42] Day's amusing device of the sleeper being awakened by one who points to the rising sun, with the punning motto 'Arise for it is day', and his other well-known but totally different and rather frightening device of a skeleton stretched on a tomb, can be seen in the books printed by him in the library.

Music printings

The small but valuable collection of early printed music in the library contains some of the best-known music printed during the sixteenth century. One of the most popular and relaxing pastimes of Elizabethan times was singing, and almost everybody from courtiers to servants took part. Madrigals were probably the most popular of all types of music. Even Archbishop Marsh was devoted to music. We have already referred to his musical activities in Oxford which he mentioned in his diary.[43] George Sampson commenting on the music of this period said, 'English music of Tudor and early Stuart times is a very noble national possession, and William Byrd is among the greatest composers of any time or place.'[44] The printed music in the library represents some of the early English music printers and the works of many of their best composers.

Thomas East (d.1608?) is probably the most renowned music printer, but he began his career printing medical and theological works in 1566. East appears to have given up this type of printing in 1588 and concentrated on printing music, for which he is chiefly remembered. Colin Clair quotes Fuller-Maitland's remarks on the frequency of East's name appearing as Este on his printings and suggests that East may well have been of Italian origin and for that reason been specifically chosen to print the great collection of Italian madrigals.[45] However, *The New Grove Dictionary of music and musicians* (2nd ed., 2001) says, 'it seems that East was born in Swavesey, Cambridgeshire'.

Thomas East printed the compositions of the great English composer whom we have already mentioned, William Byrd (d.1623).[46] Although Byrd was a Catholic he managed to write music for both the Anglican and Catholic churches, even though Catholics were generally regarded during Queen Elizabeth's reign with great suspicion. Byrd became a pupil of Thomas Tallis and was appointed with Tallis joint organist of the Chapel

---

42 Ibid., p. 76.   **43** Archbishop Marsh's diary, p. 9.   **44** George Sampson, op. cit., p. 189.   **45** Colin Clair, op. cit., p. 95.   **46** *DNB* (William Byrd).

CORONA
DELLA MORTE
DELL'ILLVSTRE SIGNORE,
IL SIG. COMENDATOR ANIBAL CARO.

AL NOBILE ET GENEROSO CAVALIERO
Il Signor Giouanni Ferro da Macerata.

Di nouo poſta in luce per Giulio Bonagionta da S. Geneſi.

CON GRATIA ET PRIVILEGGIO.

BAS   SO

IN VINEGIA,
APPRESSO GIROLAMO SCOTTO
M D LXVIII.

17 Title-page of Anibal Caro's *Corona della morte* (Venice, 1568).

Royal in 1572. In 1575 Queen Elizabeth granted to Tallis and Byrd the privilege to print and sell all musical works in England. The conferring of this privilege meant that they had the sole right to print and sell all musical works for a specified number of years, and usually the right to transfer, assign, and bequeath their privilege. Tallis died in 1585 and two years later Byrd assigned his privilege to Thomas East. There are in Marsh's Library music books printed by East as the assignee of William Byrd. Probably the most important of these is a collection of madrigals by Nicholas Yonge entitled *Musica transalpina*. These madrigals make up one of the earliest and most important collections of Elizabethan madrigals, and were chiefly collected from the works of the best Flemish and Italian composers. It was in this collection that the word madrigal was used for the first time.[47] But this collection also includes a piece composed by William Byrd, *La Verginella*, and this is believed to be the earliest English madrigal. It has four parts only, lacking quintus and sextus. These were printed by Thomas East as the assignee of William Byrd in 1588 (*STC* 26094). We also have another set of madrigals by Nicholas Yonge entitled *The second booke of madrigalles*, and these were printed by Thomas East in 1597 (*STC* 26095). This second collection of Nicholas Yonge's madrigals was donated to Marsh's by Christopher Usher in April 1727.

In 1598 a new patent was granted to William Byrd's pupil Thomas Morley, and Morley assigned licences to Thomas East, Peter Short and William Barley. Thomas Morley (*d.*1603) was organist of St Paul's Cathedral and wrote church music and madrigals, and he also contributed some music for Shakespeare's *As you like it*.[48] Morley's *A plaine and easie introduction to practicall musicke* (*STC* 18133) was printed by Peter Short in 1597; there is a copy in the library but unfortunately it is imperfect. However, it has definitely been identified as the first issue of the first edition.[49]

Earlier, in 1593, Thomas East as the assignee of Byrd printed Morley's delightful *Canzonets. Or little short songs to three voyces* (altus and cantus parts only in Marsh's, *STC* 18121). In 1595 East printed two further pieces by Morley. The first is *The first booke of Canzonets to two voyces* (*STC* 18119), and the second, *The first booke of balletts to five voyces* (cantus and quintus parts

47 J.F. Fleming Inc., *Sale catalogue of English books printed before 1640*, New York [1958], p. 147. 48 Eric Blom, *Everyman's dictionary of music*, London, John M. Dent, 1946, p. 384. 49 O.E. Deutsch, 'The editions of Morley's *Introduction*' (Bibliographical Notes) in *The Library*, 4 ser., xxiii, 1943, pp 127–9.

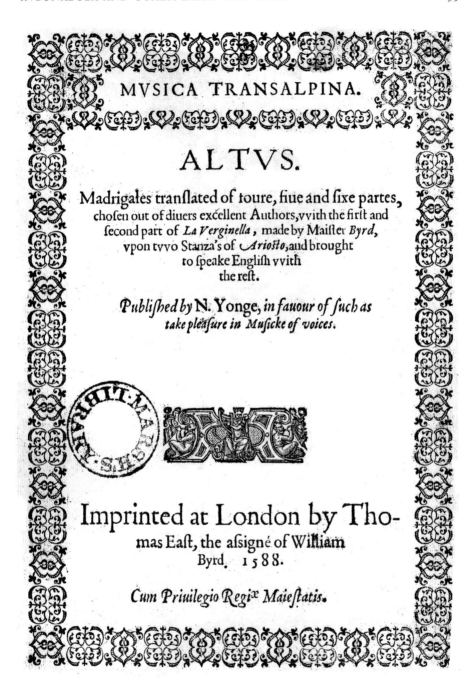

MVSICA TRANSALPINA.

ALTVS.

Madrigales tranſlated of toure, fiue and ſixe partes,
choſen out of diuers excellent Authors,vvith the firſt and
ſecond part of *La Verginella*, made by Maiſter *Byrd*,
vpon tvvo Stanza's of *Arioſto*,and brought
to ſpeake Engliſh vvith
the reſt.

Publiſhed by N. Yonge, *in fauour of ſuch as
take pleaſure in Muſicke of voices.*

Imprinted at London by Thomas Eaſt, the aſſigné of William
Byrd. 1588.

Cum Priuilegio Regiæ Maieſtatis.

18 Title-page of *Musica transalpina* (London, 1588).

only in Marsh's, *STC* 18116). Later East as the assignee of Morley began printing some of Morley's madrigals which were entitled *Madrigalls to foure voyces*, 1600 (altus and cantus parts only in Marsh's, *STC* 18128). All the title-pages of Morley's compositions printed by East are decorated with a border made by the continuous use of a small printer's ornament, and in the 1593 printing of the *Canzonets* East decorated every page of the music in this ornamental style. East also used handsome initial letters including large pictorial initials which can be seen in this collection of music books.

Other interesting madrigals in Marsh's were composed by John Farmer the sixteenth-century English composer who from some time in the early 1590s to 1599 was employed as organist in Christ Church Cathedral, Dublin.[50] Farmer's charming madrigals are entitled *The first set of English madrigals to foure voices* and were printed in 1599 by Barley, the assignee of Morley (cantus only in Marsh's, *STC* 10697).

John Bennett was another who composed madrigals at about the same period and these were also printed in 1599 by Barley. Bennet's madrigals are entitled *Madrigalls to foure voyces* and like Farmer's compositions only the cantus parts are in the library (*STC* 1882). The title-pages are decorated with the same printer's ornament which East used and many of these books of music bear the signature of William Meteyard (unidentified).

The donor who is recorded in our donations book as Christopher Usher also presented John Adson's *Courtly masquing ayres* which were composed for violins, consorts, and cornets and they included six parts. Five parts only are in Marsh's, the quintus is missing. They were printed by T.S. for J. Browne in 1621 (*STC* 153). The initials T.S. refer to Thomas Snodham to whom Thomas East's widow transferred some of his business. Thomas Snodham printed these pieces after his return from Ireland where he had been sent by the Stationers' Company to look after their business in Dublin. But, as we have already mentioned, this business was not successful and it was eventually wound up.[51]

Books printed on the Continent for the English and Scottish market

Although there was some increase in the number of printers in London during the sixteenth century, the English printers were unable to fulfil the

---

50 Eric Blom, op. cit., p. 170.   51 R.B. McKerrow, General editor, *A dictionary of printers and booksellers ... 1557–1640*, p. 251.

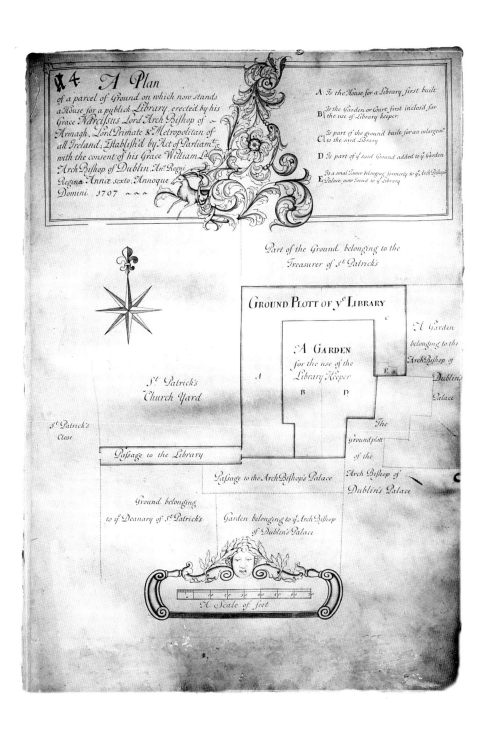

N 4. A Plan

A Is the House for a Library first built

B Is the Garden or Court first inclos'd for the use of Library keeper.

C Is part of the ground built for an inlargem.t to the said Library

D Is part of ye said Ground added to ye Garden

E Is a smal Tower belonging formerly to ye Arch Bishops Palace now Joind to ye Library

of a parcel of Ground on which now stands a House for a publick Library, erected by his Grace Narcissus Lord Arch Bishop of Armagh, Lord Primate & Metropolitan of all Ireland; Establish'd by Act of Parliam.t with the consent of his Grace William L.d Arch Bishop of Dublin An.o Regni Reginæ Anniæ sexto, Annoque Domini 1707

Part of the Ground belonging to the Treasurer of S.t Patrick's

GROUND PLOTT OF Y.e LIBRARY

A GARDEN for the use of the Library Keeper

A Garden belonging to the Arch Byshop of Dublins Palace

S.t Patrick's Church Yard

S.t Patrick's Close

The ground plott of the Arch Byshop of Dublin's Palace

Passage to the Library

Passage to the Arch Byshop's Palace

Ground belonging to ye Deanary of S.t Patrick's

Garden belonging to ye Arch Byshop of Dublin's Palace

A Scale of feet

1 Ground plan of the Library, 1707.

2 Watercolour of St Patrick's Cathedral and Marsh's Library by L.K. Bradford, 1856.

3 Portrait of Archbishop Narcissus Marsh (1638–1713) attributed to Hugh Howard.
   (In first gallery.)

4 Portrait of Dean Jonathan Swift (1667–1745). By Charles Jervas. Photograph by courtesy of the National Gallery of Ireland.

5 Engraved portrait of Bishop Edward Stillingfleet (1635–99). (In first Gallery.)

6 Photograph of the first gallery, containing the Stillingfleet collection.

7 Portrait of Professor Robert Travers, assistant keeper of Marsh's Library (1841–88). (In first gallery.)

8 Photograph of second gallery, containing the Marsh and Stearne collections.

increased demand for books, particularly for service books, and so an important trade developed between Paris, Rouen and Antwerp.[52]

The continental printers with their greater skill and cheaper raw materials were able to supply the English market with a cheaper and far better printed and illustrated book than could be produced in England.[53] There are such service books in Marsh's which were printed on the Continent for the English and the Irish markets and there are three books in the Stillingfleet collection which are good examples of this. Only one is strictly speaking a service book but the other two do have a strong religious content.

The first was written by William Lyndewode (*d.*1446), the bishop of St David's, and is entitled *Prouinciale, seu cōstitutiones Anglie … reuise.* Lyndewode's book is a digest of the synodal constitutions of the province of Canterbury and was printed by the well-known Paris printer W. Hopyl in 1505 (*STC* 17109).[54] The printing of this book was financed by William Bretton, an important businessman in Calais, for Joyce Pelgrim and Henry Jacobi, the London booksellers.[55] Lyndewode seems to have attached special importance to his very popular book. So popular did the work become that seventeen editions were printed between 1483 and 1534. He directed that after his death his body be buried in St Stephen's Chapel in Westminster and his book be chained in the chapel.[56] The copy in Marsh's is one of the few books in the library bearing a small metal clasp on the binding which indicates it was originally chained to the shelf.

The second work is Joannes de Burgo's *Pupilla oculi oī̄bus presbyteris precipue Anglicanis summe necessaria*, which was also printed by Hopyl at the expense of William Bretton in Paris in 1510 (*STC* 4115). According to Revd G.T. Stokes this celebrated medieval work was the theological handbook of the English clergy from 1300 to 1560.[57] It is still in its original binding.[58]

The third book is *This prymer of Salysbury vse* which was printed in Rouen in 1538 (*STC 16001, Hoskins* 132) for the English and Irish market. It is well illustrated with woodcuts in the French manner; it shows on the

---

52 H.G. Aldis, 'The book-trade 1557–1625' in *CHEL*, iv, p. 402. **53** Colin Clair, op. cit., p. 55. **54** *A guide to the exhibition in the king's library*, p. 87. **55** *DNB* (Joyce Pelgrim). William Bretton is not mentioned separately but in conjunction with Joyce Pelgrim. **56** *DNB* (William Lyndwood or Lyndewode). **57** G.T. Stokes, *Some worthies of the Irish church*, note on p. 126. **58** It was bound by the London binder John Reynes (*d.*1544). The book is decorated with Reynes' pineapple and half pineapple stamp and the dancing peasants roll. See J. Basil Oldham, *Shrewsbury school library bindings*, Oxford, At the University Press, 1943. See A.VII.20, Roll no. 6, page 26 and plate XLVIII, no. 64.

title-page the first printing of the invocation 'God be in my head and in my understanding'.

But the books printed on the Continent for the English market were not printed solely for religious purposes. Books on education and books which could not be safely printed in England, particularly those dealing with political and religious controversy, were also printed on the Continent.

Three important books relating to Mary, queen of Scots, and her claim to the English throne are in the library. These were written by Bishop John Leslie. Bishop Leslie (*d.*1596) was chief adviser to Queen Mary on her ecclesiastical policy and he was appointed her ambassador to Queen Elizabeth in 1569.[59] Leslie was imprisoned in the Tower because he was suspected of being involved in the Ridolfi plot. He was set free on the understanding that he would remain in exile. He wrote *A defence of the honour ... of Marie queene of Scotlande*, which was first printed in Paris (?) in 1569. The third edition of this work, with a new title, *A treatise concerning the defence of the honour of Marie of Scotland* (*STC* 15506, *A&R* 453), was printed under the pseudonym M. Philippes with a false imprint which gave the place of printing as Liege and the printer G. Morberius with the date 1571. But *Allison and Rogers* identified the place of printing as Louvain and the printer as John Fowler.[60] The copy which is in the Stillingfleet collection bears on the title-page a slightly sour annotation made by a previous owner which reads 'From wyne and woman good lord delyver us'. The second part of this work was again printed by G. L'Oyselet in Rouen in 1584 (*STC* 15507 *A&R* 455) and is also in the Stillingfleet collection. It originally belonged to the English book-collector Humphrey Dyson. But it is a little unusual; not only does it contain Dyson's signature, it also includes his printed bookstamp with a printed inscription dated 1611. Gordon Duff noted that it originally belonged to Richard Smith[61] and it appears as Item No. 513, p. 204 in Smith's auction catalogue of 1682. Another important book also written by John Leslie is *De origine, moribus, et rebus gestis Scotorum* which was printed in Rome in 1578. This first edition is particularly interesting because it contains what are believed to be the earliest medallion portraits of Queen Mary and her son James VI as a child. It also has a rare map of Scotland. It is part of the Stearne collection in the library.

---

59 *DNB* (John Leslie).   60 A.F. Allison & D.M. Rogers, op. cit., pt 1, no. 15506, p. 83, [453] [214].
61 E.G. Duff, 'Notes on a visit to Archbishop Marsh's Library', p. 138.

19 The earliest known medallion portraits of Mary queen of Scots, and her son James VI as a child. From Bishop John Leslie's *De origine, moribus, et rebus gestis Scotorum* (Rome, 1578).

An interesting edition of a Latin grammar by John Colet is also in the Stillingfleet collection. Colet (*d.*1519), dean of St Paul's Cathedral and founder of St Paul's School, wrote his Latin grammar, entitled *Aeditio*, in collaboration with William Lily, the first headmaster of the school. Colet's grammar became so popular that it was later revised by Erasmus and became the standard textbook for nearly two hundred years.[62] The edition in Marsh's was printed in Antwerp in 1539 by the widow of Martinus de Keyser.

Martinus de Keyser (or Caesar) became one of the most productive of the Antwerp printers and printed books for export to England;[63] when de Keyser died in 1536 his widow continued the printing business. Colet's *Aeditio* was often printed together with Thomas Wolsey's *Rudimenta grammatices*, a tiny four-page tract instructing the teachers of the school at Ipswich how to make practical use of Colet's grammar. The edition in Marsh's is no exception. The tract was also printed by de Keyser's widow in Antwerp in 1539 (*STC* 25947 now pt. 1 of 5543b7).

A remarkable and rare book by Nicholas Harpsfield is in the Stillingfleet collection. Harpsfield (*d.*1575) was a theologian and became the first regius professor of Greek in Oxford.[64] As a Catholic he refused to accept the prayer book and consequently was imprisoned in the Tower from 1559 until his death in 1575. While Harpsfield was in prison he wrote six Latin dialogues. In five of these dialogues he defended some of the beliefs of the Catholic Church, but in the sixth he attacked pseudomartyrs, particularly those Protestant martyrs mentioned by John Foxe. Harpsfield sent his completed manuscript to his friend Alan Cope, who published it at Antwerp under his own name, but Cope then added a colophon stating that it had been written by Harpsfield. It was printed by Christopher Plantin in 1566 and it contains a full-size drawing in brown ink of a cross which appeared in the middle of a tree in the parish of St Donats, Glamorganshire.

A slight reversal of the export business from the Continent to England occurred when an Englishman, Richard Rowlands alias Verstegen (*d.*1620), emigrated to Antwerp and set up a printing business.[65] Rowlands assumed his grandfather's name of Verstegen and he wrote *A restitution of decayed intelligence: in antiquities* which was printed by Robert Bruney in Antwerp in

---

62 George Sampson, op. cit., p. 117.   63 M.E. Kronenberg, 'Notes on English printing in the Low Countries' (Early sixteenth century) in *The Library*, 4 ser., ix, no. 2, September 1928, pp 160–1. 64 *DNB* (Nicholas Harpsfield or Harpesfeld).   65 *DNB* (Richard Rowlands alias Verstegen). Manuscript note possibly written by the previous owner, E.W. Gosse.

1605 (*STC* 21361, *A&R* 846); it was intended for sale in London. (Rowlands' book is believed to contain the earliest speculations on the possibility of the Panama canal.) The copy in the library has several unusual features including the rare plate of the Verstegen arms on page 339 and the signature of John Earle, the philologist (*d*.1903). It also contains the bookplate of Sir Edmund Gosse (*d*.1928) and it was purchased for Marsh's in 1936 to replace the copy missing from the library since 1780.

Another unusual book in Marsh's is Edward Maihew's *Trophaea*. It was printed in Rheims in 1625. Edward Maihew OSB (*d*.1625) was an English Benedictine monk who wrote a monumental history of the Benedictine Order. Although there are at least six other known copies, Marsh's is apparently the only perfect one.[66] (Curiously three volumes of this work are in the Stillingfleet collection and the fourth volume is in Marsh's collection.)

Cambridge University

John Siberch, otherwise John Laer of Siegburg, was a native of Cologne and became printer to Cambridge University in 1521. The first piece which Siberch printed in Cambridge in 1521 (1522) was by Henry Bullock, the vice-president of the university.[67] It is entitled *Doctissimi viri Henrici Bulloci … oratio ad Thomā* [Wolsey] *cardinalem archiepiscopum Eboracensem* (*STC* 4082). Henry Bullock's speech was made when Cardinal Wolsey visited the university in 1520. It is a small tract and is bound together with similar tracts including one by Papyrius Geminus entitled *Hermathena* which was also printed in Cambridge in 1522 (*STC* 11719). Both works are in the Stillingfleet collection.

Oxford and Oxford University

Printing began in Oxford in 1478–9.[68] But it was over one hundred years before the university appointed its own printer. The first printer to the university was Joseph Barnes, appointed in 1585.[69] The earliest piece printed by Barnes in the library was written by Alberico Gentili and we deal with it in the next chapter in the section on Witchcraft.

---

66 See article written by Dom Hugh Connolly OSB on Maihew's *Trophaea* in *Downside Review*, no. 142, vol. l, January, London, Sheed & Ward, 1932, pp 108–25, and correspondence in the library. **67** G.R. Barnes and others, *A list of books printed in Cambridge at the University Press 1521–1800*, CUP, 1935, pp 6–7. **68** *A guide to the exhibition in the king's library*, p. 74. **69** Falconer Maden, *The early Oxford Press, a bibliography of printing and publishing at Oxford '1468'–1640*, Oxford, At the Clarendon Press, 1895, p. 35, 1593 (3). See also article by J.W. Binns on 'Alberico Gentili in defence of poetry and acting' in *Studies in the Renaissance*, xix, 1972, pp 224–72. See also Colin Clair, op. cit., p. 138.

Another Oxford university printer whose printings can be seen in the library is William Turner (d.1644). Turner was not considered a reliable printer. On one occasion he 'borrowed' the beautiful Savile Greek type from the university and did not return it for five years.[70] Two interesting books printed by Turner are in Archbishop Marsh's collection. The first is G.J. Vossius' *Theses theologicæ et historicæ ...*, 1628. The *STC* (24883) says this edition is a variant, with the imprint Bellositi Dobunorum (i.e. Oxford). The place name in the imprint is whimsical as the Dobuni tribe once inhabited the district near Oxford. Bellositi Dobunorum was the Roman name for Oxford.[71] The second book is Johannes Combachius' *Metaphysicorum, libri duo. Editio tertia.* This was printed by Turner in 1633 (*STC* 5591).

But the most spectacular Oxford printed book in the library is William Cowper's *The anatomy of humane bodies* (*Wing* C 6698). This was printed in Oxford in 1698 for two of the best-known English publishers, Benjamin Walford and Samuel Smith. William Cowper or Cooper (d.1709) practised surgery in London and was elected a fellow of the Royal Society in 1696. His book contains enormous copperplate illustrations showing many new anatomical discoveries. These illustrations were the cause of a bitter dispute between Cowper and Dr Bidloo, a Dutch professor. Bidloo maintained that the plates in Cowper's book had been taken from his (Bidloo's) own book on anatomy and he accused Walford and Smith, the publishers, and Cowper himself of fraud.[72] This book was originally part of the Stillingfleet collection but is now kept in the 'cages' in the second gallery. (Bidloo's superb book is also in Marsh's.)

In about 1671 Dr John Fell generously provided the University Press with a foundry, printing equipment, and types which enabled the press to print some notable books.[73] In 1669 the University Press was moved to the Sheldonian Theatre and although it did not produce many books it did produce some very valuable ones. These included Edward Hyde, earl of Clarendon's *The history of the rebellion and civil wars in England*, 3 vols (1707). The copy in Marsh's of Clarendon's *History* originally belonged to Jonathan Swift and has been extensively annotated by him. These annotations are mostly insulting references to the Scottish people whom Swift regarded as traitors for the part they took in the civil war.

---

70 H.R. Plomer, *A dictionary of the booksellers and printers ... 1641–1667*, p. 182.   71 Henry Cotton, op. cit., p. 207.   72 *DNB* (William Cowper).   73 Colin Clair, op. cit., pp 139–40.

MECHANICK
EXERCISES,
OR,
The Doctrine of
Handy-works.

Began Jan. 1. 1677. *And intended to be
Monthly continued.*

By *Joseph Moxon* Hydrographer to the
Kings most Excellent Majesty.

LONDON,
Printed for *Joseph Moxon* at the sign of *Atlas* on
Ludgate-Hill, 1677.

20 Title-page of Joseph Moxon's *Mechanick exercises* (London, 1677).

In 1677 Joseph Moxon wrote the first English book on typefounding. This
was entitled *Mechanick exercises, or, the doctrine of handy-works* (*Wing* M 3013). In
1683 Moxon (*d.*1700) brought out a second volume which was devoted to the
art of printing (*Wing* M 3014). This volume describes and illustrates in great
detail all the processes of printing with an early hand press. Colin Clair noted
that while this book was 'an indispensable sourcebook on every aspect of
printing as practised in the days of the hand press', it was atrociously printed.[74]
This first English book on printing may not be a masterpiece of typography
but it is exciting to discover that the only copy of the work available in Ireland
is in Archbishop Marsh's collection.

74 Ibid., p. 141, see also D.B. Updike, op cit., ii, pp 43–4.

Later printers

While the publication of Moxon's *Mechanick exercises* may not have been a great success, it was not very long before one of the greatest English type-founders began to influence English book production. This was William Caslon (*d.*1766), who began producing founts of type in about 1720. These founts included Arabic, Hebrew, and a beautiful roman. Caslon's roman type became so successful that it was used all over England and by some of the early American printers.[75] Caslon is believed to have been financed and introduced to letter-cutting by two well-known English printers, William Bowyer I and John Watts. William Bowyer used Caslon's types and produced some of the finest books in England.

William Bowyer I (*d.*1737) and his even more famous son William Bowyer II became renowned for the fine quality of their printings. Two splendid examples of William Bowyer I's printing are in the library. The first is *The theological works*, 2 vols, of the Revd Charles Leslie which he printed in 1721. D.B. Updike, writing about this book and its interesting pieces of eighteenth-century composition, said, 'Its head and tail-pieces are splendid examples of printer's ornaments of that epoch; and the headbands of type "flowers" are handsome and cleverly managed.'[76] The second book is John Seldon's *Opera* which Bowyer printed in three volumes in 1726 for a number of London publishers. This superb printing shows Caslon's founts of roman, italic, and Hebrew types. D.B. Updike noted that although Bowyer printed the first volume of this work in two parts, the succeeding two volumes were printed by S. Palmer and T. Wood, probably to ensure that all three volumes would appear together.[77] But even though Bowyer did not print the second and third volumes, according to Updike the whole work illustrates both William Bowyer's and his son's skilful typesetting and planning. The work was edited by Dr David Wilkins and it was issued by subscription.

The next most important innovator in English printing in the eighteenth century was John Baskerville (*d.*1775). Baskerville worked in Birmingham as a writing master and stone cutter. He became interested in japanned ware and succeeded in developing a business which became a great financial success. Then Baskerville became interested in printing and type design and in all the processes of book production.[78] He developed a special new ink

---

75 D.B. Updike, op. cit., ii, p. 151.   **76** Ibid., p. 136.   **77** Ibid., pp 136–7.   **78** Ibid., pp 108.

and had paper specially made for him by James Whatman. After many years of experimentation and effort he issued his first book. This was an edition of Virgil which came out in 1757. For this book he used a special process of 'hot pressing' the sheets of paper, which gave a fine gloss appearance to every page.[79] There is an edition of Virgil printed by Baskerville in Marsh's and the title-page bears the date 1757. But because of the inferior quality of the paper it is obviously not the edition of 1757 but appears to be the much later edition of 1771 (*Lowndes*, p. 2777).[80] There is, however, another example of Baskerville's printing in the library. This is the two-volume edition of Milton's *Paradise lost* and *Paradise regained* which Baskerville printed in 1758 and for which he also wrote the preface. But unfortunately these volumes are not particularly well printed. The title-page of the first volume is laid out in Baskerville's usual style but the title-page of the second volume is cramped and ugly. While Baskerville's printing of Milton's *Paradise lost* is rather disappointing, there is no doubt that he made an outstanding contribution to printing and his designs and ideas influenced many English and continental printers.

Throughout the sixteenth and seventeenth centuries most English authors had to depend on patronage for the publication of their writings. When the copyright act was passed in 1709, an entirely different situation arose. English authors now had the exclusive right to their own property and many popular authors began to receive substantial sums of money for their writings. Some of the best-known authors such as Oliver Goldsmith and Henry Fielding were particularly well paid.[81] This new development encouraged partnerships between the printers, publishers and authors in order to keep the expenses of book production at a reasonable level.

Another characteristic of early eighteenth-century printing in England was the revival of interest in fine typography. Philip Gaskell said, 'The best of the superb work done by British printers during the astonishing eighteenth-century revival of typography, following the almost unrelieved incompetence displayed by our seventeenth century printers, is to be found in editions of the ancient Greek and Roman authors. This was because the eighteenth-century reading public believed the classics to be the most valuable source of polite learning available to it, and was prepared to pay a little extra to obtain them in a suitably dignified form.'[82] In particular Philip Gaskell

79 Colin Clair, op. cit., p. 193.   **80** W.T. Lowndes, *The bibliographer's manual of English literature*, new edition, rev. by H.G. Bohn, 4 vols, London, George Bell [1864], iv, p. 2777.   **81** S.H. Steinberg, op. cit., p. 226.   **82** Philip Gaskell, 'Printing the classics in the eighteenth century' in *The Book Collector* i, no.

mentioned that in London three splendid classical editions appeared from two or three presses and one sumptuous edition of the works of Caesar. This was published by Jacob Tonson with annotations by Samuel Clarke in 1712. There is a copy of this superb book in the Stearne collection. The title-page is beautifully set out in spaced italic capitals. It is illustrated with full-page copperplates, and magnificent engraved initial letters, headpieces and tailpieces, and it is bound in white vellum.

There are some further examples of these luxury type books in the library. But as we have already explained, since the majority of the books in Marsh's were acquired before 1745, these later additions were usually donated to the library or occasionally, whenever the tiny book fund permitted, they were purchased by the keeper.

In 1762 the keeper, Dr Thomas Cobbe, purchased the *Works* of Joseph Addison for £2 16s. 10d.[83] These books were published by Jacob Tonson. Tonson (*d*.1736) was a bookseller; he also engaged in printing and published the writings of some of the best contemporary English writers. (In about 1720 Jacob Tonson retired in favour of his nephew, also called Jacob Tonson.) Together with another publisher, John Barber, Tonson published a splendid edition of Prior's *Poems on several occasions* in 1718. It was printed for Tonson and Barber by another celebrated English printer, John Watts. (It is interesting to note that this was one of the tallest folios ever produced and is kept with similar type folios in the 'cages' in the library.) The *Works* of Joseph Addison which Tonson published in 1721 contain a preface written by Thomas Tickell. These were produced in four very handsome volumes and their purchase by Dr Cobbe made a fine contribution to the collections in the library.

Jacob Tonson in partnership with Bernard Lintot published another interesting contemporary work. This was John Gay's *Poems on several occasions* which they published in 1720. Bernard Lintot also published independently. Like Tonson, Lintot published the writings of many well-known contemporary English authors. But one of his publications led to an unfortunate dispute. This was the edition of Alexander Pope's translation of Homer's *Odyssey* which Lintot published in 1725 (vols I–III, to end of Book XIV, 3 vols in Marsh's). In order to complete this translation as quickly as possible Pope employed two assistants, William Broome and Elijah Fenton. They translated twelve books out of the twenty-four. Although Pope received a considerable sum of money for the translation, he paid his assistants badly and in the dispute that followed Pope induced Broome, unknown to Fenton, to state that they had done far less work than was generally believed.[84]

An even more controversial publication was Pope's *Literary correspondence for thirty years*, 2 vols. This was published by Edmund Curll in 1735–7. Curll (*d*.1747) had been imprisoned and fined many times for pirating various authors' writings and for the publication of indecent books. Although Pope was well aware of Curll's reputation (he had referred to him in the *Dunciad* as 'shameless Curll') he secretly arranged with Curll to publish his *Literary correspondence*. Then Pope contrived to have the publication stopped by the house of lords on the pretext that it was a breach of privilege. Henry F. Plomer suggested that Pope's reason for doing this was to gain more publicity for his own edition which appeared two years later.[85] There is a fine copy of Curll's edition in the library.

Other notable English printers of this period represented in the library are William Strahan, Thomas Cadell and John Nichols. William Strahan (*d*.1785) is chiefly remembered for his printing of Dr Johnson's *Dictionary* in 1755. Twenty-one years later Strahan in partnership with Thomas Cadell published Gibbon's *Decline and fall*. Both these works are in Marsh's but not in the first editions. John Nichols (*d*.1826) was a printer and author. In 1786 he printed his great folio edition of C.G. Woide's *Novum Testamentum Graecum*. This magnificent book, based on the Codex Alexandrinus, was printed by Nichols at the expense of the trustees of the British Museum. It is interesting to note that Marsh's is listed in the Subscribers' List in this book as St Sepulchre's Library, Dublin. The old account book in Marsh's shows that the first subscription of £1 2s. 9d. was paid by the library in July 1780 and the second subscription for the same amount in August 1786.[86]

In 1918 Miss Harriet M. Everth presented the library of her father, the Revd Godfrey Everth, to Marsh's. This library which consists of 1218 volumes is a good example of a nineteenth-century clergyman's library. It contains what would obviously have been regarded as 'good' nineteenth-century popular literature. It is for this reason also that it includes books issued by many English printers and publishers of the period. They include

---

84 *DNB* (Alexander Pope). See also John Dennis, *The age of Pope (1700–1744)*, London, G. Bell, 1925, pp 38–9. **85** H.R. Plomer, *A dictionary of the printers and booksellers ... 1668–1725*, ed. Arundell Esdaile, p. 94. **86** Old account book in the library, July 1780, f. 10 and August 1786, f. 15.

William Bulmer, Thomas Bensley, John Bell and the Chiswick Press. These printers and publishers were responsible for the revival of interest in fine typography and an improvement in the general standard of printing.

Thomas Bensley (*d.*1833) is represented in the Everth collection by his printing of *The plays* of William Shakespeare which he printed for Wynne and Scholey and J. Wallis in ten volumes from 1803 to 1805. The first volume has a charming illustration of Shakespeare watching a thunderstorm with the dramatic explanation underneath which reads, 'The poet's eye in a fine frenzy rolling'. William Bulmer (*d.*1830) worked as a printer with the London publisher, John Bell. Bulmer became one of the finest printers in England and produced some magnificent books.[87] He printed the *Works* of Ben Jonson in nine volumes in 1816 for a group of London publishers. This edition was edited by William Gifford (*d.*1826) who became celebrated as the first editor of the *Quarterly Review*. These volumes are also part of the Everth collection in the library.

John Bell (*d.*1831), whom we have already mentioned, was a publisher. But he was also a bookseller and he became deeply interested in typography. Bell set up his own foundry and produced his own type. His new ideas and designs had a considerable impact on English printers. From 1791 to 1795 Bell published a series of tragedies which were performed at the Theatre Royal, Drury Lane, and also in Covent Garden. These tragedies include Richard Cumberland's *The battle of Hastings* and *The Carmelite*. They are charmingly illustrated with portraits of the actors and actresses who played dramatic parts in the productions including such famous performers as Mr Kemble and Mrs Siddons. Another very successful publishing venture during the middle of the nineteenth century was the publication of books by H.G. Bohn for his Standard Library, 1846–55. Many of these editions were collected by the Revd Godfrey Everth and can now be consulted in Marsh's.

Charles Whittingham

In 1789 Charles Whittingham the Elder (*d.*1840), founder of the Chiswick Press, first set up a printing press in London. Whittingham began his business in a small way and later moved to Chiswick where he became interested in the production of paper. Subsequently he began to print for the publisher, John Sharpe, a series of British Classics which were illustrated with

87 Colin Clair, op. cit., p. 197.

particularly fine engravings. In fact Whittingham used some of the best engravers in England for these small books. The following are in the Everth collection: Sharpe's editions of the *British poets*, 1805–8, *Lives of the English poets*, 1805–6 and *Translations from the Greek, Roman, and Italian poets*, 1809–10. Whittingham also printed another series which he called Whittingham's *Cabinet Library* and these included such writers as Oliver Goldsmith, Edmund Burke, Benjamin Franklin and Izaak Walton. These are also part of the Everth collection in the library.

Charles Whittingham's nephew, also called Charles Whittingham (*d.*1876), was apprenticed to his uncle and eventually went into partnership with him. After some years the partnership was dissolved and Whittingham set up his own printing business and began a very successful association with the publisher, William Pickering (*d.*1854).[88] For William Pickering, Whittingham began to print a series of reprints of the *Prayer book* which ended with a final volume called the '*Victoria*' *prayer book* in 1844. This splendid book was printed in a handsome black letter type on handmade paper. It is lavishly decorated with ornamental initial letters and is rubricated throughout. Whittingham was an admirer of the great Venetian printer Aldus and he included Aldus' device of the dolphin and anchor on the title-page. But Whittingham did not use Aldus' motto which always accompanied the device. Instead, Whittingham inserted 'Aldi Discip. Anglus' (English disciple of Aldus). This beautiful book was presented to Marsh's by the keeper, the Revd N.J.D. White, in 1926. It bears the bookplate of the previous owner, Thomas Barrowclough.

Finally, to complete this short account of some of the English printings, we include a fine donation which brings us into the twentieth century. This is an edition of the *Metz Pontifical* which was edited by E.S. Dewick and printed by J.B. Nichols for the Roxburghe Club in 1902. It is bound in the special style of the Roxburghe Club, a gilt-lettered flat green leather spine and dark red paper-board sides. It was bequeathed to Marsh's by Bishop Owen Thomas Lloyd Crossley in 1926.

Scotland

Printing began in Scotland when Andrew Millar and Walter Chapman established the first printing press in Edinburgh in 1507.[89] The best-known early Scottish printer represented in Marsh's is Robert Lekpreuik. Lekpreuik began printing in Edinburgh in about 1561 and was appointed king's printer

---

88 Ibid., p. 240.   **89** *A guide to the exhibition in the king's library*, p. 93.

in 1568. Three years later Lekpreuik got into trouble with the authorities when he was suspected of printing a satire by the Scottish historian George Buchanan on Secretary Maitland of Lethington.[90] Lekpreuik fled to Stirling taking his equipment with him and so became the first printer there.

A copy of George Buchanan's book *Ane admonition direct to the trew Lordis mantenaris of the kingis graces authoritie* was printed in Stirling by Robert Lekpreuik [really London, J. Day] in 1571 (*STC* 3968, *Aldis* 99). Buchanan wrote in the Scottish dialect this attack on the house of Hamilton. The Hamiltons, who supported Queen Mary, were the principal opponents of Moray, the regent whom Hamilton of Bothwellhaugh had murdered. Buchanan appealed to the lords of Scotland to support the young king. Another book by George Buchanan (*d*.1582) entitled *Rerum Scoticarum historia* was printed by Alexander Arbuthnot in 1583 (*STC* 3992). Although the imprint of this book reads 'Edimburgi Ad exemplar A. Arbuthneti, 1583', there is a strong possibility that it was not printed in Edinburgh but may have been printed in Antwerp.[91] Buchanan's history is regarded as one of his finest pieces and Shakespeare is believed to have used it for the dramatic events in *Macbeth*.[92] Buchanan's books are in the Stillingfleet collection.

Robert Waldegrave (*d*.1604) was a London printer who came to Edinburgh as king's printer in 1590. While he was in Edinburgh, Waldegrave printed Robert Rollock's *In epistolam Pauli apostoli ad Ephesios, commentarius* in 1590 (*STC* 21278, *Aldis* 218). Robert Rollock (*d*.1599) was the first principal of Edinburgh University and was one of the earliest Scottish writers on theological subjects.[93] His book is part of the Stearne collection. Waldegrave printed theological books and the writings of the prohibited English Puritan authors. (He was fined and imprisoned several times for these offences.) Waldegrave also printed the scurrilous pamphlets which were issued under the pseudonym of Martin Marprelate.[94] Another book, *The lawes and actes of parliament, maid be king Iames the first, and his successours … (collected be J. Skene)*, Edinburgh, 1597 (*STC* 21877, *Aldis* 291) was also printed by Robert Waldegrave. It bears the signature of James Barry, Lord Santry (*d*.1673), and it also has a fascinating annotation on the endpapers

90 Colin Clair, op cit., p. 123.   **91** H.G. Aldis does not include this edition in his *A list of books printed in Scotland before 1700*, printed for the Edinburgh Bibliographical Society, MCMIV. But Pollard and Redgrave's *STC* 3992 gives [Antwerp, G. van den Rade].   **92** J.F. Fleming op. cit., no. 75, p. 20. **93** *DNB* (Robert Rollock).   **94** Colin Clair, op. cit., p. 111.

which reads, 'This book was gelben [*sic*] be my Lord Register to James Hutsone'.[95] It is part of the Stearne collection.

Edward Raban (*d.*1658) was another English printer who began printing in Edinburgh in 1620. Two years later he moved to Aberdeen and became the first printer there. Raban printed Andrew Logie's *Cum bono deo. Raine from the clouds* in Aberdeen in 1624 (*STC* 16694, *Aldis* 618). For some reason the printed date on the title-page in the copy in Archbishop Marsh's collection has been altered in an unknown hand to 1634. It is interesting to discover that Henry Cotton found that the date had been similarly altered in the copy in the Bodleian Library.[96]

Edward Raban also printed for David Melvill, the Aberdeen bookseller. For Melvill, Raban printed Daniel Tilenus (*d.*1633) *De disciplina ecclesiastica … dissertatio* in Aberdeen in 1622 (*STC* 24067, *Aldis* 584). Daniel Tilenus was a German Protestant divine who went to live in France.[97] While he was there he engaged in various controversies with the Arminians and the Remonstrants. Tilenus disapproved of Presbyterianism and wrote a letter to the Scottish people recommending the episcopal form of the reformed church, as established in England. King James so approved of Tilenus' views that he invited him to visit England.

Due to religious and political difficulties, printing in Scotland like printing in Ireland developed very slowly. These difficulties provided English and continental printers with an opportunity of supplying books for these markets.

The London printer, Valentine Simmes (*d.*1622), printed *The earle of Gowries conspiracie against the kings maiestie* in 1603 (*STC* 21467.5). This book deals with John Ruthven, the third earl of Gowrie, who opposed King James. Gowrie was killed in a fight with the king's attendants while attempting to avenge his brother's death. (This very popular work was printed many times by Simmes and this late edition is part of the Stillingfleet collection.)

When Gordon Duff visited Marsh's in 1903 he noted some important Scottish printings in the Stearne collection.[98] These included a collection of tracts written by Alexander Julius which were printed by A. Hart, T. Finlason and R. Charteris in Edinburgh between the years 1606 and 1614. Since

---

95 Sir John Skene (d.1617), Scottish statesman, clerk-register, and lord of session under the title Lord Curriehill. He prepared the revision of the Scottish laws in 1597 and it seems probable that the donor mentioned in the annotation as 'my lord register' was Sir John Skene. (From the *DNB*.)   96 Henry Cotton, *A typographical gazetteer* (footnote on page 2).   97 Alexander Chalmers, op. cit. (Daniel Tilenus).   98 E.G. Duff, 'Notes on a visit to Archbishop Marsh's Library', pp 138–9.

Gordon Duff's visit many new reference books have appeared and further copies of these works have been located in other libraries.

Another book of Scottish interest bears the signature of the remarkable Scottish historian, Hector Boece. It contains three pamphlets which were written by Paulus Orosius, Diodorus Siculus and Leonardo Bruni. These pamphlets were printed in Paris in the early part of the sixteenth century and are part of the Bouhéreau collection.

Most of the Scottish printings in the library are concerned with religious controversy and it is a relief to turn to a completely different subject. Sir Robert Sibbald (*d.*1722), the Scottish physician, became interested in botany and herbs. Sibbald wrote *Scotia illustrata* which was printed by James Kniblo and partners in Edinburgh in 1684 (*Wing* S 3727, *Aldis* 2490). Although Sibbald's book was severely criticised for being inaccurate it does contain many interesting observations on the medicinal uses of plants in Scotland. It also includes illustrations of birds, plants, fishes and trees.

LATER SCOTTISH PRINTING

Two of the greatest names in Scottish printing during the eighteenth century were the brothers Andrew and Robert Foulis.[99] Robert (*d.*1776) and Andrew (*d.*1775) were interested in bookselling and publishing. But because of the exceptionally poor standards of printing in Glasgow at this period the brothers decided to take up printing themselves.[1] They employed Alexander Wilson to cut type specially for their books and they became renowned for the excellence of their designs, lay-out and typography. One of Robert and Andrew Foulis' most splendid productions is the edition of Homer's *Iliad* and *Odyssey* which they printed in four volumes in Glasgow between 1756 and 1758. Dr Edward Hill of Trinity College presented these superb books to the library in 1778.

James Ballantyne (*d.*1833) founded the Ballantyne Press in Kelso in 1796. Later at the suggestion of Sir Walter Scott he moved the press to Edinburgh. Ballantyne was associated with Archibald Constable (*d.*1827), the founder of the *Edinburgh Review*, and both these publishers were responsible for publishing most of Sir Walter Scott's writings.

The first edition of Sir Walter Scott's *The lay of the last minstrel*, printed by James Ballantyne in 1805 for Archibald Constable and a group of London

99 Colin Clair, op. cit., p. 162.   **1** D.B. Updike, op. cit., ii, pp 117–18.

publishers, is in the library. There is also a copy of Scott's *Marmion* which Ballantyne printed for Constable and two London publishers in 1808. The collapse of Constable's publishing business in 1826 unfortunately involved both James Ballantyne and Sir Walter Scott. Sir Walter gallantly offered to pay the debts incurred by the bankruptcy and worked until his death to pay his creditors.

According to D.J. O'Donoghue, Sir Walter visited Marsh's Library in July 1825.[2]

---

2 D.J. O'Donoghue, *Sir Walter Scott's tour in Ireland in 1825*, Glasgow/Dublin, 1905, p. 32.

Chapter 4

Famous Books

E CAN IN AN ACCOUNT such as this give merely an indication of the riches of Marsh's Library. The principal emphasis in the last chapter has been on important printers and printing, but this does not give a full picture and consequently we provide in this chapter a brief outline of some other important books in the four main collections.

Bibles

The collectors usually began their collections with editions of the classical writers and Marsh's contains fine editions of all the Greek and Latin poets. But because three of the main collections were made by Protestant bishops there is understandably a very fine collection of Bibles, including the four great Polyglot Bibles. And there are Bibles in a great many different languages, including Bengali, Dutch, French, Greek, German, Hebrew, Irish, Latin, Persian, Rarotongan, Slavonic and Spanish. They range in size from enormous folios to small pocket Bibles. There are also commentaries on the Bible, and some fifteen editions of missals, breviaries and books of hours of the Sarum use. Among the Bibles and prayer books are early printings from the first half of the sixteenth century, and these are comparatively rare, many being known in only one or two copies.

Oriental

Archbishop Marsh was particularly interested in oriental literature, science, mathematics and music. A former librarian of Marsh's, Newport J.D. White, commenting on Archbishop Marsh's own collection of oriental books said:

> The printed books which Marsh left to the library … testify abundantly to the extent of his linguistic interest, if not knowledge. Besides Hebrew, Syriac and Arabic, the Armenian, Coptic, Ethiopic, Georgic, Slavonic, Persian and Turkish languages are here represented. The

Hebrew books include fine editions of the Talmud and Targums, Rabbinical commentaries, Cabbalistic treatises and liturgical works both of the Spanish and German Jews … Most of the lexicons and grammars are the work of Roman Catholic scholars and due to Roman missionary enterprise. This is certainly the case with the Roman Breviary in Slavonic, edited by order of Innocent X in 1647, the Breviary in Syriac, 1666, a Missal in Arabic and an epitome of Baronius' Annals in the same language, 1653, and Histories of Christ and of St Peter by Hieron. Xavier S.J., 1639, and the Catechism in Armenian, 1634.[1]

Religious controversy

The subject of religious controversy is well represented, particularly the Reformation and Counter-Reformation, and we have books by such writers as Erasmus, Luther, Melanchthon, and Calvin. There are also the Catholic writers, St Thomas More, Cardinals Robert Bellarmine and Caesar Baronius, St Ignatius Loyola, and members of the Jesuit Order. The most interesting from the library's point of view is Cardinal Baronius. Baronius wrote *Annales ecclesiastici* as a reply to the Protestant Centuriators of Magdeburg and this copy originally belonged to Jonathan Swift. Swift was not impressed by the cardinal's reply; he wrote on the endpaper of the first volume (Antwerp, 1612) the following annotation:

> Worst of bad writers, falsest of the false,
> Shallowest of the shallow,
> Silliest of the silly.

> This, when I had read twelve volumes and with ire and boredom was incensed, was my considered opinion.
> A.D. 1729 J.S.

English political and religious controversy

Frequently we find dealt with subjects such as the divine right of kings, the Act of Uniformity, Puritanism, Socinianism, Quakerism, Presbyterianism,

---

1 G.T. Stokes, *Some worthies of the Irish church* (no. 3. Narcissus Marsh), ed. H.J. Lawlor, London, Hodder & Stoughton, 1900, pp 72–4. (Note 3 by Newport J.D. White.)

Catholic plots and conspiracies. The library is particularly rich in this type of controversy and a good example is *A conference about the next succession to the crowne of Ingland*, which was published under the pseudonym R. Doleman in Antwerp in 1594 (1595) (*STC* 19398, *A & R* 271; it lacks the genealogical tree). This was in fact written by Robert Parsons, R. Rowlands and others. Parsons, an English Jesuit, was one of the most important and skilful men of his time. He was condemned by Queen Elizabeth and possession of his book was declared to be high treason.[2]

A very different book, *De jure regni apud Scotos dialogus,* is in the Stillingfleet collection. This was written by the Scottish historian, George Buchanan; in it he defended the Scottish Reformation and made a vigorous attack on absolutism. Buchanan firmly believed that the king held power from the people and might be judged by them.[3] This edition of *De jure regni* was printed together with another work written by Buchanan entitled *Rerum Scoticarum historia* which we have already mentioned.

There are in the Stillingfleet collection many books both written and owned by Isaac Casaubon. Casaubon was a Swiss Protestant who came to be regarded as one of the finest classical scholars in Europe in the sixteenth century. Casaubon was deeply interested in Protestant theology and church history. While he lived in France he had been involved in the great theological controversy between Philippe de Mornay, Seigneur du Plessis Marly, and Cardinal Du Perron. Casaubon came to England partly on the invitation of Bishop Lancelot Andrewes. When Casaubon came to live in England, King James I specially requested him to reply to Baronius' arguments in *Annales ecclesiastici*.[4] Casaubon did reply to Baronius' arguments, and it is fascinating that among the books which originally belonged to Casaubon in the library, there is a copy of Baronius' *Annales ecclesiastici* which contains several sheets of manuscript notes which Casaubon made. (It is interesting that this is the same work which we have mentioned in connection with Swift's annotations.)

Political sermonising

At a time when church-going was still legally enforceable in England the pulpit was an important means of communication. Since many of the

---

2 *DNB* (Robert Parsons).   **3** George Sampson, *The concise Cambridge history of English literature,* Cambridge, At the University Press, 1941, p. 215.   **4** *DNB* (Isaac Casaubon). See also Mark Pattison,

bishops held important political positions, they often used the pulpit for their political views. Many of these divines (of whose sermons we have many examples) were fine writers, and we find their influence in English letters.

Lancelot Andrewes took part in the preparation of the Authorised Version of the Bible and preached before Queen Elizabeth and the court. It was Lancelot Andrewes' Christmas sermon that T.S. Eliot used as the 'source' for his poem 'Journey of the Magi'.[5] Other writers include Richard Hooker, an outstanding example of a moderate and charitable writer for his time, and the great bishop of Down and Connor, Jeremy Taylor, considered to be one of the masters of English prose. Apart from the divines of the Church of England there was another group which is well represented in the library. These were known as the Cambridge Platonists whom Bishop Burnet claimed saved the Church of England.

Antiquarian research

But not all English scholars and divines at this period engaged in writing and answering arguments on theological and political controversy. Some remarkable contributions were made to antiquarian research and monastic scholarship. Such distinguished names as Henry Wharton, Thomas Hearne and George Hickes (whom David C. Douglas described as 'the most important single figure among the historical scholars of England in the latter half of the seventeenth century')[6] are well represented. The collections in the library also contain books written by many fine English writers who wrote chronicles and antiquarian books.

Philosophy

There are apart from the controversial and other types of books already mentioned a large number of the writings of the English and continental philosophers. They include the disputes between the Arminians and Remonstrants, the writings of Leibnitz, Malebranche, Spinoza and most important, the writings of René Descartes, the founder of modern philosophy. The English philosopher Thomas Hobbes is also included. His ideas on political absolutism influenced political thinking for many years.

Isaac Casaubon 1559–1614, London, Longmans Green, 1875.   **5** Douglas Bush, *English literature in the earlier seventeenth century 1600–1660*, 2nd ed., Oxford, Clarendon Press, 1962, p. 317.   **6** D.C. Douglas, *English scholars*, London, Jonathan Cape, 1939, p. 93.

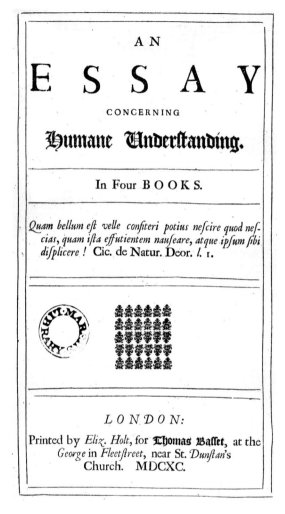

21 Title-page of John Locke's *An essay concerning humane understanding* (London, 1690).

More interesting for Marsh's is the first edition of John Locke's *An essay concerning humane understanding* (London, 1690, *Wing* L 2738). To this Edward Stillingfleet had taken great exception and engaged Locke in a famous controversy on the doctrine of the Trinity.[7]

Although we have no evidence that the Irish philosopher, George Berkeley, ever visited Marsh's, we believe there is a strong possibility that he did so. The Stillingfleet collection was known to most scholars and Berkeley would also have known many of the governors and guardians of Marsh's

---

7 *DNB* (Edward Stillingfleet) and R.T. Carroll, *The common-sense philosophy of religion of Bishop Edward Stilling fleet 1635–1699*, The Hague, Martinus Nijhoff, 1975.

Library. But Marsh's in the early part of the eighteenth century was also the only scholarly library that was open to the public. Berkeley's *Siris: a chain of philosophical reflexions and inquiries concerning the virtues of tar water* (Dublin, Margt. Rhames for R. Gunne, 1744) is in the Stearne collection, together with many of Berkeley's other writings.

The collection which belonged to the first librarian, Dr Bouhéreau, also reflects similar types of religious and political controversy. Dr Bouhéreau had attended the Protestant university of Saumur, where Moses Amyraut was the professor of Protestant theology. His writings are in the collection. Amyraut wrote a piece in which he explained the mystery of predestination and grace, according to the hypothesis of Cameron. This view almost caused a civil war amongst the Protestants and Amyraut was accused of Arminianism.[8]

The writings of many similar French divines and reformers such as Pierre Du Moulin, Charles Drelincourt, and Pierre Jurieu are in the collection. Some of the writings of one of the most important writers on Calvinism, Theodore de Bèze, and of the poet Clément Marot are also here. There is also Theodore Agrippa d'Aubigné's history of the Protestants in France, *Histoire universelle* (Maille, 1616–20). Copies of the first edition are rare because it was ordered to be burnt.[9] There is Jean Bodin's *Les six livres de la République* (Paris, 1576).[10] It was in this great work that Bodin put forward the view that property and family formed the basis of society and a limited monarchy was the best form of government.

But religious controversy was not confined to Protestantism. One of the bitterest Catholic disputes was between François de Salignac de la Mothe Fénélon and Bishop Bossuet, the great Catholic orator and writer. Fénélon had been appointed tutor to Louis XIV's grandson but had become influenced by Madame Guyon's ideas on Quietism.[11] Fénélon wrote *Explication des maximes des saints sur la vie intérieure* (Amsterdam, 1698), which was a defence of some of Madame Guyon's ideas. It was vigorously condemned by Bishop Bossuet and by the pope.

We have the writings of Antoine Arnauld who was religious director of the famous convent of Port-Royal, where his sister Marie Angélique

---

8 Peter Bayle, *The dictionary historical & critical*, translated into English, 2nd ed., London, 1734, pp 260–6. See also Alexander Chalmers, *The general biographical dictionary*, a new ed. rev. and enlar., London, 1812–17 (Moses Amyraut).   **9** Henry Cotton, *A typographical gazetteer*, 2nd ed., Oxford, At the University Press, 1831, p. 159.   **10** This edition belonged to Archbishop Marsh. A later edition belonged to Dr Bouhéreau.   **11** Geoffrey Brereton, *A short history of French literature*, London, Penguin Books, 1968, p. 89.

Arnauld was the abbess. Arnauld wrote against the Jesuits in defence of the Jansenists, and Pierre Nicole and Blaise Pascal also took part in this dispute. Books associated with the controversy on the Eucharist which again involved Port-Royal, the Jesuits, and such writers as Jean Claude and Jacques Nouet are also here.

But fortunately not all of the books in the French collection are confined to controversy and religious disputes. In the Bouhéreau collection there is a beautiful edition of the great French medieval romance, *Le rommant de la rose*, begun by G. de Lorris and finished by J. de Meung. It was printed by Galliot du Pré in Paris in about 1526. Geoffrey Brereton in his book said that the *Roman de la rose* was 'the most popular single work of the thirteenth century and perhaps of the whole medieval period'.[12]

There is also Pierre de Ronsard's *Les œuvres* (Paris, 1609). This edition has the superb architectural type title-page designed by Leonard Gaultier. Dr Bouhéreau also owned a copy of Michel Eyquem de Montaigne's *Les Essais* which was printed in Paris in 1652. Bishop Stillingfleet acquired a fine copy of Pierre Bayle's *Dictionaire historique et critique*, 4 vols (Rotterdam, 1697) which had such an enormous influence on French literature and philosophy.[13] (The first English translation of this work was donated many years later to the library.)

Another fine acquisition is Molière's *Oeuvres*, 6 vols (Paris, 1734). This edition is the first impression with illustrations by F. Boucher and engravings by L. Cars. It bears an annotation on the upper endpaper which says it was purchased for the library at Dr Stewart's sale in 1748.

Italian books

There is a small but valuable collection of Italian books in the library. About 430 of these were printed before 1600. During this early period Latin was still the language of the church and it continued to be used by the Renaissance scholars, humanists, and the great Italian poets and writers. Although some of the best editions of the writings of the Italian poets were stolen from Marsh's during the eighteenth century, there are still happily books by such writers as Boccaccio, Dante, Petrarch and Tasso.

Fortunately too, many of the well-known elegant and sometimes professional writers such as Annibale Caro, Baldesar Castiglione, Gabriello

---

12 Ibid., p. 23.   **13** *Chambers's biographical dictionary*, ed. David Patrick & Francis Hindes Groome, London & Edinburgh, W. & R. Chambers, 1897 (Pierre Bayle).

Dult reste de ce que fol pense/
Car trop y trouuay de deffense. Nota:
Quant celle part mon bras tēdit
Dangier le pas me deffendit/
Le Bilain que mau loup lestrangle.
Al sestoit musse en Bng angle
Par derriere et nous agaitoit

22 From G. de Lorris and J. de Meung, *Le rommant de la rose*, printed in Paris in
    1526.

Chiabrera, Giambattista Marino, Giovanni Della Casa, and Jacopo Sannazaro can still be read. Lodovico Ariosto's *Orlando Furioso* is regarded as one of the greatest works of the Italian Renaissance, and it is not very surprising to find several editions of this work in the library. Dr Bouhéreau owned an edition which was printed by Paulo Zanfretti in Venice in 1582 and there is also a French translation; and Sir John Harington's English translation was recently presented to the library.

Similarly, *Il Pastor Fido* by Giovanni Battista Guarini became one of the best-known Italian poems and was translated into several languages. From an examination of the catalogue in Marsh's it also appears, unfortunately, to have been a great favourite with Dublin thieves. Our catalogue records four different editions printed before 1700, but sadly the two earliest editions entered in the catalogue are marked missing.

The wide and scholarly tastes of all four collectors are again illustrated by the inclusion of so many Italian writers on historical, political, and antiquarian subjects, and by the writings of such scholars and humanists as Marsilio Ficino, Giovanni Pico della Mirandola and the controversial Lorenzo Valla. The fanatical and powerful Dominican preacher Savonarola seems to have interested both Dr Bouhéreau and Bishop Stillingfleet, but not, for some reason, Archbishop Marsh. It seems clear, however, that all four collectors were interested in the Venetian historian and theologian Paolo Sarpi. There are five different editions of Sarpi's *Historia del concilio Tridentino* in the library, including the edition in Italian printed in London in 1619 (*STC* 21760). Paolo Sarpi acted as adviser to Venice in the bitter dispute with Pope Paul V on the question of clerical immunities.[14] Because of his opposition to the church, Sarpi was excommunicated by the pope. He retired from public life and wrote his masterpiece on the history of the council of Trent.

It is not very surprising to find editions of the writings of Machiavelli in the library (*Tutte le opere di Nicolo Machiavelli … s.l.,* 1550), but it is amusing to find a small volume of sixteenth-century licentious comedies in Dr Bouhéreau's collection. This volume includes plays by such writers as Bernardo Accolti, Pietro Aretino, Agnolo Firenzuola, as well as Machiavelli's satirical comedy, Mandragola. The renewed Italian interest in the early Greek and Latin writers, and in the remains of Roman antiquity, which

---

14 J.H. Whitfield, *A short history of Italian literature*, London, Penguin Books, 1969, pp 186–7.

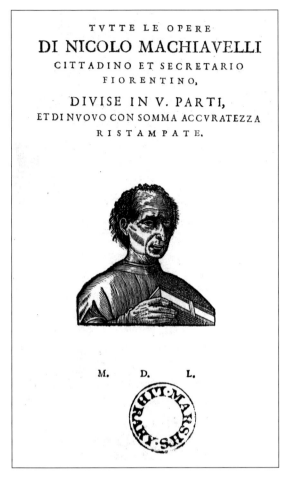

23 Title-page of Niccolo Machiavelli's *Tutte le opere* (s.l., 1550).

became such an important part of the new movement in scholarship, also spread into many other areas, one of the most notable being architecture.

Andrea Palladio was considered to be the founder of modern Italian architecture and his influence spread all over Europe.[15] Palladio's *I quattro libri dell' architettura*, which we have in the library, was printed in Venice in 1581 and it is a reprint of the first edition of 1570. It was donated to Marsh's by Archbishop Arthur Smyth. Smyth was an eighteenth-century archbishop of Dublin and his small but valuable donation consisted of some books of architectural interest, but he also bequeathed an edition of Albrecht Dürer's *Della simmetria dei corpi humani* (Venice, 1591).

15 Nikolaus Pevsner, *An outline of European architecture*, rev. and enlar. ed., London, Penguin Books, 1945,

Apart from the books which we have already mentioned there are also Italian books on law, science, medicine and travel in the collections. Cardinal Bembo's *Prose nellequali si ragiona della uolgar lingua* (Venice, 1525) is the most important Italian book in the Stillingfleet collection. Cardinal Bembo wrote books in both Italian and Latin and he became one of the most celebrated authors of the sixteenth century. Bembo in this book for the first time used the Tuscan language as the equal of Greek and Latin. J.H. Whitfield wrote of Cardinal Bembo's work as follows: 'Here with gravity and lucidity Italian is finally put forward as preferable to Latin, and the difficulty of dialects removed by pointing to Florentine as the norm.'[16]

Mathematical, scientific and astronomical books

Mathematics was one of the most popular studies in the seventeenth century. Scholars were absorbed in the various arguments on the different methods of squaring the circle, philosophers attempted to use mathematics as a method of reasoning, and geometry and algebra were used for scientific, astrological and experimental purposes.[17]

Archbishop Marsh as we have already mentioned was particularly interested in mathematics. He recorded in his diary the mathematical problems which he had solved, and some examples of these problems can be seen in the extensive annotations which he made in his mathematical and scientific books. Marsh's own book, *Institutiones logicae*, also shows some mathematical interest.

Bishop Stillingfleet collected similar types of mathematical and scientific books. Like all the other special subjects in the library the collections usually begin with the very earliest writers on the particular subject. The earliest mathematical, scientific and astronomical authors such as Hero of Alexandria, Claudius Ptolemy, Apollonius of Perga, Archimedes, and Aristarchus of Samos are all represented in the different collections.

A copy of Euclid's *Geometricorum elemētorum libri XV* (with commentaries by I. Campanus and others) is in Archbishop Marsh's collection. It was printed by Henri Stephanus in Paris in 1516 and it is in fact the very first printing of Euclid in France. It was edited by J. le Fèvre.

Archbishop Marsh must have been particularly pleased when he purchased the Stillingfleet library and discovered that there were so many mathematical

REGINA   VIRTVS

IL TERZO
LIBRO
DELL'ARCHITTETVRA
Di Andrea Palladio.

NEL QVALE SI TRATTA
delle Vie, de' Ponti, delle Piazze,
delle Basiliche, e de' Xisti .

IN VENETIA,
Appresso Bartolomeo
Carampello.
1581.

24   The title-page from the 1581 edition of the Italian architect Andrea Palladio's
influential book, *I quattro libri dell'architettura*, first published *c*.1570.

books in it. A fine example from this collection is Isaac Newton's *Philosophiae naturalis principia mathematica* (London, 1687). (There were two editions in 1687 and this edition bears the Smith imprint, *Wing* N 1049.) In 1952 A.N.L. Munby noted the existence in Marsh's Library of this Smith copy of the first edition. (He also said that the tool used on this binding did not conform with that on the group which Halley had bound up. Munby was referring to Newton's friend Edmund Halley who had originally published Newton's work.) William Gilbert's *De magnete* (London, 1600, *STC* 11883) was the first English scientific treatise to be printed and Gilbert is regarded as the founder of electrical science.[18] This work is also in the Stillingfleet collection.

Robert Recorde was the first writer in English on arithmetic, geometry and astronomy. Recorde also had the distinction of introducing algebra into England.[19] Recorde's *Arithmetick* was first printed in London in about 1646. The edition of Recorde's *Arithmetick* (London, 1662 *Wing* R 646) was augmented by John Dee and others. Dee became Queen Elizabeth's astrologer and spy, and he was also a very fine mathematician. An interesting scientific book entitled *Compilatio de astrorum scientia* (Venice, 1520) has another connection with Dee. It bears his signature on the title-page and the date '9 Feb. 1551'. It is interesting to note that John Dee was lecturing with great success on Euclid in Paris during the period 1550–1. Both these last mentioned books are in Marsh's collection.[20]

In the Stillingfleet collection is Thomas Salusbury's (or Salisbury's) *Mathematical collections and translations* (London, printed by William Leybourne for George Sawbridge, 1667, *Wing* S517A). A note in our catalogue made by a previous librarian says that part of the original edition of 1661 was destroyed in the Great Fire of London.

It seems inevitable that when mathematics and science became such popular subjects in the seventeenth century they would also attract pseudo-scientific quacks. Such a man was Richard Saunders. His book, *Physiognomie and chiromancie*, is a most extraordinary piece of work. Saunders gives fanciful interpretations for a great many things including moles on people's bodies, lines on faces and hands, and interpretations of dreams. It also contains some highly entertaining illustrations. This popular work was first printed in 1653.

Kline, *Mathematics in western culture*, London, Penguin Books, 1972.   **18** Eric Quayle, *The collector's book of books*, London, Studio Vista, November Books, 1971, p. 65.   **19** *DNB* (Robert Recorde).   **20** C.F. Smith, *John Dee 1527–1608*, London, Constable, 1909, pp 11–12.

F. Villamoena Fecat.

25 The portrait of Galileo from *Le operationi del compasso geometrico, e militare* (Bologna, 1656).

The edition in the library is the 'much enlarged' second edition of 1671 (*Wing* S 755) and it is, rather surprisingly, in Marsh's own collection.

New discoveries and developments in mathematics were of enormous importance to navigation. Probably one of the most important contributions in this area was made by Edmund Gunter.[21] Gunter's *Canon triangulorum, sive tabulæ sinuum et tangentium artificialium* published in 1620 was the first table of its kind. In these tables Gunter applied to navigation, and other branches of mathematics, his admirable rule 'the Gunter'. The second edition of this important work is in the Stillingfleet collection (London, 1623, *STC* 12517).

The collections also contain many of the writings of the great continental mathematicians and scientists. Many of these books are superbly illustrated with diagrams, plans, and remarkable title-pages. We also have works in the library by Tycho Brahe, Galileo Galilei, Johann Kepler, Marin Mersenne, Christopher Clavius, Petrus Ramus (Pierre de la Ramée), and Franciscus Vieta.

In Philip de La Hire's book *Sectiones conicae in novem libros distributae* (Paris, 1685), we recently discovered two sheets of mathematical calculations. These were made by Archbishop Marsh. It seems possible that Marsh may have been interrupted while he was working on these problems, and left them in this book where they have lain undisturbed for nearly three hundred years.

The Franciscan priest, Marin Mersenne, was deeply interested in philosophy and mathematics. Mersenne became a friend of Descartes and was a great admirer of Descartes' new ideas. Mersenne's *Quaestiones celeberrimae in Genesim* (Paris, 1623) was intended by Mersenne to interest mathematicians, philosophers and musicians. Although it has hardly anything of mathematical value, it does have one curious feature. Mersenne in this book attempted to show the number of atheists in Paris.[22] After his book was published, Mersenne regretted the information which he had given, and he tried to have the particular pages suppressed. He was only partly successful. One of the great delights of Marsh's Library is to find so many books which were at one time prohibited, suppressed, or ordered to be burnt, and Mersenne's book is no exception. The copy of Mersenne's book in the Stillingfleet collection contains the suppressed leaves intact.

In comparison to the very large number of English and continental writers on mathematics, science and astronomy in the library, there are

---

21 *DNB* (Edmund Gunter).   **22** Alexander Chalmers, *The general biographical dictionary* (Marin Mersenne).

unfortunately very few books of Irish interest going back to Marsh's time. There are plenty of later books of Irish interest. The lack of Irish material at this particular period was due to the almost complete absence of educational opportunities for the majority of the Irish people, and also due to the difficult religious and political situation. But there are some Irish writers who wrote on scientific and mathematical subjects. These writers, however, came almost entirely from the Protestant establishment and were members of the Dublin Philosophical Society.

Archbishop Marsh as we have already explained was one of the first members of the Dublin Philosophical Society founded by William Molyneux in 1683. The Dublin Philosophical Society was strongly influenced by the Royal Society in England, and many members of the Dublin Philosophical Society, including Marsh, had their papers published in the English Society's *Philosophical Transactions*.

William Molyneux became a friend of Archbishop Marsh and presented Marsh with a copy of his book *Dioptrica nova*. This was the first English book on optics when it was published in London in 1692 (*Wing* M 2405). Bishop Stearne also seems to have been interested in Molyneux's writings; a copy of *Sciothericum telescopicum* (Dublin 1686, *Wing* M 2406A, *Dix* p. 220) is bound up with thirteen similar pamphlets in his collection. (It is very difficult to say with complete certainty whether the Molyneux pamphlet definitely belonged to Bishop Stearne. Unbound pamphlets from the major collections in the library were often bound up together for convenience sake, and at least one of these pamphlets belonged to Marsh, and another pamphlet belonged to Bishop Stillingfleet's wife, Elizabeth.) William Molyneux seems to have been a very generous author. He also presented Dr Bouhéreau with a copy of his best-known book, *The case of Ireland's being bound by acts of parliament in England stated* (Dublin, 1698, *Wing* M 2402, *Dix* p. 298).

Bishop Edward Wetenhall was another member of the Dublin Philosophical Society who wrote on scientific as well as religious subjects. Wetenhall, like Marsh, was an Englishman, who had been sent to take an important position in Ireland. In 1672 he was made master of the Blue Coat School in Dublin, and some years later was appointed bishop of Kilmore and Ardagh. Wetenhall's book *A judgement of the comet ... 1680* (Dublin, 1682, *Wing* W 1503A, *Dix* p.195) is a discourse on the significance of the famous comet which appeared over Dublin in 1680 and which interested so many members of the Dublin Philosophical Society including Archbishop Marsh.[23] The book bears a charming dedication to the countess of Ardglass and Viscountess Blessington, and it is in Archbishop Marsh's collection.

Sir William Petty was made physician-general to the Cromwellian army in Ireland in 1652. Before he came to Ireland, Petty had been one of the group that later founded the Royal Society in England, and he contributed many scientific papers to that society. He afterwards joined the Dublin Philosophical Society, and was appointed its first president in 1684. In 1654 Petty was asked by the government to survey some of the forfeited lands in Ireland. He employed soldiers to carry out this survey, which became known as the 'Down Survey', because it was measured 'down' on maps. It was also a remarkable contribution to Irish cartography. Dr John Andrews commenting on Petty's maps said, 'By the standards of the time they were extraordinarily accurate'. He also said, 'It was the first direct survey of Ireland comprehensive enough to serve as the basis for a new small-scale map of the whole country.'[24] There are a large number of Petty's writings in the Stearne collection including maps based on the Down Survey and entitled *Hiberniae delineatio* ([London, 1685] *Wing* P 1928) and his *Observations upon the Dublin-bills of mortality, MDCLXXXI ...* (London, 1683, *Wing* P 1929). The copy of *Hiberniae delineatio*, is unfortunately imperfect; it lacks both the portrait and the title-page. Petty also wrote *A geographicall description of ... Ireland* ([London] published by Fra. Lamb, [1689] *Wing* P 1927), which was originally in the Stillingfleet collection. This present copy was purchased in 1925 to replace the copy missing from the original collection.

Another Irishman who contributed to astronomy and surveying was Henry Osborne. There is very little information on him but it is known that he lived at Dardistown, Co. Meath, and that he became friendly with the members of the Dublin Philosophical Society.[25] He wrote an important pamphlet on land surveying, *A more exact way to delineate the plot of any ... land* (Dublin, 1654, *Wing* o 524, *Dix* p. 95). Osborne's pamphlet is in the Stearne collection, and it is the only copy of this work in Ireland.

---

23 Archbishop Marsh's letter to Dr Smith dated April 9 1681. In Bodleian Library, MS Smith 45. Photostat in Marsh's Library.   **24** *Ireland in maps: an introduction* by John Andrews, Dublin, Dolmen Press, 1961, p. 10.   **25** K.T. Hoppen, *The common scientist in the seventeenth century*, London, pp 13, 113–14. See also *A list of such of the names of the nobility ... attainted of high treason*, London, 1690. *Wing* L 2409. On page 28 of this list the name John Osborne of Dardistown appears. Possibly Henry Osborne's father?

The most famous and best-known Irish scientist throughout this period was the Hon. Robert Boyle. Boyle, as we have already mentioned, was a friend of Archbishop Marsh, and he was also a leading member of the Royal Society in England. He is chiefly remembered for his discovery of a proportional relation between elasticity and pressure, known as 'Boyle's Law'. But Boyle was a prolific writer on scientific and also on theological subjects. Unfortunately his writings in Marsh's seem to have been particularly attractive to thieves. Two copies of his best-known work, *The sceptical chymist*, are missing, but we still have the first complete edition of his collected *Works*, with his correspondence and Life by Dr Birch, 5 vols (London, 1744).

The increase in the later part of the eighteenth century in the number of Irish writers on scientific and mathematical subjects in Ireland is in great contrast to the poverty of the earlier period. The Royal Irish Academy was incorporated in 1785 and the Dunsink and Armagh Observatories were founded between 1770 and 1790. Many of the professors in Trinity College were interested in scientific subjects, and they published their ideas and discoveries. There are books in the library by such well-known writers as Edward Beatty, Bishop Thomas Elrington, William Hales, Humphrey Lloyd, Andrew Reid and Robert Steell. Robert Steell's book, *A treatise of conic sections* (Dublin, 1723), was dedicated to the provost, fellows, and scholars of Trinity College.

One of the greatest Irish mathematicians at this period was Sir William Rowan Hamilton. Hamilton became president of the Royal Irish Academy and he published many of his writings in the Academy's *Proceedings*. These journals and similar type journals are available in the library.

In 1925 E.R. McClintock Dix presented to the library a copy of a very interesting continental mathematical work. This is entitled *The use of the bean table*, and it was based on Johann Heinrich Pestalozzi's principles. Pestalozzi was a famous Swiss educational theorist whose novel ideas aroused great controversy both on the Continent and also in educational circles in Ireland. This edition of Pestalozzi's book was printed in Ireland, and it has an imprint which reads 'Dublin, Sold by R.M. Tims, 1820. Bull, Printer; Roundwood, Wicklow'.

Medical books

One of the largest single collections in the library relating to a particular subject is the collection of medical books. This collection includes books on chemistry, surgery, anatomy, obstetrics and herbal remedies. The majority of the medical books belonged to Dr Bouhéreau and Bishop Stillingfleet, but Archbishop Marsh and Bishop Stearne were also interested in medical subjects, and they collected similar types of medical books.

The collectors began their collections with the earliest classical writers such as Hippocrates, Dioscorides Pedanius, Galen, and Aulus Cornelius Celsus. Many of these early medical writers also wrote philosophical discourses. Such writers include Averroes, Avicenna, and the Jewish rabbi, Moses ben Maimon (Maimonides).

Maimonides was born of Jewish parents in Spain in 1135. He studied Aristotelian philosophy and Greek medicine from Arab teachers. His book *Moreh nevukhim* (Guide for the perplexed) is regarded as his finest work, and it had an enormous influence on many European universities. The copy in the Stillingfleet collection is also interesting from the printing point of view.[26] It was printed in Sabionetta in Austrian Italy in 1553.

The English medical writers are also well represented in the collections. A man who considered himself an authority on many subjects including medicine was Sir Kenelm Digby. Digby's book *A late discourse made in a solemne assembly … touching the cure of wounds by the powder of sympathy* (London, 1658, *Wing* D 1436) was translated into French and German. Most of Digby's medical suggestions and ideas were quite useless, but he did discover the necessity of oxygen for the life of plants.[27]

The writings of the great William Harvey who discovered the circulation of the blood, and of Francis Glisson who became famous for his work on rickets are in the library. Glisson also wrote on another disease. In his book *Anatomia hepatis* (London, 1654, *Wing* G 853) Glisson gave such a comprehensive description of the liver that the sheath of the liver was afterwards known as 'Glisson's capsule'. Some further English writers include Richard Banister, who wrote on diseases of the eyes, and Philip Barrough (or Barrow) whom we have already mentioned.

There are also in the library the writings of such well-known English physicians as John Caius (the co-founder of Gonville and Caius College, Cambridge), Thomas Linacre, William Cole, and Thomas Sydenham.

---

26 Henry Cotton, *A typographical gazetteer*, quotes De Rossi who said that Sabionetta was famous for its Jewish printing chiefly carried on in the house of Tobias Foa. De Rossi also said that the press reached perfection in 1553 under the direction of a famous printer named Adel-kind, pp 246–7. **27** *DNB* (Sir Kenelm Digby).

26 The 'Plague doctor'. From Thomas Bartholin's *Historiarum anatomicarum &*
    medicarum (Copenhagen, 1661).

Some of the most important advances in medicine in the seventeenth century were made in the universities of Padua and Leiden. The development of medical knowledge, and new studies in anatomy, botany, and other branches of medicine attracted Irish and English students to these continental universities. The collectors in Marsh's appear to have been familiar with many of these continental writers and included their writings in their collections.

The Dutch doctor, Isbrandus de Diemerbroeck, wrote on the plague, measles and small pox. Nicholas Steno, the Danish expert on anatomy, also wrote on the nature of fossils and the earth's crust. The strange Swiss called Paracelsus, whose real name was Theophrastus Bombastus von Hohenheim, revolted against the accepted views of both Galen and Avicenna and introduced some new pharmaceutical methods including the use of 'tincture of opium'. Marie Fouquet wrote a charming book of medical prescriptions which contains remedies for almost every illness. Madame Fouquet suggested at least one excellent remedy for a complaint which she called 'Contre le miserere' (sic). Her book was printed in Dijon for sale in Paris in 1678. Our copy originally belonged to Dr Bouhéreau.

Bishop Stillingfleet seems to have been the only collector in the library who was interested in the Belgian chemist, Jean Baptiste van Helmont. Van Helmont studied gases and he invented the word 'gas'. But Archbishop Marsh, as well as Stillingfleet, was interested in the Dutch microscopist Anton van Leeuwenhoek. Van Leeuwenhoek ground his own lenses for his instruments;[28] he also contributed important papers to the *Philosophical Transactions* of the Royal Society in England.

Similarly Dr Bouhéreau collected many of these continental authors' writings, but he also collected specially for his own use medical books such as the chemistry books written by Nicasius Le Febvre and Nicolas Lemery. Indeed it is interesting to note the difference between the books collected by a practising doctor and the books purchased by scholarly collectors. In contrast to the other collectors Dr Bouhéreau annotated his medical books. Important authors' descriptions of various diseases are noted, the pharmaceutical books are particularly annotated, and in the case of many of his medical books Dr Bouhéreau carefully noted inside each cover the price which he had paid.

---

28 Eric Quayle, op. cit., p. 66. For information on the medical writers I have consulted, Arturo Castiglioni, *A history of medicine*, translated from the Italian and edited by E.B. Krumbhaar, 2nd ed., London, Routledge & Kegan Paul, 1947.

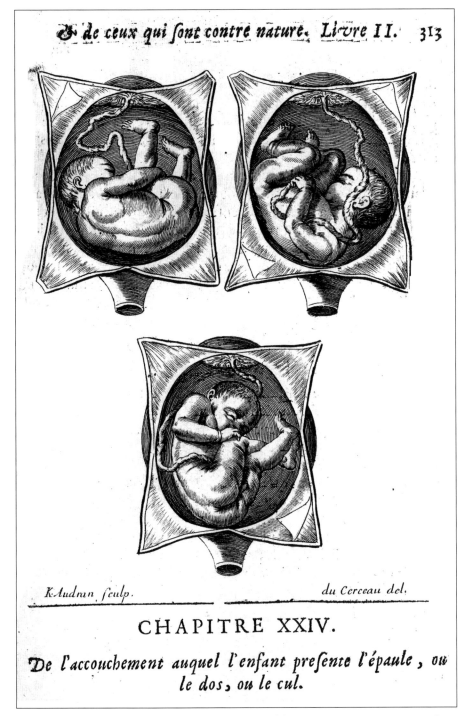

& de ceux qui sont contre nature. Livre II. 313

K. Audran *sculp.*   *du Cerceau del.*

CHAPITRE XXIV.

*De l'accouchement auquel l'enfant presente l'épaule, ou
le dos, ou le cul.*

27 Abnormal presentations of the foetus probably requiring a Caesarean section.
From François Mauriceau's *Traité des femmes grosses* (Paris, 1675).

Johann Rudolph Glauber was the German chemist who discovered hydrochloric acid and he also gave his name to the popular domestic remedy 'Glauber's Salt'. His book, *Furni novi philosophici, sive descriptio artis destillatoriae novae,* which was first printed in Amsterdam in 1651, contains many illustrations of distilling processes and our copy has been annotated by Dr Bouhéreau. Archbishop Marsh was also interested in Glauber's writings and owned a copy of *Pharmacopoea spagyrica* (Amsterdam, 1654).

Georgius Agricola's *De re metallica* was regarded as one of the most valuable contributions to practical chemistry when it was first published in 1556.[29] The edition in the Stillingfleet collection was printed over one hundred years after the first edition; it contains nearly 300 woodcut illustrations of chemical processes, mechanical devices, and valuable advice on geology and chemistry.

There are some medical books of Irish interest in the collections and probably the best known is a remarkable work on anatomy. This was written by Allen Mullen (or Molines). Mullen's pamphlet entitled *An anatomical account of the elephant accidentally burnt in Dublin, on Fryday, June 17 in the year 1681* (London, 1682, *Wing* M 3057) gives a vivid and detailed description of the remains of the elephant. In the second part of this work Mullen gives an account of his discovery of the vascularity of the lens of the eye. According to K. T. Hoppen, Mullen's publication on the elephant was 'to remain the standard work in English on its subject for many years'.[30] Mullen was a very active member of the Dublin Philosophical Society and became acquainted with Archbishop Marsh. (Mullen's pamphlet is in Marsh's collection.) When Mullen visited London in 1682 Marsh gave him an impressive letter of introduction to the Hon. Robert Boyle.[31] Boyle was responsible for having Mullen admitted to the Royal Society and he (Boyle) cooperated in many joint scientific experiments with Mullen. Later Mullen went on a fortune-hunting expedition to the West Indies but unfortunately died from the effects of intoxication.

Charles Allen's *Curious observations in that difficult part of chirurgery, relating to the teeth* (Dublyn, 1687, *Wing A 1019, Dix* p. 224) is a very early work on the subject of dentistry.[32] Allen's book which is in the Stearne collection

---

29 Eric Quayle, op. cit., p. 65.   30 K.T. Hoppen, op. cit., p. 20.   31 Ibid., pp 37–8.   32 M. Pollard, formerly of Trinity College Library (Older Printed Books and Special Collections Dept.), says that this edition is a reissue of *The operator for the teeth*, Dublin, A. Crook & S. Helsham, 1686, with cancellan title fold.

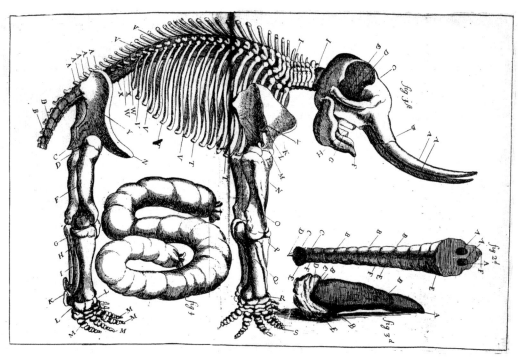

28   From Allen Mullen's *An anatomical account of the elephant accidentally burnt in Dublin, on Fryday, June 17 in the year 1681* (London, 1682).

gives detailed accounts of tooth decay, and Allen also put forward suggestions for transplanting animal teeth to humans. But he was very careful about this suggestion and cautiously added the warning 'that the thing be undertaken and carried on by one that at least knows something of Anatomy'.

Two further books of Irish medical interest are Edmund Meara's *Examen diatribæ Thomæ Willisii … de febribus* (London, 1665, *Wing* M 1577) in the Stillingfleet collection and Bernard Connor's *Evangelium medici* (London, 1697, *Wing* C 5886) in Marsh's collection. Edmund Meara was born in Co. Tipperary, the son of a doctor. He engaged in a controversy on the neurological theories of Thomas Willis and published this book on the controversy. (This edition also includes a treatise written by his father, Dermod Meara.) Bernard Connor was born in Co. Kerry and studied medicine on the Continent. He was appointed physician to the court of King John Sobieski and wrote a history of Poland. Connor's *Evangelium medici* was an extraordinary book. In this work he put forward the theory that the miracles performed by Our Lord and his Apostles could be explained by natural means. His book caused a sensation. While we are certain that Archbishop Marsh would have strongly disapproved of Connor's ideas, he must have been sufficiently interested to have acquired a copy for his collection.

Botanical and Natural History books

There are books on botany and natural history in all the collections in the library. The collection is a small but valuable one and was primarily intended for specialists and scholars. Many of these books are particularly well illustrated and for this reason are probably visually the most exciting books in the library. The oldest botanical work in the collection is *Libri de re rustica, M. Catonis lib. I. M. Terentii Varronis libri III*. This edition was printed by Aldus and his father-in-law in Venice in 1514 and is in the Stillingfleet collection.

Pliny's *Historiarum naturae libri xxxvii* (Paris, 1532) belonged to Dr Bouhéreau, who seems to have been particularly interested in scholarly botanical works. A good example of the type of scholarly works collected by Dr Bouhéreau can be seen in the books written by the French scholars, Jacques Dalechamp and Jean Des Moulins.

The English and continental sixteenth-century writers on botany seem to have been particularly popular with the collectors in Marsh's. Probably one of the best-known writers was Leonhard Fuchs. Fuchs who is regarded as the founder of German botany has another unique distinction. The celebrated French botanist, Fr Plumier, paid Fuchs the compliment of naming the fuchsia after him. A copy of Fuchs' superb book, *De historia stirpium commentarii* (Paris, 1543), is in Archbishop Marsh's collection and his *Herbarum ac stirpium historia* (Paris, 1549) is in Bishop Stearne's collection. The latter work contains the names of the plants in Greek, Latin, and French. Two previous owners or readers have made copious annotations in this book. The majority of these annotations are in Latin, but the English names of the plants have also been added in some instances.

The Swiss doctor, Caspar Bauhinus, made some of the most important advances in the general system of classification. In his *Pinax theatri botanici* (Basle, 1623) Bauhinus gave descriptions of 6000 different species of plants,[33] many of which had been incorrectly named in earlier botanical books. It originally belonged to Archbishop Marsh and bears his motto on the title-page.

33 Eric Quayle, op. cit., p. 81.

The French botanist and traveller, Joseph Pitton de Tournefort, studied medicine and anatomy at the famous university of Montpellier. But Tournefort also developed a passion for collecting plants, and he travelled throughout Greece and Asia collecting an enormous number of specimens which he brought back to France.[34] Tournefort's *Institutiones rei herbariae*, 3 vols (Paris, 1719) is in the Stearne collection. Tournefort also contributed to Pierre Pomet's book, *A complete history of druggs* (London, 1725). This work is lavishly illustrated with over 400 'copper cutts' of seeds, flowers, fruits, animals, metals, and minerals. It originally belonged to Bishop Stearne.

Marcello Malpighi, the renowned Italian anatomist, was a pioneer in the development of microscopic anatomy, animal and vegetable. His books, which are lavishly decorated with superb illustrations, can be seen in the Stearne and Stillingfleet collections.

The Swedish botanist, Carl Linnaeus, is regarded as the founder of modern botany because of his further development of the classification system. Dr Robert Travers donated copies of two of Linnaeus' most important books to the library. They are *Species plantarum*, 2 vols (Stockholm, 1762) and *Systema plantarum*, 4 vols (Frankfurt, 1779–80). Dr Travers, whom we have already mentioned, was assistant librarian of Marsh's Library (1841–88) and donated some books to the library. These donations by Travers are an indication of his attempts to extend the scope of Marsh's by including books which incorporated new ideas and discoveries.

Many of the finest English writers on botany and natural history are included in the collections. There are such writers as John Ray (who is regarded as the 'father' of natural history in England), John Evelyn, Nehemiah Grew, Edward Topsell, Francis Willughby and Leonard Plukenet. Plukenet's books which were printed at his own expense included descriptions of exotic and rare plants and the contents of his own herbarium.

Two of the best-known works of Irish interest in the library relating to botany are John K'Eogh's *Botanalogia universalis Hiberniae* (Corke, 1735), and Walter Wade's *Catalogus systematicus plantarum indigenarum in comitatu Dublinensi .... pars prima* (Dublin, 1794). Wade was a lecturer on botany and made extensive botanical tours in Ireland. He was the first person to find the pipe-wort (*Eriocaulon*), and he played a very important part in the development of the Botanic Gardens in Glasnevin.[35] Wade donated his book to Marsh's in 1795.

34 Alexander Chalmers, op. cit. (J.P. de Tournefort).   **35** *DNB* (Walter Wade).

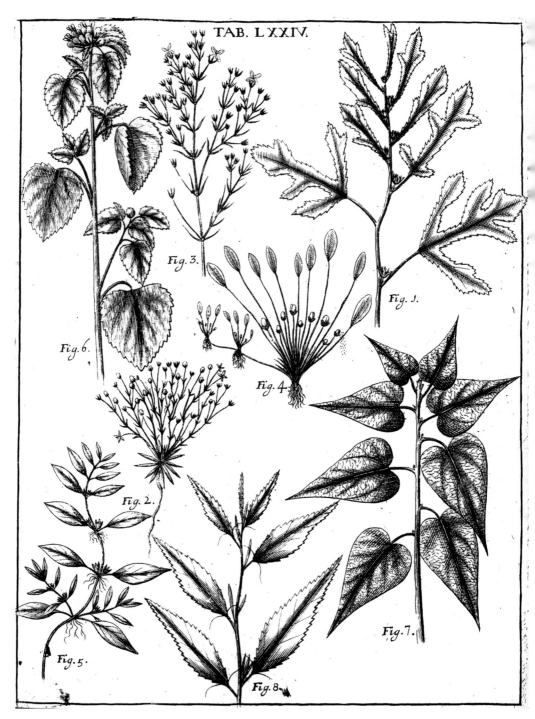

29 One of the fine engravings from Leonard Plukenet's *Phytographia, pars prior*
    (London, 1691).

A very different type of book connected with both medicine and botany is the herbal. Such books were enormously popular in the seventeenth century and they provided remedies for almost every disease. One of the best-known and most popular was written by John Gerard. Gerard's extraordinary book contains illustrations of plants and herbs, and it also provides remedies for thousands of ailments from freckles to the plague. Gerard gives prescriptions 'to procure or stir up bodily lust', and then provides a remedy 'to restraine bodily lust'. His book, *The herball*, was first published in 1597, but the edition in Marsh's collection is the 'very much enlarged' edition by T. Johnson (London, 1633, *STC* 11751).

It was inevitable that the popular success of the herbals would attract unscrupulous quacks. A man who fits into this category is William Salmon who, although he practised as a doctor, and considered himself an authority on every known disease, was really only a quack. He cast horoscopes and practised alchemy; he wrote medical books, religious discourses, a prophetic almanac, and eventually a herbal. Salmon's *Botanologia, The English herbal* (London, 1710), was produced in two volumes, but only the first volume is in Bishop Stearne's collection. It is however a little unusual since it does not have the bishop's bookplate inside the cover, but instead bears his signature on the title-page.

Many of the finest continental writers on natural history such as Ulisse Aldrovandi, Conrad Gesner and René Antoine Ferchault de Réamur are also in the library. Guillaume Rondelet's *Libri de piscibus marinis* (Lyon, 1554) contains the most delightful illustrations on natural history. Rondelet's illustrations for the 'Monkfish' and the 'Bishopfish' are both clothed in their full religious attire. Whatever about the monkfish, the bishopfish is unfortunately entirely fictitious. Rondelet was a French doctor and was regarded as eccentric. He became obsessed with the study of anatomy and on the death of one of his children his friends were scandalised to discover that he had dissected the body of his own child.[36]

As we have already said, these early books on natural history and botany were intended for scholars and specialists. It was not until the middle of the eighteenth century that the first popular books on this subject appeared.[37] *Histoire naturelle* by George Louis Leclerc, Comte de Buffon, appeared in 44 volumes between 1749 and 1804 and was a great success. There is an English

[36] Alexander Chalmers, op. cit. (Guillaume Rondelet).   [37] Eric Quayle, op. cit., p. 81.

De Pifce monachi habitu.

30 The 'Monkfish' from
Guillaume Rondelet's
Libri de piscibus marinis
(Lyon, 1554).

translation of this work by W. Smellie, edited by W. Wood in the Everth collection. It was printed in London in 1812 and published in 20 volumes.

Thomas Bewick was an Englishman who contributed to books on natural history but he also magnificently revived the old art of wood engraving.[38] Bewick's *A history of British birds*, which first appeared between 1797 and 1804 in two volumes, was instantly recognised for its superb quality. In fact it has never really been surpassed. The edition of Bewick's *A history of British birds*, 2 vols, in the Everth collection is the later edition printed in Newcastle by E. Walker in 1821.

---

38 D.B. Updike, *Printing types*, Cambridge, Mass. The Belknap Press of Harvard University Press, 1966, ii, pp 146–7. See also Colin Clair, *A history of printing in Britain*, London, Cassell, 1965, p. 186.

De Pifce Epifcopi habitu.

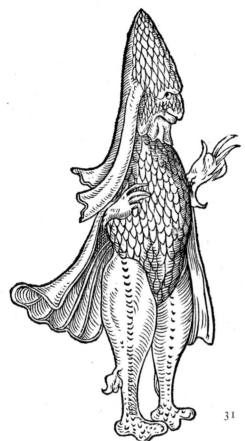

31   The 'Bishopfish' from Guillaume
Rondelet's *Libri de piscibus marinis*
(Lyon, 1554).

While it is pleasant to have such books on natural history in the library, we think pride of place in this collection must go to two volumes which were presented to Marsh's in 1803. These volumes consist of exquisite water colour paintings on vellum which were used to illustrate Eleazar Albin's *Natural history of birds*. They originally belonged to Lady Margaret Cavendish Harley who married William Bentinck, the second duke of Portland. Margaret Cavendish Harley was celebrated as a child when Matthew Prior, the English poet, referred to her as 'My noble, lovely little Peggy'.[39]

39 *DNB* (Matthew Prior). See also Muriel McCarthy, 'Eleazar Albin's watercolours of birds' in *Irish Arts Review Yearbook*, ii, 1995, pp 88–95.

TAB.XXIV

Merula aquatica
The Water Ouzell.

Upupa
The Hoopoe.

Ispida.
The Kingfisher.

Merops.
The Beeeater.

Guira guainumbi.

Jaguacati guacu.

32   Illustration from Francis Willughby's *Ornithologiae libri tres* (London, 1676).

Books on travel

There are about three hundred books on travel in the library. Like the books on natural history, these travel books are among the most entertaining and best illustrated that we have in the library. They give accounts of voyages and explorations to such places as Africa, China, India, the Far East and the New World. They often include descriptions of the inhabitants of these countries together with accounts of their religions and customs. But sometimes, too, these early travel books give accounts of the hostile way in which visitors were treated. Many were captured and imprisoned, and some were tortured, or sold into slavery. Occasionally a few lucky prisoners managed to escape or were ransomed and allowed to return home, some to write of their experiences.

While initially most of these journeys were undertaken to discover new lands for trading purposes, it was not long before the great missionary orders became interested in converting the inhabitants to Christianity. The French Jesuits and the Capuchins were particularly interested in China and the Far East. Priests such as Fr Philip Avril, Fr Guy Tachard and Fr Ferdinand Verbiest wrote accounts of their travels, and many of these authors' writings are included in the collections in the library.

Other famous French travellers include Francois Bernier, Jean de Thévenot, Melchisedec Thévenot, Jean Baptiste Tavernier, Le Chevalier de Chaumont, Simon de La Loubére, and the French botanist whom we have already mentioned, Joseph Pitton de Tournefort. There is also the French army engineer Amédé François Frézier who was sent by the French court to examine the colonies in Peru and Chile. His book, *Relation du voyage de la mer du Sud* (Paris, 1716), gives fine descriptions of the inhabitants of these countries, and Frézier also gives an account of the Jesuits in Paraguay. The book contains 37 engraved plates which include plans and views of Conception, Santiago, Lima, San Salvador and Valparaiso. It was donated to Marsh's by Archbishop Richard Whately in 1846 and it bears the bookplate of the Calwich Library.

Some of the earliest English sailors and buccaneers wrote accounts of their travels and expeditions. The writings of the Elizabethan adventurers, Sir Humphrey Gilbert and Martin Frobisher, are in the library. Humphrey Gilbert's tract, *A discourse of a discouerie for a new passage to Cataia* [ed. G. Gascoigne], (London, 1576, *STC* 11881), has been described as 'amongst the

33 'A very active game call'd *La Chueca*, wherein the men show their greatest
    Agility and Nimbleness ...' Illustration from Alonso d'Ovalle's *Historia relatione
    del regno di Cile* (Rome, 1646).

most notable literary contributions to the subject of exploration'.[40] There
are accounts of the later voyages of exploration which were made by Sir
John Narborough, Lord George Anson and Captain James Cook.

Captain James Cook is still regarded as one of England's greatest sailors.[41]
His historic voyages were responsible for the development of navigational
aids, and his humanitarian approach to his sailors led to new improvements
in their living and working conditions while at sea.

Peter Martyr of Anghiera's book, *De orbe novo*, gave the first account of
the discovery of America. The first *Decade* of *De orbe novo* was published at

40 C.N. Robinson and John Leyland, 'The literature of the sea. From the origins to Hakluyt' in *CHEL*,
iv, p. 74.   41 Sir Maurice Holmes, 'Captain James Cook, R.N., F.R.S.' in *Endeavour*, viii, no. 29, January
1949, pp 11–17.

Seville in 1511. (A secret version first appeared at Venice in 1504.) Three of the *Decades* were published at Alcalá in 1516. Peter Martyr of Anghiera was born in Italy but went to Spain in 1487. He was appointed to an important position in the council of the Indies in the government of the Spanish colonies. Peter Martyr compiled an account of the discovery of America from the reports which Columbus sent back to the council in Spain. There is an edition of *De orbe novo* (Paris, 1587) in the Stillingfleet collection which was edited by the English travel writer, Richard Hakluyt.

John Smith was one of the best-known and one of the most colourful of the early settlers in America. He was an English soldier who went to Virginia in 1606 and after two years was appointed head of the English colony. The most romantic and exciting of adventures are associated with Smith's life, including the story of his capture by the Indian king, Powhatan. He was rescued through the intervention of King Powhatan's daughter, Princess Pocahontas. Smith's book, *The generall historie of Virginia* (London, 1632, *STC* 22790d), was a great success when it was first published in 1623. This late edition in the Stillingfleet collection contains illustrations of Smith's heroic adventures among the Indians in America, and it also includes an illustration of King Powhatan ordering Smith to be flayed alive, while his daughter Princess Pocahontas pleads for Smith's life.

Daniel Denton's *A brief description of New-York* (London, 1670, *Wing* D 1062) was written specifically to encourage English people to settle in America. Denton gave lyrical descriptions of New York in 1670 and wrote: 'Where besides the sweetness of the Air, the Countrey itself sends forth such a fragrant smell, that it may be perceived at Sea before they can make the Land.' He also said, 'the Land floweth with milk and honey'. Denton gave vivid and sometimes sad descriptions of the Indians in America. He noticed how few Indians there were at this time and he said they were being wiped out by wars and disease. Denton also remarked that the Indians left were 'no ways hurtful but rather serviceable to the *English*'.

Edward Heawood in his book *A history of geographical discovery in the 17th and 18th centuries* said that the brilliant geographical achievements in North America were all the work of Frenchmen.[42] Heawood particularly mentioned two outstanding French explorers, René Robert Cavelier Sieur de La Salle and Fr Louis Hennepin.

---

42 Edward Heawood, *A history of geographical discovery in the seventeenth and eighteenth centuries*, Cambridge, At the University Press, 1912, p. 117.

An account of Monsieur de la Salle's last expedition (London, 1698, *Wing* A
210A) in the Stillingfleet collection gave descriptions of La Salle's remarkable
adventures and discoveries in North America. There are also accounts of
several Indian tribes and their customs, and a description of La Salle's
murder on an expedition overland to the Mississippi while he was trying to
bring back relief from Canada. (This work was originally under Henri de
Tonti in the *Wing* catalogue, T 1890.)

Fr Louis Hennepin's book, *A new discovery of a vast country in America*
(London, 1698, *Wing* H 1450), also in the Stillingfleet collection, gave details
of the customs, ceremonies, habits, and religion of the Iroquois Indians. It
also contains illustrations of La Salle's murder, 'unheard of crueltys of the
Iroquois' and a fine illustration of a magnificent buffalo.

Theodore de Bry was an eminent Belgian engraver who worked in
Germany. He and his family were particularly noted for the fine illustrations
which they provided for books on travel. De Bry's *Historiae Americae*, 2 vols
(Frankfurt, 1590–1602), contains superb illustrations of the Spanish explorations
in South America. Many of these illustrations show the horrifying and
barbarous cruelties carried out by the Spanish conquerors. Other writers on
North and South America represented in the library include J. Esquemeling,
Thomas Gage, Marc Lescarbot and Gabriel Thomas.

Jean Leon's *Historiale description de l'Afrique*, 2 vols (Lyon, 1556), in Dr
Bouhéreau's collection, is a particularly fascinating travel book. Leon was a
Cordovan Moor who had travelled in Africa and Asia Minor and was
afterwards captured by Venetian corsairs. He was taken to Rome where he
lived for twenty years. Eventually he managed to escape to Africa and died
in Tunis in 1552. He was also known under a completely different name,
that of Hasan Ibn Muhammad. Leon's book was for a long time the chief
source of information on the geography of Africa.[43]

The edition of *Nouus orbis regionum ac insularum veteribus incognitarum*
(Paris, 1532), in the Bouhéreau collection, is regarded as the first general
history of travels. It includes descriptions of the voyages of Columbus, Vespucci
and Marco Polo and it also contains a map by the French mathematician
Oronce Finé. Although this book is catalogued under Grynaeus, it was in fact
compiled by John Huttich; Grynaeus wrote only the preface.

---

43 Alexander Chalmers, op. cit. (Jean Lyon). See also M. Pollard's notes for An exhibition: French
renaissance books, held in Marsh's Library in June 1959 (unpublished).

34 'An Eastern Sheep drawing his fatt Tayle in a cart weighing 40 pound weight
or More.' From Hiob Ludolf's *A new history of Ethiopia* (London, 1682).

Giovanni Battista Ramusio's *Primo (-terzo) volume delle nauigationi et viaggi*
(Venice, 3 vols in 2, 1563, 1559, 1565) is regarded as the first great systematic
collection of voyages. Ramusio's book, which is in the Stillingfleet collection,
became the model for many later collections of books on travel. These volumes
contain maps, and illustrations of cities, animals, islands, and ships at sea
surrounded by ferocious sea monsters about to devour everything in sight.

Richard Hakluyt was one of the best-known English compilers of travel
stories. Hakluyt when he was chaplain to the English ambassador at the French
court was distressed by an insulting reference to the lack of adventure shown by
English sailors.[44] He was determined to write and publish accounts of English
explorations. Hakluyt's *The principal navigations, voiages … and discoueries of the
English nation*, 3 vols (London, 1598–1600, *STC* 12626), is in the Stillingfleet
collection. The first volume contains the following words on the title-page:
'… and the famous victorie atchieued at the citie of Cadiz 1596 are described'.
The account of this voyage was ordered to be suppressed by Queen Elizabeth
after the disgrace of the earl of Essex in 1599. Hakluyt's collection was an
enormous success. George Sampson said that 'Hakluyt's great compilation
preserves for us a noble and valiant body of narrative literature of the highest
worth, both for its own sake and for its interpretation of the Elizabethan age.'[45]

44 George Sampson, op. cit., p. 184.   45 Ibid., p. 185. See also *CHEL*, iv, pp 66–85. And further
information in, Foster Watson, *Richard Hakluyt*, London, Sheldon Press, 1924.

35 'The wilde man at the
court of Prester John.'
From Edward Webbe's
*The rare and most
wonderfull things which
E. Webbe hath seene …*
(London, 1590).

Most of the books which we have already mentioned are by well-known travel writers, but there are also in the library smaller and even more fascinating individual accounts of travels and adventures. A book which contains twelve pamphlets mainly relating to travel includes the courageous adventures of two Englishmen, Edward Webbe and Richard Hasleton.

Edward Webbe's pamphlet *The rare and most wonderfull things which E. Webbe hath seene …* (London, 1590, STC 25152) gives an exciting account of Webbe's extraordinary adventures in Jerusalem, Egypt and Russia.[46] Webbe was a master gunner on an English ship which was captured by the Turks, and consequently was forced to become a galley slave. When Webbe's skill as a gunner was discovered, he was compelled to fight with the Turks against the Persians. Webbe described his imprisonment and slavery and some of the terrible sufferings and tortures which he saw. His pamphlet

---

46 For a modern edition see *Edward Webbe, chief master gunner, his trauailes, 1590,* carefully edited by Edward Arber, London, Alex. Murray, 1868.

contains an illustration of a 'wilde man' which Webbe apparently saw at the court of Prester John, and there are also two charming woodcuts of a 'unicorn' and an elephant.

Richard Hasleton's *A discourse of the miserable captiuitie of an Englishman* (London, Abel Jeffes, 1595, *STC* 12924.5) is a very similar adventure to the one mentioned above. Hasleton was another sailor who was captured and sold into slavery to the Turks. He managed to escape but was again recaptured by the Spanish, who discovered he was a Protestant. Hasleton was forced to appear before the officers of the Inquisition. He gave a fascinating account of his interrogation before the Inquisition and his firm refusal to conform to the Catholic Church in return for his freedom. Hasleton managed to escape and after many more adventures he eventually returned safely to England. This pamphlet is also illustrated, and Lowndes in his *Bibliographer's manual* says the woodcuts in this book were copied from the Poliphilo.[47] Both of these pamphlets bear the signature of the English book-collector, Humphrey Dyson. They may possibly have originally been in the Stillingfleet collection but they are now kept in the 'cages' in the second gallery.

Cornelius Geraldson's *An addition to the sea journal of the Hollanders vnto Jaua* (London, 1598, *STC* 11747) is also part of this group of pamphlets on travel and it is a very rare work. It deals with the first Dutch expedition to the East Indies and includes a description of the Island of Bali together with a dictionary of the languages of Malacca and Madagascar. It also contains a fine woodcut of the Emu bird and eight full-page illustrations of the inhabitants of Bali.

Books on navigation

None of these voyages or explorations would have been possible without the help of navigational aids. In the sixteenth and seventeenth centuries primitive and elementary instruments were still being used by sailors and navigators. The Portuguese were the first to make use of the astrolabe and invented a quadrant fitted with sights, but developments were very gradual and speed was estimated by throwing a knotted rope overboard and observing how fast it ran out to the rear. It was not until the eighteenth century that the method of calculating longitude was discovered.

---

47 W.T. Lowndes, *The bibliographer's manual of English literature* (new ed.), London, H.G. Bohn, [1864], ii, G–N, pp 1009–10.

Elephant avec sa Chaise pour la Princesse Reyne.

Elephant avec sa Chaise pour les Étrangers.

36 Elephants with chairs for carrying royalty and foreigners. Illustration from
Voyage de Siam, des pères Jésuites [By Guy Tachard] (Paris, 1686).

Guillaume de Nautonier's *Mécométrie de l'eymant* (Venes, 1603), in Dr
Bouhéreau's collection, has been described by Dr J. de Courcy Ireland as 'an
interesting curiosity in the history of the art of navigation'. Dr de Courcy
Ireland also said that

> Guillaume de Nautonier thought that longitude could be deter-
> mined by compass variation … he worked out tables giving the
> calculated variation at every degree of latitude and longitude, on the
> old assumption that a complete and symmetrical network of
> magnetic meridians and parallels, to which the compass needle
> conformed, could be identified on the globe.[48]

Nautonier's views were devastatingly refuted by Dounod of Bar-le-Duc in
France and by Wright in England. In spite of its incorrect assumptions
Nautonier's work did stimulate fruitful research.

Pedro de Medina's *L'art de nauiguer* (Lyon, 1569) was regarded as the first
book dealing specifically with navigation when it was published in Valladolid
in 1545. The copy in Dr Bouhéreau's collection was translated into French
by Nicolas de Nicolai and he was also the illustrator and cartographer.

William Bourne's *A mate for mariners* (London, 1641, not in *Wing*) was a
very good practical handbook. Bourne had been a ship's carpenter and
gunner and had a sound knowledge of seamanship. E.G.R. Taylor in her
book on William Bourne's writings said that Bourne was 'the successful
writer of a new type of text-book, one intended for a new type of reader.
Neither a scholar nor of gentle birth, he intruded into the field of authorship which was still generally regarded as the preserve of the scholar and the
gentleman.'[49] Bourne was severely criticised for daring to enter the preserve
of scholars and gentlemen, but his books were a great success and were
'simply written, knowledgable, and above all practical'.

William Bourne's work is in Bishop Stearne's collection and it is bound
together with two important pieces relating to navigation, Martin Cortes,
The arte of nauigation (London, 1572, *STC* 5799), and Thomas Addison's
Arithmeticall navigation (Radcliffe, 1625, *STC* 150). Thomas Addison's work
contributed to the application of logarithms as an aid to navigation.

---

48 Note in Marsh's Library written by Dr J. de Courcy Ireland on this work.   **49** William Bourne,
A regiment for the sea, ed. E.G.R. Taylor, Cambridge University Press, published for the Hakluyt Society,
1963. Second series, no. CXXI, issued for 1961, pp xiii, xiv, General Introduction. See also pp 456–7 for
bibliographical description of copy in Marsh's Library.

37   The construction and use of old northern warships. From Olaus Magnus,
     Historia de gentibus septentrionalibus (Rome, 1555).

Books on clocks

The development of watches and similar instruments was another important
aid to navigation in the seventeenth century. Christiaan Huygens in his
Horologium oscillatorium (Paris, 1673) gave a complete description of his new
invention, the pendulum clock. William Derham's *The artificial clock-maker*
(London, 1696, *Wing* D 1099), seems particularly to have interested Archbishop
Marsh. Marsh made some interesting additional calculations and corrections
in the margins of this book. Derham in the preface to his book said he
wrote it 'only to please myself, and divert the vacant hours of a Solitary
Country Life', and he also intended it for the coarser sort of persons of
quality, who had too much time on their hands, and it might 'hinder their
commission of many sins, which are the effects of idleness'.

Maps and atlases

While these new developments and discoveries helped to make seafaring and travel much safer, another great improvement was in the art of mapmaking.

R.A. Skelton commenting on the development of maps said:

> New map projections were devised, mainly to give a more faithful representation of high latitudes. The extent and relationship of the continents and the possible existence of navigable passages through or around them were anxiously studied and conjecturally laid down on the maps ... The gradual accretion of new maps to augment the twenty-seven Ptolemaic maps anticipated the appearance of the atlas, the typical product of synoptic cartography, as an index to contemporary knowledge of the world.[50]

The first volume of uniform-sized maps, planned to provide the most up-to-date information, was made by Abraham Ortelius in Antwerp in 1570. They were a superb achievement. The edition of these maps, *Theatrum orbis terrarum*, in Dr Bouhéreau's collection is unfortunately lacking the title-page. It appears to be the much later edition of 1590 or 1598, and it includes the historical atlas which was not added to the *Theatrum* until 1579. There are also maps in the library by Judocus Hondius, Herman Moll, Gerard Mercator, John Speed and the Ordnance Survey maps of Ireland dated 1839–46.

Sebastian Münster's *Cosmographiae uniuersalis* was first published in Basle in about 1544. Although the edition of this work in the Stillingfleet collection is the much later edition printed in Basle in 1634, it still contains the delightful illustration of 'ducks in trees': Münster said ducks were born and lived in trees. An edition of Ptolemy's maps (Basle, 1552) in Dr Bouhéreau's collection also includes maps made by Sebastian Münster. Münster's map of the 'New World' shows parts of South America inhabited by cannibals.

The finest collection of maps in Marsh's is the eleven folio volumes of Joan Blaeu's *Grand Atlas* (Amsterdam, 1662). Professor C. Koeman said that these sumptuous volumes were designed in the golden age of the young Republic of the United Netherlands. Blaeu's maps were designed on such

---

50 R.A. Skelton, *Maps: a historical survey of their study and collecting*, 2nd impression, Chicago & London, University of Chicago Press, 1975, p. 14.

high standards of scholarship and such superb typography that they were 'a traditional gift presented on behalf of the United Republic to royal and other personages'.[51] They were 'the most expensive printed book that money could buy in the latter half of the 17th century'.[52] Many of the maps are beautifully coloured and they were described by S.H. Steinberg as 'master-pieces alike of geographical science, typographical skill and the engravers art'.[53] The Blaeu maps are part of the Stillingfleet collection and they are all bound in yellow vellum with simple gold tooling. They were rebacked with calf leather, possibly in the latter half of the eighteenth century.

Books on witchcraft

One of the most curious and bizarre collections of books in Marsh's is the small collection which deals with the subject of witchcraft. The majority of these are in the Stillingfleet collection and they include some of the best-known continental and English writers on this subject.

Although the witchcraft movement had begun some years earlier, it was not until December 1484, when Pope Innocent VIII issued the papal bull *Summis desiderantes affectibus*, that the real persecution began. This papal bull authorised the two Dominican inquisitors, Heinrich Institor (Krämer) and Jakob Sprenger, to begin the campaign against witchcraft.

The witchcraft craze of the sixteenth and seventeenth centuries was an extraordinary occurrence. It was a vicious, hysterical movement which swept over Europe and the unfortunate people who were accused of witchcraft had to endure tortures of the most revolting kind. The majority of the cases occurred in Germany, where the rack, the whip, the thumb-screw, and even more refined instruments of torture were freely used to extract confessions.[54] These tortures were justified on the grounds that the devil protected witches. During the period of the witchcraft movement over one hundred thousand people were burnt or hanged in Europe.

H.R. Trevor-Roper (later Lord Dacre) in his book *The European witch-craze of the 16th and 17th centuries* commented on this extraordinary move-ment and said, '[It] is a perplexing phenomenon: a standing warning to

---

51 Ir. C. Koeman, *Joan Blaeu and his Grand Atlas*, London, George Philip & Son, 1970, pp 41–2. **52** Ibid., p. 46.   **53** S.H. Steinberg, *Five hundred years of printing*, 3rd ed., London, Penguin Books, 1974, p. 185.   **54** Bertrand Russell, *History of western philosophy*, p. 489. And Ronald Seth, *In the name of the devil: great witchcraft cases*, Arrow Books, 1970, pp 10, 14–15 in the introduction.

those who would simplify the stages of human progress'. Trevor-Roper suggested that the craze was not separable from the intellectual and spiritual life of those years. It was helped by the popes of the Renaissance, by the Protestant reformers and by the saints of the Counter-Reformation.[55] He also suggested that its origins came from social pressures, and the similarity between the persecution of Jews and the persecution of witches suggests that the pressure behind both was social. 'The witch and the Jew both represent social nonconformity.'[56] The persecution of witches was not confined to the Catholic Church; the Reformers were even more bitter opponents of witches than Catholics.

The witchcraft craze spread to England, Scotland, and Ireland but it never reached the same degree of viciousness in England or Ireland as it did in Europe. In Scotland, however, some of the most barbaric trials were accompanied by the use of horrible tortures. King James VI of Scotland, a firm believer in witchcraft, personally presided at some of the trials.[57] He wrote an influential treatise on witchcraft which is included in an edition of his *Workes* (London, 1616, *STC* 14344) in the Stillingfleet collection. By the time King James ascended the English throne some years later he appears to have changed his mind about the existence of witches and witchcraft.

The most famous case of witchcraft in Ireland was that of Dame Alice Kyteler in Kilkenny in 1324. Dame Alice was lucky and managed to escape to England. But Ireland was unique in one respect. It was the only country where witches were persecuted by the church as heretics,[58] and Ireland also seems to have been the last country in which penalties were retained in statute law.[59]

Belief in witchcraft was almost universal in the sixteenth and seventeenth centuries and it was understandable if unfortunate that some of the most distinguished European scholars and writers took an active part in the campaign. There were some brave and outstanding exceptions, scholars who as a consequence suffered condemnation and had their books burnt.

---

55 H.R. Trevor-Roper, *The European witch-craze of the 16th and 17th centuries*, London, Penguin Books, 1969, pp 11–12.   **56** Ibid., p. 33.   **57** Ronald Seth, *In the name of the devil*, p. 24.   **58** *A contemporary narrative of the proceedings against Dame Alice Kyteler*, ed. Thomas Wright, London, printed for the Camden Society, 1843. Introduction, p. ix. See also St John D. Seymour, *Irish witchcraft and demonology*, Dublin, Hodges Figgis, 1913, pp 25–45 (Alice Kyteler).   **59** *Encyclopaedia Britannica*, xxiv, Edinburgh, Adam & Charles Black, 1888 (Witchcraft). See also Joseph Glanvill, *Saducismus triumphatus*, London, 1682. Glanvill gives Valentine Greatrake's account of an Irish witch, Florence Newton, in Youghal, Co. Cork, pp 137–55, and 'An Irish story of one that had like to have been carried away by spirits …', pp 203–7.

The book of Heinrich Institor (Krämer) and Jakob Sprenger, *Malleus maleficarum* or 'The hammer of witches', became the first great encyclopedia on demonology when it was printed in 1486. There are two copies of this work in the library. The first copy is in the Stearne collection, printed in Lyon in 1584; the second copy, printed in Frankfurt in 1588, is in the Stillingfleet collection.

Malleus maleficarum is a terrifying and cruel book. When it was first published it bore on the title-page the dreadful warning: 'Haeresis est maxima opera maleficarum non credere'(To disbelieve in witches is the greatest of heresies).[60] The Dominican inquisitors amongst other quaint beliefs suggested that witchcraft was more natural to women than men because of the inherent wretchedness of their hearts.

John Wier's (or Weyer's) *De praestigiis daemonum* (Basle 1568) caused a storm of criticism when it was first published in 1563. Wier was physician to the duke of Cleves-Jülich-Berg-Marck, William V, and he is regarded as the founder of modern psychiatry. Although Wier did believe in witches he thought that witches' confessions were caused by illusions brought on by disease. Wier's book was ordered to be burnt by the Lutheran university of Marburg and it was put on the *Index* by the duke of Alba. But Wier's book, which is in the Stillingfleet collection, does have another fascinating aspect. It was in this book that the first account of the 'Pied piper of Hamelin' was given.[61]

Jean Bodin's *De la démonomanie des sorciers, et réfutation des opinions de Jean Wier* (Paris, 1580) was a ferocious attack on Jean Wier's views on witches. Bodin was regarded as one of the greatest French intellectual writers of his day, although he was also a firm believer in witchcraft. Bodin believed that any person accused of sorcery must never be acquitted, and he accused Jean Wier of being 'a criminal accomplice of the devil'.[62] Bodin's book is part of the Bouhéreau collection.

Dr Bouhéreau collected two further particularly interesting books on this subject for his collection. The first is a tiny tract written by Mark Duncan. Duncan was born in Scotland and went to live in France and became rector and professor of philosophy in the university of Saumur. Duncan's *Discours de la possession des religieuses Ursulines de Lodun* (Loudun) was printed in 1634.

---

60 H.R. Trevor-Roper, op. cit., p. 42. **61** C.F. Smith, *John Dee*, p. 269. **62** H.R. Trevor-Roper, op. cit., p. 74.

13. Booke.   The difcouerie

To cut off ones head, and to laie it in a platter,
which the iugglers call the decollation of Iohn Baptift.

The forme
of ỹ planks,
&c.

The order
of the acti-
on, as it is
to be fhew-
ed.

What order is to be obferued for the practifing hereof
with great admiration, read page 349.350.

¶ The

38 Reginald Scot's *The discouerie of witchcraft* (London, 1584). Illustration of the
juggler's trick of how 'To cut off ones head, and to laie it in a platter'.

It consists of an evaluation and criticism of the famous case of possession by the devil, brought against the Catholic curate, Urbain Grandier, and the Ursuline nuns at the convent in Loudun. Duncan was also a practising physician and he believed that the nuns were suffering from melancholia and were not possessed by the devil. Laubardemont, the commissary who investigated the case, treated Duncan's opinion with deep suspicion, and his position in the university of Saumur was put in question.[63] But fortunately for Duncan he was protected by an influential patron and managed to avoid dismissal. The unfortunate Urbain Grandier was convicted on the evidence of the 'possessed' nuns and was sentenced to be burnt alive.

The second book is Pierre de Lancre's (or L'Ancre's) *Tableau de l'inconstance des mauvais anges et démons* (Paris, 1612). Pierre de Lancre was described by Trevor-Roper as 'an enchanting writer', because he wrote such charming accounts of his country house at Loubens.[64] But de Lancre also wrote vitriolic attacks on both Jews and witches. When de Lancre became a counsellor of the Parlement of Bordeaux he is believed to have been personally responsible for burning over one hundred people who had been condemned for witchcraft.

The German scholar Cornelius Agrippa opposed the contemporary witchcraft craze and was himself attacked for being a witch. Agrippa was known as a cabalistic philosopher. Agrippa's *Opera* (Lyon, [1550] one volume only) contains many chapters on witchcraft, magic, and necromancy, and is part of the Stillingfleet collection.

Balthasar Bekker's *Le monde enchanté* (Amsterdam, 1694) was another brave attempt to stop the witchcraft craze. Bekker, a Dutch Protestant minister, believed that the devil had been locked up in hell and was therefore incapable of interfering in human affairs. Because of the ill feelings caused by these views, Bekker was eventually driven out of the ministry. Bekker's work was published in four volumes and is part of the Stillingfleet collection.[65]

Trevor-Roper noted that it was a most extraordinary phenomenon that some of the men who were responsible for many of the most atrocious witch

---

63 Alexander Chalmers, *The general biographical dictionary* (Mark Duncan). Dr Bouhéreau added a fascinating annotation to the endpapers of this book. He noted that in a book written by Balthasar de Monconys entitled *Journal des voyages* (Lyon, 1665), (in the Stillingfleet collection), Monconys gave a description of a visit which he (Monconys) made to the superior of the Ursuline convent at Loudun. Maconys described a curious incident which occurred during his visit to the convent which illustrated the deceitful behaviour of the superior in the convent.   64 H.R. Trevor-Roper, op. cit., pp 80 and 36.
65 At the end of the Epistle in each of these four volumes the signature J. Bekker appears. Possibly a relative of the author.

hunts were themselves 'harmless scholarly characters'.[66] Nicolas Remy certainly fits into this category; he was a scholar, a historian and an elegant Latin poet. His *Dæmonolatreiae* (Lyon, 1595) in the Stillingfleet collection was considered to be the greatest Catholic encyclopedia on witchcraft since the publication of the *Malleus maleficarum* over one hundred years earlier. Remy's book has been extensively annotated with many cross-references to other writers on witchcraft. Bishop Stillingfleet may have been responsible for these annotations and similar type annotations in Bishop Binsfeld's *De confessionibus maleficorum* (Trier, 1591) and also in Philippo Elich's *Daemonomagia* (Frankfurt, 1607). Bishop Binsfeld was a notorious witch-hunter and carried out an enormous number of executions.

Martin del Rio's (or Delrius) *Disquisitionum magicarum* (Lyon, 1608) was another massive encyclopedia on witchcraft. Del Rio gave ludicrous details on how to identify witches and on what parts of the body the witch's mark could be found. Yet Del Rio was a great Jesuit scholar and was described by Justus Lipsus as 'the miracle of our age'. There are two editions of this work in the library; the first is in the Stillingfleet collection and there is a later edition in the Bouhéreau collection. Both editions have the engraved title-page with illustrations from the Book of Exodus. It is in the text of the Book of Exodus (22.18) that one of the judicial laws of Moses 'thou shalt not suffer a witch to live' appears.

Lambert Daneau was an eminent French Protestant divine. According to Trevor-Roper, Daneau was one of the most important French Huguenot preachers after Calvin and Beza. But the Huguenots were persecuted for their religious beliefs and, after the massacre on St Bartholomew's Day, Daneau sought refuge in Geneva. For these reasons one might have supposed that Daneau would have been sympathetic to the people who were being persecuted for witchcraft. But Daneau's *De veneficis … Dialogus* ([Geneva] 1574) was just as nonsensical as any of the other books written against witches at this period. (In 1575 Daneau's book was translated into English and published in England, being the first manual on witch-beliefs in that country.[67] Only the Geneva edition is in the Stillingfleet collection.)

One of the most popular English theological writers of the sixteenth century was William Perkins. Perkins had strong Calvinist opinions and Keith Thomas in his *Religion and the decline of magic* said that Perkins believed

---

66 H.R. Trevor-Roper, op. cit., p. 79.   **67** Ibid., p. 66. See also *STC* 6226.

that there was 'no difference whatsoever between the practices of English
witches and those of France, Spain, Italy or Germany'.[68] Perkins also urged
that all witches without any exception be executed. His *A discourse of the
damned art of witchcraft* (Cambridge, 1608? *STC* 19697) is in the Stillingfleet
collection but unfortunately it is very imperfect and lacks the title-page, and
much else.

Another distinguished English writer who believed in witches and
witchcraft was Joseph Glanvill. Glanvill's *The vanity of dogmatizing* (London,
1661, *Wing* G 834) has been described as 'a noble appeal for freedom of
thought and experimental science'.[69] Matthew Arnold found the inspiration
for his poem *The scholar gypsy* in a chapter in this book. Yet in spite of
Glanvill's great intellectual gifts his book on witches, *A philosophical endeavour
towards the defence of the being of witches and apparitions* (London, 1666, *Wing* G
817A), was a strong attack on all those who did not believe in witchcraft.[70]
Glanvill again defended his belief in witchcraft in his *Saducismus triumphatus*
(London, 1681). The edition in Archbishop Marsh's collection was printed
in 1682 (*Wing* G 823).[71] Lecky when commenting on Glanvill's opinions
and writings on witchcraft said *Saducismus triumphatus* was 'the ablest ever
published'.[72] It also has an engraved frontispiece and title by W. Faithorne
and remarkable illustrations of demons and witches. Glanvill's writings were
collected by Bishops Stearne and Stillingfleet and by Archbishop Marsh.

Reginald Scot's *The discouerie of witchcraft* (London, 1584, *STC* 21864) was
another courageous attempt to prevent the cruel persecution of the
unfortunate people accused of witchcraft in England. Scot believed that it
was the poor, the aged and the simple-minded who were being arrested for
witchcraft and he felt they were unable to defend themselves. His book is
a manual of tricks used by magicians and conjurers to deceive innocent

---

68 Keith Thomas, *Religion and the decline of magic*, London, Penguin University Books, 1973, p. 523.
69 Chambers's *Biographical dictionary* (Joseph Glanvill).   **70** This book seems to have caused some
confusion. The first edition of *A philosophical endeavour ...* (London, 1666), in Marsh's. An examination
of the book entitled *Some philosophical considerations touching the being of witches* (1667, *Wing* G 832)
reveals that apart from tiny textual changes it is the same work as *A philosophical endeavour ...* (1666). It
has of course a different title and it is a different printing.   **71** The first edition of this work with the
title *Saducismus triumphatus* was printed in London in 1681, *Wing* G 822. Another edition was printed
in 1682, and the second edition was also printed in 1682, *Wing* G 823.   **72** J.B. Mullinger, 'Platonists
and Latitudinarians' in *CHEL*, viii, p. 291.   **73** H.V. Routh, 'The progress of social literature in Tudor
times' in *CHEL*, iii, p. 112. See also *DNB* (Joseph Glanvill), and Maggs Bros. Sale Catalogue no. 921,
Witchcraft and Magic, December 1969, Item no. 48, p. 14.

39 Illustration from Joseph Glanvill's *Saducismus triumphatus*, on the subject of witchcraft, published in London in 1681.

people. Scot's book infuriated King James I and he is said to have ordered every copy to be destroyed. But Scot's book is regarded as 'the first great English contribution to this European controversy'.[73] Shakespeare is believed to have used it when he was writing *A midsummer night's dream* and *Macbeth*. It is part of the Stillingfleet collection and contains the two rare woodcut leaves which are so often missing from this work. It bears the signature of Rob. Johnson on the title-page; this may be Robert Johnson, the musician, who set to music several of the songs in Shakespeare's *Tempest*.

From Samuel Harsnet's *A declaration of egregious popish impostures* (London, 1603, *STC* 12880), Shakespeare apparently took the names of the devils mentioned by Edgar in *King Lear*.[74] Harsnet was archbishop of York and like Reginald Scot did not believe in witchcraft. In fact Harsnet had earlier been involved in the notorious fraudulent cases of exorcism which had been organised by John Darrell. Harsnet's book was written by order of the privy council, and it was described by Keith Thomas as 'a scathing work of polemic'.[75] The copy in the Stillingfleet collection is the first edition of 1603, but for some unknown reason the title-page of the second issue of 1604 has been pasted over the original title-page.

We have already mentioned in the section on printing Alberico Gentili's treatise, *Ad tit. C. de maleficis … commentarius* [Commentary on the title of the (Justinian) code on magicians and astrologers and others like them] (Oxford, 1593, *STC* 11732). Gentili's work is in two parts; the first part is a defence of poetry and acting and both pieces are in outward form commentaries on the Justinian code.[76] Alberico Gentili was an Italian who became a Protestant and was forced to leave Italy. He came to England where he became professor of law in Oxford university. These are just some of the writers who wrote on this extraordinary subject and whose books are in the library. But there are other equally well-known writers whose work is available, such as Meric Casaubon, Thomas Cooper, Sir Robert Filmer, Ludovico Lavatero, Pierre Le Loyer, Cotton Mather, Gabriel Naudé and John Wagstaffe.

Books relating to Ireland

The majority of the books in the library relating to Ireland are kept in a special room. Most of these books were printed in the nineteenth and the

74 *DNB* (Samuel Harsnet).   **75** Keith Thomas, *Religion and the decline of magic*, p. 583.   **76** J. W. Binns, 'Alberico Gentili in defence of poetry and acting' in *Studies in the Renaissance*, xix, 1972, p. 225.

early part of the twentieth century. Among them are histories of Ireland, including ecclesiastical histories, biographies, the journals of the Royal Irish Academy, the Royal Society of Antiquaries, the Celtic Society, the Parish Register Society, etc. They also include Sir John Gilbert's *Calendar of ancient records of Dublin*, and various issues of John Watson's *Gentleman and citizen's almanack* from 1733.

In the early part of the last century two valuable donations of Irish interest were presented to the library. The first was bequeathed by Lord Cloncurry in 1929. It consists of papers and notebooks which belonged to his sister, the writer, Emily Lawless. The bequest includes 44 volumes of her writings.

The second donation was made in 1941 by the Revd C.A. Webster, dean of Ross. The Webster donation contains a collection of material relating to Irish antiquities together with about eighty deeds (mostly on parchment, with many seals remaining) of the sixteenth and seventeenth centuries relating to the city and county of Cork and formerly owned by another well-known antiquarian, Dr R. Caulfield. The Webster donation also includes a number of notebooks containing manuscript material (transcripts, indexes, etc., some in the Irish language) written by or for the use of Bishop William Reeves.

There are also books relating to Ireland in the main collections in the library. They were printed in the seventeenth and eighteenth centuries and they deal with some of the political and religious events of that period.

Many of the well-known Catholic writers and English Protestant writers who wrote political, historical and antiquarian books on Ireland are also represented in the main collections. These writers include Edmund Borlase, Gerard Boate, Thomas Carte, John Colgan, Francis Grose, Geoffrey Keating, Richard Lawrence, William Molyneux, Fynes Moryson, Hugh Reilly, Roderic O'Flaherty, Edward Ledwich, John Rutty, Sir Thomas Stafford, Richard Stanihurst and Sir James Ware. Bishop John Stearne seems to have been particularly interested in some of these writers, possibly because of the fact that of the original collectors who formed the library he was the only Irishman.

There are also a surprising number of books in the main collections written by Irish Catholic priests. Many of the Irish priests who had been banished because of the penal laws were employed as teachers and professors in European universities and colleges. Some wrote scholarly theological and religious books which were printed on the Continent.

Although the collectors in Marsh's would have been unsympathetic to these Catholic writers' ideas, they were, nevertheless, deeply interested in controversial theological arguments and disputes, and they collected books written by writers who held totally different ideas from their own beliefs. These authors included many of the banished Irish priests who formed part of the 'society of scholars' in Europe.

Fr Benignus Millett commenting on these Irish Catholic writers said:

> Latin learning and literature not only survived but indeed flourished among the Irish, particularly among the Irish abroad … The extensive spiritual movement of the counter-reformation, gathering momentum during the sixteenth and into the seventeenth century, revitalised studies, and especially theology, in many catholic centres of western Europe. More remarkable even than the great influx of Irish pupils and teachers to continental universities and colleges was the flowering of scholarship among them at a high level of literary productivity.[77]

Archbishop Peter Lombard was the Catholic archbishop of Armagh, but like so many Irish prelates during the seventeenth century he lived in Rome. Lombard became the leading adviser in Rome on Irish affairs and he was regarded as one of the most important theologians at the papal court. His book, *De regno Hiberniae … commentarius* (Louvain, 1632, *Walsh* 284), was an historical commentary on Ireland. According to Professor T.W. Moody it 'was intended to enlist the support of Pope Clement VIII on [Hugh] O'Neill's side'.[78] Although this work seems an unlikely subject to have interested Archbishop Marsh, he did have a copy in his collection.

Archbishop Lombard never returned to Ireland, and Bishop David Rothe was made Lombard's deputy. Rothe was appointed bishop of Ossory in 1618 and lived in Kilkenny. He was recognised as a great scholar and a notable peacemaker, particularly between Archbishop Rinuccini and the different factions at the confederation of Kilkenny. Rothe's *Analecta sacra nova et mira* (Cologne, 1617–19, 3pts., *Walsh* 466 and 467), issued under the pseudonym T.N. Philadelpho, gives an account of the sufferings of the Irish Catholics at the hands of the English government. It is part of the Stillingfleet collection and it has been annotated by a previous owner or possibly by Bishop Stillingfleet. Rothe's other book (issued under the pseudonym, Donato

77 Benignus Millett, 'Irish literature in Latin, 1550–1700' in Moody, Martin, and Byrne, ed., *A new history of Ireland*, iii, *Early modern Ireland 1534–1691*, Oxford, At the Clarendon Press, 1976, p. 585.
78 T.W. Moody, *A new history of Ireland*, Introduction, p. lvi. See also M.J. Brenan, OSF, *An ecclesiastical*

Roirk Hiberno), *Hibernia resurgens* (Rouen, 1621, *Walsh* 470), is a defence of Ireland and its saints and was written in answer to the Scottish writer, Thomas Dempster. (Dempster's writings are also in the library.) Both Bishop Stillingfleet and Bishop Stearne had copies of *Hibernia resurgens* in their collections. The copy in the Stillingfleet collection bears the signatures of Arthur Annesley and Richard Arthur. Arthur Annesley, earl of Anglesey, was vice-treasurer for Ireland, 1660–7 and was then made lord privy seal. He was dismissed for adverse criticism of the government in 1682, the year in which he purchased this book for three shillings and seven pence. Richard Arthur was probably the seventeenth-century Catholic bishop of Limerick who was a friend of Bishop David Rothe. From an annotation on the endpaper it appears that Bishop Rothe presented it to him.[79]

Some of the most famous writers who were banished from Ireland at this period were members of the Jesuit Order. Richard Archdekin SJ was born in Co. Kilkenny and like so many Irish students went to study theology in Louvain. He became professor of philosophy and theology at Antwerp and Louvain and wrote theological works. His *Praecipuae controversiae fidei* (Louvain, 1671, *Walsh* 5) became so successful that, when a few copies reached Prague, transcripts were made in order that as many copies as possible would be available for the students. Fr Benignus Millett described Archdekin's book as 'a seventeenth-century best-seller'.[80] There are three different editions in the Stillingfleet collection including the edition already mentioned. The second copy of this work is entitled, *Theologia tripartita*, 3 vols (Antwerp, 1682, *Walsh* 9).[81] It bears Samuel Foley's signature and the date 1691 and the price 7/6.

One of the cleverest priests who engaged in theological disputes at this period in Dublin was Fr Henry Fitzsimon SJ. Fitzsimon was born in Dublin and studied in Oxford, Paris and Douai.[82] He became a Jesuit in 1592 and was sent back to Ireland in 1596 or 1597. He was engaged in many

history of Ireland, a new ed., Dublin, James Duffy, 1864, pp 490–2.   **79** I am grateful to Revd Professor Donal Cregan for information on Bishop Richard Arthur.   **80** Benignus Millett, op. cit., p. 575. **81** According to M.ON. Walsh, 'Irish books printed abroad 1475–1700' in *The Irish Book*, ii, no. 1, 1963, p. 5, Archdekin's *Praecipuae controversiae fidei* was issued in Louvain in 1671. Another edition of this work with a different title, *Theologia quadripartita*, was published in Prague without the author's consent (Prague, 1678, *Walsh* 6, 2nd ed.). The edition in Marsh's is that printed in Antwerp by Michael Knobbaert in a 12mo format in 3 volumes, *Walsh* no. 9.   **82** Information from Revd Edmund Hogan's *Distinguished Irishmen of the sixteenth century*, London, Burns & Oates, 1894, pp 196–310. See also *DNB* (Henry Fitzsimon, SJ), and Charles McNeill, 'Publications of Irish interest published by Irish authors on the Continent of Europe prior to the eighteenth century' in *The Bibliographical Society of Ireland*, iv, 1930, pp 27–8.

polemical disputes, the most famous being with John Rider, the dean of St Patrick's Cathedral. Fitzsimon's *A catholike confutation of M. John Riders clayme of antiquitie* (Roan, [false imprint] Douai, 1608, *STC* 11025, *A & R* 319, *Walsh* 218; part 1 only) is in Bishop Stearne's collection.

Christopher Holywood SJ (Christophorus a Sacrobosco) was born in Artane Castle in 1559. He studied on the Continent and became professor of divinity at Dole and Padua.[83] He returned to Ireland and was made superior of the Jesuit mission. Holywood worked tirelessly under conditions of great hardship in Ireland; he was condemned by James I for his recommendation to Irish parents that they should send their children to be educated on the Continent. His *Defensio decreti Tridentini et sententiae Roberti Bellarmini* (Antwerp, 1604, *Walsh* 272) is regarded as the most important of his writings. The copy in the Stillingfleet collection contains the treatise *The nag's head fable* which first appeared in print in this work (in the treatise at the end, pp 17–19).

Fr Peter Wadding SJ was born in Co. Waterford and was a cousin of the famous Franciscan, Luke Wadding. Fr Wadding studied classics in Ireland, but the whereabouts of the particular school which he attended is not known. It may have been in Waterford or Kilkenny. He continued his studies at Douai and was ordained a Jesuit in 1609. Fr Wadding had a distinguished academic career and became professor of theology in Louvain, later in Antwerp, and eventually chancellor of the university of Prague.[84] Unfortunately he became involved in an academic row between the Ferdinandea and the Carolina universities and was ordered by his superior to leave Prague. He continued to teach canon law in Graz university where he died in 1644. Wadding's *Tractatus de incarnatione* (Antwerp, 1636, *Walsh* 629), which is in Archbishop Marsh's collection, was regarded as an important book and it was highly appreciated in its time.

Professor T.W. Moody when commenting on the valuable contribution made to Irish history by many of these writers at this period said: 'Seventeenth-century Europe saw the beginnings of modern historical scholarship, with its insistence on the critical use of primary sources.' Professor Moody mentioned the writings of Ussher, Ware, Colgan, and Wadding as among those who 'may be regarded as contributors to the new historiography'.[85]

---

83 Information from Revd Edmund Hogan's *Distinguished Irishmen of the sixteenth century*, pp 395–501, and *DNB* (Christopher Holywood SJ).   **84** Paul O'Dea, 'Father Peter Wadding, SJ, Chancellor of the University of Prague 1629–1641' in *Studies*, xxx, no. 119, September 1941, pp 337–48. See also Benignus Millett, op. cit., p. 575.   **85** T.W. Moody, op. cit., Introduction, p. lxi.

The mention of Luke Wadding is a reminder that the Franciscans made a particularly important political and academic contribution to Irish affairs in the seventeenth century. We have already mentioned the two volumes of John Colgan's work in a different section. Colgan's monumental work on the Irish saints was regarded as one of the great achievements of the Irish priests and scholars in Louvain.

Luke Wadding's *Annales Minorum*, 7 vols (Lyon, 1628–48, *Walsh* 596–601 and 603), and his *Scriptores Ordinis Minorom* (Rome, 1650, *Walsh* 610) are both in the Stillingfleet collection. Wadding's enormous history of the Franciscan Order took thirty years to write and the Franciscan Order paid the costs.[86]

Patrick Fleming was born in Co. Louth and became a friar of the Strict Observance in the college of St Anthony in Louvain in 1618. Appointed first superior of the Irish seminary in Prague,[87] during the religious wars in Bohemia, he fled from the city and was tragically killed by a group of armed peasants. His *Collectanea sacra seu S. Columbani Hiberni abbatis …* (Louvain, 1667, *Walsh* 228) is in the Stearne collection.

Another Irish Franciscan, Francis Porter, lived in Rome and was appointed president of St Isidore's college. Porter was recognised as a distinguished campaigner in the anti-Jansenist controversy which reached Rome in the middle of the seventeenth century. His book, *Securis evangelica* (Rome, 1674, *Walsh* 434), which is in the Stillingfleet collection, was described by Fr Benignus Millett as 'a fine piece of controversial reasoning'.[88]

Other well-known religious and lay writers who published their writings on the Continent and whose books are in the library include Bishop Nicholas French, John Callaghan (MacCallaghan), Thomas Messingham, Don Philip O'Sullivan Beare, and the poet friar Aodh Mac Aingil or Hugh Mac Caghwell, archbishop of Armagh, whose writings on Joannes Duns Scotus are also in the library.

Finally we would like to mention one of the best-known of all the Franciscan friars, Peter Walsh. Walsh was born in Co. Kildare and was educated in Louvain where he joined the Franciscans.[89] He returned to Ireland and was appointed a divinity lecturer in Kilkenny convent. Walsh became deeply involved in Irish politics and he opposed the proposals put forward by the papal nuncio, Archbishop Rinuccini. He conceived the idea

86 Benignus Millett, op. cit., p. 583.   **87** Charles McNeill, 'Publications of Irish Interest', pp 14–15, and see *DNB* (Patrick Fleming). **88** Benignus Millett, op. cit., pp 578–9.   **89** J.G. Simms, 'The Restoration, 1660–85' in *A new history of Ireland*, iii, p. 429, and *DNB* (Peter Walsh).

of a 'loyal remonstrance' which was an attempt to show the government that while Catholics were obedient to Rome in spiritual matters they would be equally loyal to the king in temporal matters. The 'loyal remonstrance' was not acceptable to Rome or the Irish clergy and Walsh returned to London. In 1670 he was excommunicated by the Franciscan chapter-general in Valladolid. Walsh's *The history & vindication of the loyal formulary* ([London and Dublin] 1674, *Wing* W 634) is in the Stillingfleet collection. When Peter Walsh lived in London he became involved in the controversy between Bishop Stillingfleet and the Jesuits. Walsh attacked Stillingfleet's arguments in a book entitled *An answer to three treatises* (London, 1678 *Wing* W 628). There are two copies of this work in the library.

Archbishop Peter Talbot, the brother of Richard Talbot, earl of Tyrconnell, made a bitter attack on Peter Walsh. He accused Walsh of being vain, insolent, and extravagant, and of publishing a book 'stufft with errors, no less dangerous to the state, then (*sic*) damnable to the soul'. Talbot's *The friar disciplind* (Gant, 1674, *Wing* T 116, *Walsh* 543) is now in Marsh's collection although it was originally part of the Stearne collection. (This book was published under the name of Robert Wilson.)

A book which deals with the registration of the Catholic clergy under one of the penal laws also provides interesting information on where many of these priests were educated and ordained. This book is entitled *A list of the names of the popish parish priests* (Dublin, 1705), and it originally belonged to Bishop Stearne. It is divided into various headings which list the Catholic priests in all the counties of Ireland, together with their addresses, parishes, and the dates and places of their ordination and the ordaining bishop. A great many of these priests were ordained on the Continent by continental bishops, but it is interesting to note how active St Oliver Plunkett and some of the Irish bishops were at that difficult time in Ireland.

There are books in the Stearne collection which deal with Oliver Plunkett's condemnation and trial, and there is a copy of his own work, *Jus primatiale ...* ([London], 1672, *Wing* P 2623). Plunkett's book is a defence of the primacy of the see of Armagh,[90] against the argument put forward by the archbishop of Dublin, Peter Talbot, that, because Dublin was the capital city, it should be the seat of the primacy and not Armagh.

90 Charles McNeill, 'Publications of Irish interest', p. 32.

While the list of registered parish priests provides valuable information on the Catholic priests working in the seventeenth century in Ireland, evidence of the changing fortunes of the Protestants during the time of King James II is provided in a book in Archbishop Marsh's own collection. This is entitled, *A list of such of the names of the nobility, gentry and commonalty of England and Ireland ... attainted of high treason* (London, 1690, *Wing* L 2409). The first name on the list is that of Archbishop Francis Marsh (no relation), who was Narcissus Marsh's predecessor as archbishop of Dublin. Narcissus Marsh as bishop of Ferns and Leighlin is listed on page 24. Marsh appears to have been particularly interested in this list. He counted the number on every page and he noted that the final total amounted to 2620 people attainted for high treason.

We have already mentioned some of the leading Irish Protestant scholarly writers such as Archbishop Ussher and Sir James Ware under a different heading, but there are naturally a large number of these writers in the collections, including Roger Boyle and Henry Dodwell.

Catholic writers have been given more prominence in this chapter because we often find that since Marsh's Library was founded by a seventeenth-century Protestant archbishop, visitors and students expect the contents of the library to be exclusively related to Protestant theology or religious affairs. We hope we have been able to demonstrate how important for four seventeenth-century Protestant collectors were the writings of the Catholic authors who belonged to the 'society of scholarship'.

In the early years of the last century the library managed to purchase from its small book-buying fund (never increased) a collection of pamphlets on trade, education, and politics. Many of these pamphlets had originally belonged to Thomas Davis and some bear his signature.

During the eighteenth and nineteenth centuries books were purchased or donated by writers who were concerned with the Irish language such as Owen Connellan, Edward Lhuyd, Patrick Lynch, Edward O'Reilly and Charles Vallancey.

The library benefited from the generosity of E.R. McClintock Dix who donated a collection of eighteenth-century Dublin printed and bound novels in 1905. His donation also included some beautiful examples of eighteenth-century Irish bookbindings.

Probably the most important eighteenth-century donations to Marsh's were made by the speakers of the Irish house of commons, Lord Shannon and the Rt Hon. John Ponsonby. They consist of *The journals of the house of commons of the kingdom of Ireland, from 11th James I to 25 George II*, etc.[91]

Although Archbishop Marsh left some schoolbooks which he and his brother, Onesiphorus, had used in England, there are two books in his collection which are particularly interesting in relation to Irish education. The first is entitled *Sacri lusus. In usum scholae Kilkenniensis* (Dublin, 1676?, *Wing* S 224A, *Dix* p. 158, *Alden* p. 36). This little book consists of Latin poetry in elegiac measure, chiefly on scripture subjects. Unfortunately it is imperfect and ends on page 64 and the title-page has been mutilated. The second book, *Adminiculum puerile* (Dublin, 1694, *Wing* D 447, *Dix* p. 264), was compiled by the master of St Patrick's School, Paul Davys. It was intended for the use of the school and consists of fundamental Latin exercises for teaching purposes. Davys' book seems to have been the cause of a most unfortunate event. He was shot by his pupils shortly after the introduction of the book into St Patrick's School. It is not altogether clear whether the boys shot Davys because they resented the introduction of this Latin grammar or because of a 'barring-out'. (A 'barring-out' such as that in which Davys was shot was a schoolboys' strike.) Rex Cathcart said that Davys' pupils barred him out and refused him admittance to the school, and that when he attempted to enter forcibly they shot him with a pistol.[92] Davys dedicated his book to Archbishop Marsh.

These little books are an indication of what was taught in Irish schools in the seventeenth century and the book used in the Kilkenny school may be one of the textbooks used by Berkeley and by Swift.

91 *The Journals of the house of commons of the kingdom of Ireland, from 11th James I to 25 George II*, in eight volumes and also volumes 9–16, including *Index volume* and *Appendix*. *Journal of the Irish House of Commons* 9 Nov. 1641 to 26 March 1647, A. Bradley, 1753–71. *The Journal ... 22 October 1765*, vols 8–15 (11 in 2 pts), pr. G. Grierson, 1797, vols 16–17 (2 pts), J. King, A. Bradley, 1795, vols 18–19 (2 pts), A. Bradley King, 1799–1800, Dublin 1795–1800. We also have the *Statutes of Ireland*, 1310–1800, 21 volumes, 1786–1801.   **92** H.R. Cathcart, 'Peter Davys: the master they shot' (ii) in *The Patrician*, 1950, no. 9, pp 16–17.

Bibliography

THIS BIBLIOGRAPHY contains books of reference and other works consulted. It does not include full bibliographical details of the works described in the text.

BOOKS

Aldis, H.G., *The printed book*, 2nd ed., rev., by John Carter and E.A. Crutchley, Cambridge, At the University Press, 1941.

Andrews, John, *Ireland in maps: an introduction*, Dublin, Dolmen Press, 1961.

Armstrong, Elizabeth, *Robert Estienne, royal printer; an historical study of the elder Stephanus*, Cambridge, At the University Press, 1954.

Ball, F.E. *The judges in Ireland, 1221–1921*, 2 vols., New York, E.P. Dutton, 1927.

Baynton-Williams, Roger, *Investing in maps*, London, Barrie & Rockliff, Cresset Press, 1969.

Beckett, J.C., *The making of modern Ireland 1603–1923*, London, Faber & Faber, 1969.

Berry, H.F., *A history of the Royal Dublin Society*, London, Longmans Green, 1915.

Birch, Thomas, *History of the Royal Society*, 4 vols., London, 1756–7. See also *The works of the Hon. Robert Boyle. To which is prefixed the life of the author by T. Birch*, 5 vols., London, A. Millar, 1744.

Birrell, T.A., *The library of John Morris: the reconstruction of a seventeenth-century collection*, London, British Museum Publications, 1976.

Blades, William, *The biography and typography of William Caxton*, repr., and ed. J. Moran, London, Frederick Muller, 1971.

Bourne, William, *A regiment for the sea*, ed. E.G.R. Taylor, Cambridge University Press, Hakluyt Society, 1963. (Second series, no. cxxi, issued for 1961.)

Brady, W.M., *The episcopal succession in England Scotland and Ireland 1400–1875*, 3 vols., Rome, Tipografia Della Pace, 1876–7.

Breathnach, Deasún, *Bedell and the Irish version of the Old Testament*, Baile Átha Cliath, Clódhanna, 1971.

Brenan, M.J., *An ecclesiastical history of Ireland*, new ed., Dublin & London, James Duffy, 1864.

Brereton, Geoffrey, *A short history of French literature*, London, Penguin Books, 1968.

Bush, Douglas. *English literature in the earlier seventeenth century 1600–1660*, 2nd ed., Oxford, Clarendon Press, 1962.

Calmet, Dom Augustin. *Dictionary of the holy Bible*, 3 vols., trans. Samuel D'Oyly and
  John Colson, London, 1732.

Carleton, William. *The autobiography of William Carleton*, rev. ed., with preface by Patrick
  Kavanagh, London, Macgibbon & Kee, 1968.

Carroll, R.T., *The common-sense philosophy of religion of Bishop Edward Stillingfleet 1635–1699*,
  The Hague, Martinus Nijhoff, 1975.

Carter, John, *ABC for book-collectors*, repr. and corr., London, R. Hart-Davis, 1967.

Carty, James, compiler and ed., *Ireland from the Great Famine to the Treaty 1851–1921: a
  documentary record*, Dublin, C.J. Fallon, 1951.

Castiglioni, Arturo, *A history of medicine*, 2nd ed., trans. and ed. by E.B. Krumbhaar,
  London, Routledge & Kegan Paul, 1947.

Chappell, Warren, *A short history of the printed word*, London, Andre Deutsch, 1972.

Childers, E.S.E. and Robert Stewart, *The story of the Royal Hospital, Kilmainham*,
  amplified and republished by R.F. Nation, London, Hutchinson, 1921.

Clair, Colin, *A history of printing in Britain*, London, Cassell, 1965.

Cotton, Henry, *Fasti ecclesiae Hibernicae: the succession of the prelates and members of the
  cathedral bodies of Ireland*, 6 vols., Dublin, Hodges & Smith; London & Oxford, J.H.
  Parker, 1847–78. (Vol. v contains general *Indexes* to the whole work, by J.R.
  Garstin; the sixth volume is a *Supplement* to 31 December 1870 by C.P. Cotton.)

D'Alton, John, *The history of the county of Dublin*, Dublin, Hodges & Smith, 1838.

—— *The memoirs of the archbishops of Dublin*, Dublin, Hodges & Smith, 1838.

Davenport, C.J.H., *English heraldic book-stamps*, London, Constable, 1909.

Davies, H.W., *Devices of the early printers*, London, Grafton, 1935.

De Courcy, Catherine, *The foundation of the National Gallery of Ireland*, Dublin, National
  Gallery of Ireland, 1985.

Dennis, John, *The age of Pope (1700–1744)*, London, G. Bell & Sons, 1925.

[Donnelly, Nicholas], bishop of Canea, *Short histories of the Dublin parishes* (pt XI),
  Dublin, Catholic Truth Society of Ireland, 1912.

Douglas, D.C., *English scholars*, London, Jonathan Cape, 1939.

Du Trieu, Philippus, *Manuductio ad logicam*, Oxoniae, typis & impensis Guil. Hall,
  prostant Venales apud F. Oxlad & S. Pocock, 1662.

Ehrenpreis, Irvin, *Swift: the man, his works, and the age*, 3 vols., London, Methuen, 1983.

Esdaile, Arundell, *A student's manual of bibliography*, London, George Allen & Unwin, and
  the Library Association, 1931.

Fagan, Patrick, *Dublin's turbulent priest: Cornelius Nary 1658–1738*, Dublin, Royal Irish
  Academy, 1992.

Fairbank, Alfred, *A book of scripts*, rev. and enlar. ed., London, Penguin Books, 1968.

Fletcher, W.Y., *English book collectors*, ed. Alfred Pollard, London, Kegan Paul, Trench,
  Trübner, 1902.

Ford, A., J. McGuire, and K. Milne, ed., *As by law established*, Dublin, Lilliput Press, 1995.

Fry, C.B., *Hannington: the records of a Wiltshire parish*, Gloucester, John Bellows, 1935. (This
  book contains references to Archbishop Marsh and his family, pp 11–14.)

Gaskell, Philip, *A new introduction to bibliography*, repr. with corr., Oxford, At the Clarendon Press, 1974.

Goldberg, G.Y., *Jonathan Swift and contemporary Cork*, Cork, Mercier Press, 1967.

Heawood, Edward, *A history of geographical discovery in the seventeenth and eighteenth centuries*, general ed. F.H.H. Guillemard, Cambridge, At the University Press, 1912.

Hill, C., B. Reay, and W. Lamont, *The world of the Muggletonians*, London, Temple Smith, 1983.

Hobson, Anthony, *Great libraries*, London, Weidenfeld & Nicholson, 1970.

Hogan, Edmund, *Distinguished Irishmen of the sixteenth century*, London, Burns & Oates, 1894.

Hoppen, K.T., *The common scientist in the seventeenth century*, London, Routledge & Kegan Paul, 1970.

Hyman, Louis, *The Jews of Ireland*, London, Jewish Historical Society of England; Jerusalem, Israel Universities Press, 1972.

Irwin, C.H., *A history of presbyterianism in Dublin*, London, Hodder & Stoughton, 1890.

Johnson, A.F., *The first century of printing at Basle*, London, Ernest Benn, 1926.

—— *The Italian sixteenth century*, London, Ernest Benn. 1926.

—— *French sixteenth century printing*, London, Ernest Benn, 1928.

Joyce, James, *Ulysses. With a foreword by M.L. Ernst and the decision of the United States District Court rendered by Judge M. Woolsey*, New York, The Modern Library, 1946.

Kelly, James, and Dáire Keogh, ed., *History of the Catholic diocese of Dublin*, Dublin, Four Courts Press, 2000.

Killen, W.D., *The ecclesiastical history of Ireland*, 2 vols., London, Macmillan, 1875–6.

Kilroy, Phil, *Protestant dissent and controversy in Ireland 1660–1714*, Cork University Press, 1994.

King, Sir C.S., ed., *A great archbishop of Dublin. William King, D.D. 1650–1729*, London, Longmans Green, 1906.

King, William, *The remembrance of the righteous: a [funeral] sermon* (Archbishop Narcissus Marsh, Nov. 6, 1713), Dublin, Andrew Crooke, 1714.

[Kirkpatrick, James], *An historical essay upon the loyalty of Presbyterians*, [Belfast, James Blow], 1713.

Kline, Morris, *Mathematics in western culture*, London, Penguin Books, 1972.

Koeman, Ir. C., *Joan Blaeu and his Grand Atlas*, London, George Philip & Son, 1970.

Landa, L.A., *Swift and the Church of Ireland*, Oxford, At the Clarendon Press, 1954.

Lawler, John, *Book auctions in England in the seventeenth century 1676–1700*, ed. H.B. Wheatley, London, Elliot Stock, 1898.

Loeber, Rolf, *A biographical dictionary of architects in Ireland 1600–1720*, London, John Murray, 1981.

Lynam, E.W., *The Irish character in print 1571–1923*, With introduction by Alf MacLochlainn, Shannon, Irish University Press, 1969.

McCarthy, Muriel, *Archbishop Marsh and his Library*, Dublin, National College of Art and
  Design, 1977. (Reprint, with illustrations, of article in *Dublin Historical Record*, xxix,
  no. 1, Dec. 1975.)

McDowell, R.B. and D.A. Webb, *Trinity College Dublin 1592–1952*, Cambridge University
  Press, 1982.

McGuinne, Dermot, *Irish type design*, Dublin, Irish Academic Press, 1992.

McGuinness, P., A. Harrison, and R. Kearney, ed., *John Toland's Christianity not mysterious*,
  Dublin, Lilliput Press, 1997.

McKerrow, R.B., *An introduction to bibliography*, 2nd imp., Oxford, At the Clarendon
  Press, 1928.

McMurtrie, D.C., *The book: the story of printing and bookmaking*, 3rd rev. ed., 10th
  printing, London, New York, Toronto, Oxford University Press, 1972.

Macray, W.D., *Annals of the Bodleian Library, Oxford, 1598–1867*, London, Rivingtons, 1868.

MacRobert, T.M., *Printed books: a short introduction to fine typography*, London, V. & A.
  Museum, HMSO, 1957.

Maittaire, Michael, *Annales typographici ab artis inventae origine ad annum M D*, 5 vols.,
  Hagae-Comitum, Apud Isaacum Vaillant, 1719. (Vols 2 and 3 have the imprint:
  Hagae-Comitum, Apud Fratres Vaillant & Nicolaum Prevost, 1722. Vols 4 & 5 have
  the imprint, pasted on: Amstelodami, Apud Petrum Humbert, 1726.)

Mant, Richard, *History of the Church of Ireland*, 2 vols. (i, 2nd ed.), London, J.W. Parker,
  1841,40.

[Marsh, Narcissus], *Institutiones logicae. In usum juventutis academicae Dubliniensis*, Dublini,
  Apud Sam: Helsham, 1679.

—   *The charge given to his clergy at his primary visitation held in the Cathedral Church of St
  Patrick in Dublin June 27th 1694*, Dublin, Joseph Ray, 1694.

Mason, W.M., *The history and antiquities of the collegiate and Cathedral Church of St Patrick,
  near Dublin*, Dublin, W. Folds, 1820.

Maxwell, Constantia, *A history of Trinity College, Dublin, 1591–1892*, Dublin, The
  University Press, Trinity College, 1946.

Meehan, C.P., *The rise and fall of the Irish Franciscan monasteries*, 4th ed., Dublin, James
  Duffy, Sons, 1877.

Murphy, Denis, ed. and trans., *Triumphalia chronologica monasterii sanctae crucis in Hibernia*,
  Dublin, Sealy, Bryers & Walker, A. Thom, 1891.

O'Donoghue, D.J., *Sir Walter Scott's tour in Ireland in 1825*, Glasgow, Gowans & Gray;
  Dublin, O'Donoghue, M.H. Gill, 1905.

—   *The life and writings of James Clarence Mangan*, Edinburgh, Dublin, Chicago, Peabody,
  Mass., 1897.

Oldham, J.B., *Shrewbury School library bindings*, Oxford, At the University Press, 1943.

O'Regan, Philip, *Archbishop William King of Dublin (1650–1729)*, Dublin, Four Courts
  Press, 2000.

Painter, G.D., *William Caxton: a quincentenary biography of England's first printer*, London, Chatto & Windus, 1976.

Palmer, Samuel, *A general history of printing*, Completed by George Psalmanaazaar, London, A. Bettesworth, C. Hitch and C. Davis, 1733.

Pattison, Mark, *Isaac Casaubon 1559–1614*, London, Longmans Green, 1875.

Pevsner, Nikolaus, *An outline of European architecture*, rev. and enlar. ed., London, Penguin Books, 1945.

Plomer, H.R., *A short history of English printing 1476–1898*, Preface by A.W. Pollard, London, Kegan Paul, Trench, Trübner, 1900.

Plot, Robert, *The natural history of Oxfordshire*, Printed at the Theater in Oxford, 1677.

Quayle, Eric, *The collector's book of books*, London, Studio Vista, November Books, 1971.

Rooke, Henry, *Gleanings from the past*, Dublin, William McGee, 1895.

Russell, Bertrand, *History of western philosophy*, London, Unwin University Books, George Allen & Unwin, 1961.

Sampson, George, *The concise Cambridge history of English literature*, Cambridge, At the University Press, 1941.

Scholderer, Victor, *Johann Gutenberg: the inventor of printing*, London, BM, 1963.

Seth, Ronald, *In the name of the devil: great witchcraft cases*, Arrow Books, 1970.

Seymour, Edward, *Christ Church Cathedral, Dublin*, [London, s.n.], 1882.

Seymour, St J.D., *Irish witchcraft and demonology*, Dublin, Hodges Figgis, 1913.

Shuckburgh, E.S., ed., *Two biographies of William Bedell, bishop of Kilmore*, ed. with notes by E.S. Shuckburgh, Cambridge, At the University Press, 1902.

Simms, J.G., *The Treaty of Limerick*, Dundalk, Dundalgan Press, 1965.

— *Huguenot Portarlington: record of the commemorations 23rd August 1972* ('The Huguenot contribution to Ireland with special reference to Portarlington'), second printing, 1977.

Skelton, R.A. and David Woodward, ed., *Maps: a historical survey of their study and collecting*, 2nd imp., Chicago & London, University of Chicago Press, 1975.

Smith, C.F., *John Dee, 1527–1608*, London, Constable, 1909.

Steinberg, S.H., *Five hundred years of printing*, 3rd ed., rev. by James Moran, London, Penguin Books, 1974.

Stewart, Robert, see Childers, E.S.E.

Stokes, G.T., *Some worthies of the Irish church*, ed. H.J. Lawlor, London, Hodder & Stoughton, 1900. Contains: (1) Richard Lingard DD. (2) Dudley Loftus DCL. (3) Narcissus Marsh DD. (4) William King DD. (5) St Colman of Lindisfarne and Innisbofin. (6) Additional lecture.

Stubbs, J.W., *The history of the University of Dublin*, Dublin, Hodges Figgis; London, Longmans Green, 1889.

Swift, Jonathan, *Journal to Stella*, ed. Harold Williams, 2 vols., Oxford, Clarendon Press, 1948.

Swift, Jonathan, *Miscellaneous and autobiographical pieces, fragments and marginalia*, ed. Herbert Davis, Oxford, Basil Blackwell, 1962.

Thomas, Keith, *Religion and the decline of magic*, London, Penguin Books, 1973.

Townsend, Horatio, *An account of the visit of Handel to Dublin*, Dublin, James McGlashan, 1852.

Trench, Richard Chevenix, *Letters and memorials*, [ed. Maria Trench], 2 vols., London, Kegan Paul, Trench, 1888.

Trevor-Roper, H.R., *The European witch craze of the 16th and 17th centuries*, London, Penguin Books, 1969.

Updike, D.B., *Printing types, their history, forms, and use*, 2 vols., (2nd printing of 3rd ed.), Cambridge, Mass., The Belknap Press of Harvard University Press, 1966.

Wall, Maureen, *The penal laws, 1691–1760*, Dundalk, Dundalgan Press, 1967.

Wallis, Ninian, *Britannia libera*, Dublin, S. Powell, 1710.

Ward, R.E., ed., *Prince of Dublin printers: the letters of George Faulkner*, Lexington, The University Press of Kentucky, 1972.

Ware, Sir James, *The whole works of Sir James Ware concerning Ireland*, 3 vols in 2, ed. Walter Harris, Dublin, E. Jones, 1739, S. Powell, 1745, A. Reilly 1746.

Watson, Foster, *Richard Hakluyt: Empire builders*, ed. W.B. Worsfold, London, The Sheldon Press, 1924.

Webbe, Edward, *Edward Webbe, chief master gunner, his trauailes 1590*, Carefully edited by Edward Arber, London, Alex. Murray, 1868.

Whately, E.J., *Life and correspondence of Richard Whately DD*, 2 vols., London, Longmans Green, 1866.

White, Newport J.D., *Four good men*, Dublin, Hodges Figgis, 1927. Contains: (1) Luke Challoner (2) Jeremy Taylor (3) Narcissus Marsh (4) Elias Bouhéreau of La Rochelle, first public librarian in Ireland. (Reprinted with some corrections, omissions, and additions, from *Proceedings of the Royal Irish Academy*, xxvii, C 4, 1908.)

—— *An account of Archbishop Marsh's Library, Dublin ... With a note on autographs by Newport B. White*, Dublin, Hodges Figgis, 1926. (Repr. and rev. from *The Library Association Record*, March, 1899.)

—— *Some recollections of Trinity College, Dublin*, Dublin, Hodges Figgis, 1935. (See also under Catalogues.)

White, T. de V., *The parents of Oscar Wilde: Sir William and Lady Wilde*, London, Hodder & Stoughton, 1967.

Whitfield, J.H., *A short history of Italian literature*, London, Penguin Books, 1969.

Wigoder, M.J., *My life*, trans. L.E. Wigoder, ed. Samuel Abel, Leeds, Porton & Sons, 1935.

Wilson, T.G., *Victorian doctor*, New York, L.B. Fischer, 1946.

Winnett, A.R., *Peter Browne: provost, bishop, metaphysician*, London, SPCK, 1974.

Wolpe, Berthold, ed., *Vincent Figgins type specimens 1801 and 1815*, Reproduced in facsimile, ed. with an introduction and notes by Berthold Wolpe, London, Printing Historical Society, 1967.

Woodward, David, see Skelton, R.A.

Wright, Thomas, ed., *A contemporary narrative of the proceedings against Dame Alice Kyteler*, London, Camden Society, MDCCCXLIII.

COOPERATIVE WORKS, COMPOSITE WORKS, JOURNALS AND PERIODICALS

Aldis, H.G., 'The book-trade, 1557–1625' in Sir A.W. Ward and A.R. Waller, ed., *CHEL*, iv, *Prose and poetry*, pp 378–414.

Barnard, Toby, 'Improving clergymen, 1660–1760' in A. Ford, J. McGuire and K. Milne, ed., *As by law established*, Dublin, Lilliput Press, 1995, pp 136–51.

Beckett, J.C., 'The government and the Church of Ireland under William III and Anne' in *Irish Historical Studies*, ii, no. 7, March 1941, pp 280–302.

Binns, J.W., 'Alberico Gentili in defence of poetry and acting' in *Studies in the Renaissance*, xix, 1972, pp 224–72.

British Magazine, July–August, 1845. 'Narcissus Marsh's Diary with notes by J.H. Todd.'

C., G.E. [i.e. George E. Cokayne], compiler, *Some notice of various families of the name of Marsh,* Exeter, W. Pollard, 1900 [*The Genealogist*, n.s., vol. 16, suppl.]

Cathcart, H.R., 'Peter Davys: the master they shot' (ii) in *The Patrician*, no. 9, 1950, Church of Ireland Printing Co., pp 16–17.

Christian Examiner and Church of Ireland Magazine, no. lxxv, Sept. 1831, pp 645–50. Contains biographical details of Marsh together with some extracts from his Diary by 'Omicron'.

— No. xxiv, Nov. 1833, pp 761–72. Letters from Narcissus Marsh to Dr Smith giving details of the arrangements for the preparation of Bishop Bedell's manuscript of the *Old Testament* for printing.

Church of Ireland Gazette, 9 Dec. 1927, pp 712–14.

Connolly, Dom Hugh, 'A rare Benedictine book Father Edward Maihew's *Trophaea*' in *Downside Review*, 142, l, Jan. 1932, pp 108–25.

Connolly, S.J., 'Reformers and highflyers: the post-revolution church' in A. Ford, J. McGuire and K. Milne, ed., *As by law established*, Dublin, Lilliput Press, 1995, pp 152–65.

Deutsch, O.E., 'The editions of Morley's *Introduction*' in *The Library*, 4 ser., xxiii, Sept.–Dec. 1942, pp 127–9.

Dix, E.R. McC., 'The earliest Dublin printers and the Company of Stationers of London', A paper read before the Bibliographical Society, March, 16, 1903, London, Reprinted by Blades, East & Blades from the *Society's Transactions,* 1904.

— 'The first printing of the New Testament in English at Dublin' in *PRIA*, xxix, C, no. 6, July 1911, pp 180–5.

— 'Printing in the city of Waterford in the seventeenth century' in *PRIA*, xxxii, C, no. 21, Jan. 1916, pp 333–44.

— 'History of early printing in Ireland' in *Reports and Proceedings of the Belfast Natural History and Philosophical Society*, Session 1916–17, [1918], pp 5–29.

Dowden, Edward, 'An Elizabethan MS Collection: Henry Constable' in *The Modern Quarterly of Language and Literature* (now *Modern Language Quarterly*), i (1898), 3–4.

Duff, E.G., 'Notes on a visit to Archbishop Marsh's Library, Dublin [in July 1903]' in *Publications of the Edinburgh Bibliographical Society*, vi, Edinburgh, MCMVI, pp 133–40.

— 'The library of Richard Smith' in *The Library*, 2 ser., no. 30, viii, April 1907, pp 113–33.

— 'The introduction of printing into England and the early work of the press' in Sir A.W. Ward and A.R. Waller, ed., *CHEL*, ii, *The end of the middle ages*, pp 310–31.

Esposito, Mario, 'St Patrick's "Confessio" and the Book of Armagh' in *Irish Historical Studies*, ix, no. 33, March 1954, pp 1–12.

Faulkner, Anselm, ed., 'Papers of Anthony Gearnon, OFM' in *Collectanea Hibernica: Sources for Irish history*, nos. 6 & 7, 1963–64, pp 122, and 212–24.

Gaskell, Philip, 'Printing the classics in the eighteenth century' in *The Book Collector*, i, no. 2, Summer 1952, pp 98–111.

Giblin, Cathaldus, 'The Stuart nomination of Irish bishops 1687–1765' in *Irish Ecclesiastical Record*, Jan.-June 1966, cv, 5 series, 1966, pp 35–6.

Glendinning, Victoria, 'Mary, Mary quite contrary' in *Irish Times*, 7 March 1974.

Gwynn, R.M., 'Newport John Davis White' in *Divinity, A Church of Ireland Quarterly Review*, v, no. 12, Sept. 1951, pp 3–6.

Hammond, J.W., 'The king's printers in Ireland 1551–1919, part II' in *Dublin Historical Record*, xi, no. 2, March–May 1950, pp 58–64.

Hayton, D.W., 'The High Church Party in the Irish Convocation 1703–1713' in Real and Stöver-Leidig, ed., *Reading Swift: Papers from the Third Münster Symposium on Jonathan Swift*, Munich, 1998, pp 117–39.

Holmes, Sir Maurice, 'Captain James Cook, R.N., F.R.S.' in *Endeavour*, viii, no. 29, Jan. 1949, pp 11–17.

Irish Builder, xix, no. 415, 1 April 1877, p. 93.

Irish Builder, xxi, no. 471, 1 August 1879, p. 236.

Irish Builder, xxvii, no. 607, 1 April 1885, p. 108. (Articles on Marsh's Library probably written by Dr Robert Travers.)

Irish Builder, xxxvii, no. 857, 1 Sept. 1895, pp 209, 216. (Photographs of Marsh's Library.)

Irish Builder, xxx, no. 691, 1 Oct. 1888. Genealogy of the Cradock family, pp 251–2.

Irish Ecclesiastical Journal, v, 1848–9. (Marsh's Diary with notes by J.H. Todd.)

Jackson, W.A., 'Edward Gwynn' in W.H. Bond, ed., *Records of a bibliographer*, no. 8, 1934, Harvard University Press, 1967, pp 115–19.

— 'Humphrey Dyson's library, or, some observations on the survival of books' in W.H. Bond, ed., *Records of a bibliographer*, no. 10, 1949, Harvard University Press, 1967, pp 135–41.

Johnson, A.F., 'Italian sixteenth-century books' in *The Library*, 5 ser., xiii, no. 3, Sept. 1958, pp 161–74.

Johnston, Elsie, 'The diary of Elie Bouhéreau', repr. from the *Proceedings of the Huguenot Society of London*, xv, no. 1, London, Spottiswoode, Ballantyne, 1934.

Kingston, John, 'Catholic families of the Pale' in *Repertorium Novum*, 1, no. 2, 1959–60, pp 254–5.

Kleinstuber, 'The letters of Paul Bauldry and Élie Bouhéreau' in *Lias* 22 (1955) 1, pp 119–46.

Kronenberg, M.E., 'Notes on English printing in the Low Countries' (Early sixteenth century) in *The Library*, 4 ser., ix, no. 2, Sept. 1928, pp 139–63.

Lass, David, 'A brief account of Nicholas de Lyra's *Tractatus de differentia nostrae translationis ab hebraica littera veteris testamenti*, in the edition printed at Rouen Ca. 1494–1497' in *Serif, Quarterly of the Kent State University Libraries*, 10, no. 2, Summer 1973, pp 19–36.

Le Fanu, T.P., 'Archbishop Marsh and the Discipline of the French Church of St Patrick's Dublin, 1694', repr. from the *Proceedings of the Huguenot Society of London*, xii, no. 4, London, Spottiswood, Ballantyne, 1922.

Lucas, P.J., 'John Capgrave and the *Nova legenda Anglie*: a survey' in *The Library*, 5 ser., xxv, no. 1, March 1970, pp 1–10.

McCarthy, Muriel, 'Eleazar Albin's watercolours of birds' in *Irish Arts Review Yearbook*, 11, 1995, pp 88–95.

McCarthy, Muriel, 'Swift and the Primate of Ireland. Marsh's Library in the early eighteenth century' in *Dublin Historical Record*, xxvii, no. 3, June 1974, pp 109–12.

— 'Archbishop Marsh and his Library' in *Dublin Historical Record*, xxix, no. 1, Dec. 1975, pp 2–23.

McNeill, Charles, 'Publications of Irish interest published by Irish authors on the Continent of Europe prior to the eighteenth century' in *The Bibliographical Society of Ireland*, iv, 1930.

MacRobert, T.M., 'Jean de Tournes (1504–1564)' in *Motif*, 2, Feb. 1959, pp 10–11.

Marsh, Narcissus, 'Essay touching the (esteemed) sympathy between lute or viol strings' in Robert Plot, *The natural history of Oxford-shire*, Oxford, 1677, pp 289–99.

— 'An introductory essay to the doctrine of sounds containing some proposals for the improvement of acousticks' in *Philosophical Transactions*, 156, Feb. 20, 1683/4, pp 471–88.

Meagher, John, 'Glimpses of eighteenth century priests' in *Repertorium Novum*, ii, no. 1, 1957–8, pp 129–47.

Medical Press, 4 April 1888 (Obituary notice of Robert Travers, p. 364).

Millett, Benignus, 'Irish literature in Latin, 1550–1700' in T.W. Moody, F.X. Martin, and F.J. Byrne, ed., *A new history of Ireland*, iii, *Early modern Ireland 1534–1691*, Oxford, At the Clarendon Press, 1976, pp 561–86.

Moody, T.W., 'Introduction' in T.W. Moody, F.X. Martin, and F.J. Byrne, ed., *A new history of Ireland*, iii, *Early modern Ireland 1534–1691*, Oxford, At the Clarendon Press, 1976, pp [xxxix]–lxiii.

Mullinger, J.B., 'Platonists and Latitudinarians' in Sir A.W. Ward and A.R. Waller, ed., *CHEL*, viii, *The age of Dryden*, pp 273–92.

Nankivell, James, 'Edward Stillingfleet, Bishop of Worcester, 1689–99' (A lecture to the Worcestershire Archaeological Society), [s.l., Dec. 1946] pp 1–20. (Copy presented by the author to Marsh's Library in 1947.)

Nixon, H.M., 'Early English gold-tooled bookbindings' in *Estratto del volume III di Studi di bibliografia e di storia in onore di Tammaro de Marinis*, Verona, 1964, pp 283–308.

Notes and Queries, 150, no. 23, 5 June 1926, pp 405–6. (Contains an annotation in a book in the Stillingfleet collection which gives details of money spent on a journey to Cambridge.)

O'Dea, Paul, 'Father Peter Wadding, S.J., Chancellor of the University of Prague 1629–1641' in *Studies*, xxx, no. 119, Sept. 1941, pp 337–48.

O'Neill, T.P., 'A bad year in the Liberties' in Elgy Gillespie, ed., *The Liberties of Dublin*, Dublin, E. & T. O'Brien, 1973, pp 76–83.

Ó Seanóir, S. and M. Pollard, 'A great deal of good verse' in *Hermathena*, nos. cxxx and cxxxi, 1981, pp 7–36.

Pittion, J.-P., 'Notes for a Saumur bibliography: XVIIth century bibliographical documents in Marsh's Library, Dublin. Part I, Introduction' in *Long Room, Bulletin of the Friends of the Library, Trinity College Dublin*, 3, Spring 1971, pp 9–22.

— 'Notes for a Saumur bibliography: Part II. The printer as publisher' (1) in *Long Room*, 5, Spring 1972, pp 11–16.

— 'Notes for a Saumur bibliography: Part II. The printer as publisher' (2) in *Long Room*, 7, Spring 1973, pp 7–17.

— 'Notes for a Saumur bibliography: Part III: a check list of Saumur printings, 1600–85' in *Long Room*, 10, Autumn–Winter, 1974, pp 7–24.

Pollard, M., 'The provost's logic: an unrecorded first issue' in *Long Room, Bulletin*, 1, 1970, (n.s.), pp 38–40.

Purcell, Mary, 'Those were the days …' in *The Bulletin*, Dublin Diocesan Press Office, 8, no. 8, Oct. 1974, pp 8–9.

Raftery, Deirdre, 'Frances Power Cobbe' in Mary Cullen and Maria Luddy, ed., *Women, power and consciousness in 19th century Ireland*, Dublin, Attic Press, 1995.

Robinson, C.N. and John Leyland, 'The literature of the sea from the origins to Hakluyt' in Sir A.W. Ward and A.R. Waller, ed., *CHEL*, iv, *Prose and poetry*, pp 66–85.

Routh, H.V., 'The progress of social literature in Tudor times' in Sir A.W. Ward and A.R. Waller, ed., *CHEL*, iii, *Renascence and reformation*, pp 83–114.

Sainty, J.C., 'The secretariat of the chief governors of Ireland, 1690–1800' in *PRIA*, 77, C, no. 1, 1977, pp 1–33.

Shields, Hugh, 'Bishop Turpin and the source of *Nycodemus gospell*' in *English Studies*, 53, 6, December 1972, pp 1–6.

Simmons, J.S.G., 'Early-printed Cyrillic books in Archbishop Marsh's Library, Dublin' in *The Irish Book*, ii, no. 2, Spring 1963, pp 37–42.

Simms, J.G., 'The restoration, 1660–85' in T.W. Moody, F.X. Martin, and F. J. Byrne, ed., *A new history of Ireland*, iii, *Early modern Ireland 1534–1691*, Oxford, At the Clarendon Press, 1976, pp 420–53.

Simms, J.G., 'John Toland (1670–1722), A Donegal Heretic' in *Irish Historical Studies*, xvi, no. 63 (March 1969), pp 304–20.

Strickland, W.G., 'The royal hospital at Kilmainham and its architect' in *JRSAI*, liii, vol. xiii, 6 ser., 1923, Miscellanea, pp 101–04.

White, H.V., *Bishop Berkeley as a missionary: a paper*, Dublin, Office of the Irish Auxiliary of the S.P.G. in Foreign Parts, 1900 (Appendix B, p.36).

White, Newport B., 'Manuscript and printed music in Marsh's Library' in *Music of Ireland, a symposium*, ed. Aloys Fleischmann, foreword by Sir Arnold Bax, Cork University Press, and Oxford, B.H. Blackwell, 1952, pp 319–21.

White, Newport J.D., 'Gleanings from the correspondence of a great Huguenot: Élie Bouhéreau of La Rochelle' repr. from the *Proceedings of the Huguenot Society of London*, ix, no. 2, London, Spottiswoode, 1910.

UNPUBLISHED THESES

Carpenter, A.P. Isdell, Archbishop King and Dean Swift, 2 vols., PhD thesis in Department of English, University College, Dublin, March 1970.

Martin, George, An edition of the English poems, Marsh's Library MS Z3.5.21, MA thesis in the University of Waterloo, Canada, September 1971.

Pittion, J-P., Intellectual life in the Académie of Saumur, 1633–1685. A study of the Bouhéreau Collection, PhD thesis in French Dept., Trinity College, Dublin, 1970.

NEWSPAPERS

Evening Press, 12 Sept. 1969, Article by Andrew Marsh on Dr Wilde and Mary Josephine.

Freeman's Journal, 7 Sept. 1887, Editorial on Marsh's Library.

Irish Independent, 4 June 1968, Article in the series Treasures of Ireland on 'Archbishop Marsh's ancient library' by M. Pollard.

Irish Independent, 5, 6, 7, 11 August 1969, Articles by Rex Mac Gall (Deasún Breathnach) on Bishop Bedell's translation of the Bible into Irish.

Irish Times, 14 Dec. 1864, The Mary Josephine Travers–Sir William Wilde, Lady Wilde libel action.

Irish Times, 7 March 1974, Article 'Mary Mary Quite Contrary' by Victoria Glendinning. (This article refers to Mary Tighe, née Blachford, the daughter of the keeper of Marsh's Library, William Blachford.)

BIOGRAPHIES, DICTIONARIES, DIRECTORIES

Bayle, Pierre, *The dictionary historical and critical*, 2nd ed., rev., corr., and enlar. by Mr Des Maizeaux, with the life of the author, 5 vols., London, 1734–38. (The first French edition and the first English translation of this work are also in the library.)

Blom, Eric, compiler, *Everyman's dictionary of music,* London, J.M. Dent & Sons, 1946.

Chalmers, Alexander, *The general biographical dictionary*, A new ed., rev., and enlar., 32 vols., London, 1812–17.

Cotton, Henry, *A typographical gazetteer*, 2nd ed., corr. and enlar., Oxford, At the University Press, MDCCCXXXI.

Cross, F.L., *The Oxford dictionary of the Christian Church*, 3rd ed. by E.A. Livingstone, Oxford University Press, 1997.

Dictionary of Irish literature, revised and expanded edition, Robert Hogan, editor-in-chief, 2 vols, London, Aldwych Press, 1996.

Encyclopædia Britannica, 9th ed., i–xxiv and *Index* volume, Edinburgh, Adam & Charles Black, 1875–89.

McKerrow, R.B, general ed., *A dictionary of printers and booksellers in England, Scotland, and Ireland, and of foreign printers of English books 1557–1640*, London, Bibliographical Society, Blades, East & Blades, 1910.

The new Grove dictionary of music and musicians, 2nd. ed., 29 vols, London, Macmillan, 2001.

Patrick, David and F.H. Groome, ed., *Chambers's biographical dictionary*, London & Edinburgh, W. & R. Chambers, 1897.

Plomer, H.R., *A dictionary of the booksellers and printers who were at work in England, Scotland and Ireland from 1641 to 1667*, London, Bibliographical Society, Blades, East and Blades, 1907.

Plomer, H.R., and others, Arundell Esdaile, ed., *A dictionary of the printers and booksellers who were at work in England, Scotland and Ireland from 1668 to 1725*, Oxford University Press, Bibliographical Society, 1922.

Stephen, Leslie and Sidney Lee, ed., *Dictionary of national biography*, 66 vols., London, Smith, Elder, 1885–1901.

Thom's Irish Almanac and Official Directory, Dublin, 1863.

Ware, Henry and W.C. Piercy, ed., *A dictionary of Christian biography and literature*, London, John Murray, 1911.

CATALOGUES

Abbott, T.K., *Catalogue of fifteenth-century books in the Library of Trinity College, Dublin, and in Marsh's Library, Dublin, with a few from other collections*, Dublin, Hodges Figgis, 1905.

Adams, H.M. *Catalogue of books printed on the continent of Europe, 1501–1600 in Cambridge libraries*, 2 vols., Cambridge, At the University Press, 1967.

A guide to the exhibition in the king's library illustrating the history of printing, music-printing and bookbinding, British Museum, printed by order of the trustees, 1926.

Alden, John, *Bibliographica Hibernica: additions and corrections to Wing*, Charlottesville, Bibliographical Society of the University of Virginia, 1955.

Aldis, H.G., *A list of books printed in Scotland before 1700*, Edinburgh Bibliographical Society, MCMIV.

Allison, A.F. and D.M. Rogers, *A catalogue of Catholic books in English printed abroad or secretly in England 1558–1640*, 2 vols., Bognor Regis, Arundel Press, 1956.

— *The contemporary printed literature of the English counter-reformation between 1558 and 1640*, 2 vols., Aldershot, Hants., Scolar Press, 1989.

An exhibition of printing at the Fitzwilliam Museum, Cambridge, At the University Press, 1940.

Barnes, G.R., compiler with others, *A list of books printed in Cambridge at the University Press 1521–1800*, Cambridge University Press, 1935.

Bernard, Edward, *Catalogi librorum manuscriptorum Angliae et Hiberniae*, Oxoniae, E. Theatro Sheldoniano, MDCXCVII.

Brunet, J.C., *Manuel du libraire et de l'amateur de livres*, 4th ed., 5 vols., A Paris, 1842–44.

Campbell, M.F.A.G., *Annales de la typographie Néerlandaise au XVe siècle*, La Haye, Martinus Nijhoff, 1874. Supplement (1–4), La Haye, Nijhoff, 1878–90.

Catalogue of the Cashel Diocesan Library, Co. Tipperary, Ireland, compiled by Jean McK. Miller, Boston, Mass., G.K. Hall, 1973.

Dix, E.R. McC., compiler, *Catalogue of early Dublin-printed books 1601–1700*, with an historical introduction and bibliographical notes by C.W. Dugan, second issue, with additions, Dublin, Sealy, Bryers & Walker, 1898–1912.

— *The earliest Dublin printing, with list of books, proclamations, etc., printed in Dublin prior to 1601*, Dublin, O'Donoghue, 1901.

— *Printing in Dublin prior to 1601*, 2nd ed., Dublin, Colm Ó Lochlainn, 1932.

Gesamtkatalog der Wiegendrucke: hrsq. ven der Kommission für den Gesamtkatalog der Wiegendrucke, 8 vols, Leipzig, 1925–40.

Hain, L.F.T., *Repertorium bibliographicum, in quo libri omnes ab arte typographica inventa usque ad annum 1500 typis expressi, ordine alphabetico …*, 2 vols., Stuttgartiae, I.G. Cottae; Lut. Pars. Iul. Renouard, 1826–38. See Copinger, W.A., *Supplement to Hain's Repertorium bibliographicum*, 1895–1902.

Hawkins, R.C., *Catalogue of books mostly from presses of the first printers showing the progress of printing with movable metal types through the second half of the fifteenth century*. Collected by R.C. Hawkins, catalogued by A.W. Pollard, Oxford University Press, 1910.

Hayes, R.J., ed., *Manuscript sources for the history of Irish civilisation*, 11 vols., Boston, Mass., G.K. Hall, 1965.

Hoskins, Edgar, *Horae beatae Mariae virginis, or, Sarum and York primers, with kindred books and primers of the reformed Roman use*, London, Longmans Green, 1901.

*List of such of the names of the nobility, gentry and commonalty of England and Ireland …
attainted of high treason*, London, for R. Clavel and J. Watts, 1690.

Pollard, A.W. and G.R. Redgrave, compilers with others, *A short-title catalogue of books
printed in England, Scotland and Ireland and of English books printed abroad 1475–1640*,
London, Bibliographical Society for Bernard Quaritch, 1926.

— Second ed., rev. & enlarg., begun by W.A. Jackson & F.S. Ferguson. Completed by
K.F. Pantzer, ii, I–Z, London, Bibliographical Society, 1976.

Pollard, M., An exhibition: French Renaissance books: Marsh's Library Dublin, June
1959. (Unpublished.)

— Italian Renaissance printing in Marsh's Library, May 1960. (Unpublished.)

*Printing and the mind of man: catalogue of the exhibitions at the British Museum and at Earls
Court, London. 16–27 July 1963*, F.W. Bridges & Sons and the Association of British
Manufacturers of Printers' Machinery (Proprietary), 1963.

Proctor, R.G.C., *An index to the early printed books in the British Museum. … to the year
MD (1500)*, London, Kegan Paul, 1898–9.

Ramage, David, compiler with others, *A finding-list of English books to 1640 in libraries
in the British Isles*, Durham, published by the Council of the Durham Colleges, G.
Bailes & Son, 1958.

Scott, J.R., compiler, and Newport J.D. White, ed., *Catalogue of the manuscripts remaining
in Marsh's Library, Dublin*, Dublin, A. Thom, [1913].

Sweeney, Tony, *Ireland and the printed word. A short descriptive catalogue of early books,
pamphlets, newsletters and broadsides relating to Ireland, printed 1475–1700*, Dublin,
Éamonn de Búrca for Edmund Burke Publishers, 1997.

Todd, H.J., *A catalogue of the archiepiscopal manuscripts in the library at Lambeth palace*,
London, Law & Gilbert, 1812.

Todd, J.H., ed., *Catalogus librorum impressorum qui in Bibliotheca Collegii sacrosanctæ et
individuæ Trinitatis reginæ Elizabethæ …*, Dublinii, E Typographeo Academico,
1864–87, 9 vols., i edited by J.H. Todd, ii–ix by H.D. Hutton.

Walsh, M. ON., 'Irish books printed abroad 1475–1700: check list' in *The Irish Book*, ii,
no. 1, Winter 1962–63.

White, Newport J.D., *A short catalogue of English books in Archbishop Marsh's Library
Dublin, printed before MDCXLI*, Oxford University Press, Bibliographical Society,
1905 (Contains a Supplement listing Incunabula separately, taken from T.K.
Abbott's catalogue [Dublin, 1905]).

— compiler, *A catalogue of books in the French language, printed in or before A.D. 1715,
remaining in Archbishop Marsh's Library, Dublin*, Dublin, University Press, Ponsonby
and Gibbs, 1918.

Wing, Donald, *Short-title catalogue of books printed in England, Scotland, Ireland, Wales, and
British America and of English books printed in other countries 1641–1700*, 3 vols., New
York, Index Society, Columbia University Press, 1945–51. (Supplement on Ireland
by J.E. Alden, 1955.)

AUCTION AND SALE CATALOGUES

Fleming, J.F. Inc., *Sale catalogue of English books printed before 1640*, New York, [1958]. (With an introduction by J.G. McManaway.)

Maggs Bros., *Sale catalogue No. 921. Witchcraft and magic*, London, Dec. 1969.

Sharpe, Charles, *Bibliotheca Marsiana. Catalogue of books, the duplicate copies of the public library, Dublin … to be sold by auction on Wednesday May 8th 1833. By Charles Sharpe*, [compiled by Robert Travers], Dublin, R.D. Webb, MDCCCXXXIII.

— *Catalogue of the library of Robert Travers, Esq. … to be sold by auction on Friday, the 18th March 1836 and following days, by Charles Sharpe*, Dublin, R.D. Webb, [1836].

CALENDAR OF TREASURY BOOKS

Calendar of treasury books, Prepared by W.A. Shaw. xiv, 1 Sept. 1698 to 31 July 1699, London, 1934, p. 170, Oct. 28 and p. 212, Dec. 7. See references to the case of Patience Bond against Epaphroditus Marsh. See also p. 378, June 1 and p. 414, July 11 for payments made to Archbishop Marsh. (One entry mistakenly refers to Marsh as archbishop of London.)

— xvi, 1 Oct. 1700 to 31 Dec. 1701, London, 1938, pp 282–3, June 11, 1701. Royal Warrant to Lords Justices to insert in the Civil List the salary of £200 for Elias Bouhéreau.

— xix, Jan. 1704 to March 1705, London, 1938, p. 24, 1704, April 21. Reduction of Bouhéreau's pension from £200 to £100, p. 260, 1704, May 31. To report on Archbishop Marsh's petition regarding payment of the quarter's rent.

— xxiii, part II, 1709, London, 1949, p. 103, 1708–9, March 14. Treasurer Godolphin to the Lord Lieutenant of Ireland to report on the enclosed petition (missing) of Dr Elias Bouhéreau praying that his pension of £200 per an., lately payable to him as library keeper of St Sepulchre's, Dublin may be continued for two years from his admission to the place of 'chorister' of St Patrick's Cathedral (the word chorister in this text is a mistake. Bouhéreau was installed as precentor of St Patrick's Cathedral in March 1709), p. 191, 1709, May 28. Royal warrant dated St James's to same to continue on the establishment of Ireland for two years from 1708 Xmas the pension of £200 per an., to Dr Elias Bouhéreau keeper of the Public Library near St Sepulchre's Dublin.

— xx, part II, April 1705 to Sept. 1706, London, 1952, p. 239, 1705, April 30. Royal Warrant to pay Marsh the remainder of the quarter's rent. (This was a reduced amount because a portion of this rent had already been paid to the Blue Coat School. This reference says the Blue Coat School in London but other references say the Blue Coat School in Dublin.)

— xxix, part II, Aug. 1714–Dec. 1715, London, 1957. See p. 585 and see also xxxi part II, Jan.–Dec. 1717, London, 1957, p. 520. In the lists of pensions in these books Dr Bouhéreau's son John is listed as receiving £30 as underkeeper of the Public Library at Dublin, during pleasure.

CALENDAR OF TREASURY PAPERS

Calendar of treasury papers, Prepared by Joseph Redington, 1697–1701–2, lxxiv, 1701, May and June, London, 1871, pp 488–9, 1701, May 6, no. 7. Letter from Archbishop Marsh to the lord lieutenant of Ireland which gives details for the erection of a public library etc.

— 1702–7, lxxxvi, 1703, June–July, London, 1874, pp 174–5, July 1 & 11, 1703, no. 107. Contains a letter from the bishop of London to the lord high treasurer describing Archbishop Marsh's pathetic financial circumstances and Archbishop Marsh's petition appealing for the rent due to him in his diocese of Armagh. See also xciii, 1705, Jan–Mar., pp 334–5, Mar. 31, no. 134. Letter from Mr Southwell to Mr Taylor, dated Dublin, Mar. 11, 1705. Southwell has added the following to this letter: 'P.S. Pray let me desire you to further the Primate's request about getting £500 in order for buying Dr Stillingfleet's library, unless you are afraid we should grow too learned.' (Marsh does not appear to have received this money.)

— 1708–14, cxii, 1709 Jan.–Feb., London, 1879. p. 92, 1708–9, Jan. 22, no. 22. The earl of Galway's letter to the lord high treasurer testifying to Elias Bouhéreau's great merits and learning. It is accompanied by Bouhéreau's petition for the continuance of his pension.

CALENDAR OF STATE PAPERS

In the *Calendar of state papers* for the years 1699–1700, 1700–4 (Domestic Series) Archbishop Marsh's name appears frequently, particularly for payments as a lord justice; Dr Bouhéreau's name also appears.

BIBLIOGRAPHIES

Lowndes, W.T., *The bibliographer's manual of English literature*, new ed., rev. corr. & enlar. by H.G. Bohn, 4 vols., London, George Bell & Sons, [1857–64].

Madan, Falconer, *The early Oxford press: a bibliography of printing and publishing at Oxford '1468' to 1640*, Oxford, At the Clarendon Press, 1895.

Teerink, Herman, *A bibliography of the writings of Jonathan Swift*, 2nd ed., rev. & corr., ed. Arthur Scouten, Philadelphia, University of Pennsylvania Press, 1963 [i.e. 1964].

PARLIAMENTARY PAPERS

9th William III, 1697, An act for banishing all papists exercising any ecclesiastical jurisdiction, and all regulars of the popish clergy out of this kingdom. In *The Statutes at large passed in the parliaments held in Ireland*, Dublin, Boulter Grierson, MDCCLXV, chap. I, pp 339–43.

6th Queen Anne, 1707, An act for settling and preserving a publick library for ever, in the house for that purpose built by his grace Narcissus, now lord archbishop of Armagh, on part of the ground belonging to the archbishop of Dublin's palace, near to the city of Dublin. In *The Statutes at large passed in the parliaments held in Ireland,* Dublin, Boulter Grierson, MDCCLXV, chap. XIX, pp 169–79.

Anno quadragesimo primo Georgii III Regis, An act for granting to his majesty several sums of money for defraying the charge of certain permanent services in that part of the United Kingdom called Ireland 30 April 1801, Cap. XXXII, To the under Library Keeper of Marsh's Library at Saint Patrick's Dublin £27.13s.10½d English. £30 Irish, London, George Eyre and Andrew Strahan, 1801.

The Journals of the house of commons of the kingdom of Ireland, from 11th James I to 25th George II, in eight volumes; and volumes 9–14. Also *An essay towards a general index and abridgement … in the eleven volumes of the Journals of the house of commons of Ireland. The Journals … from 9 November 1641 to 26 March 1647*, Dublin, Abraham Bradley, 1753–71.

The Journals … from 22 October 1765, volumes 8–15, 11 in 2 parts, Printed by George Grierson, 1797, volumes 16 and 17 (2 parts), J. King and Abraham Bradley, 1795, volumes 18 and 19 (2 parts), Abraham Bradley King, 1799–1800, Dublin, 1795–1800.

The Statutes (Ireland), 1310–1800, 21 vols., 1786–1801.

REPORTS

Report from the select committee on public libraries, 2 vols., Ordered, by the house of commons, to be printed, 9 Feb. 1849 and 1 Aug. 1850.

Reports from the commissioners respecting the public records of Ireland, With supplements and appendixes, 1810–15, Ordered, by the house of commons, to be printed, 1813, 1814, 1815.

— *The sixth, seventh, eighth, ninth, and tenth reports from the commissioners respecting the public records of Ireland, With supplements and appendixes 1816–20*, Ordered, by the house of commons, to be printed, 1819 and 1820.

The thirtieth report of the deputy keeper of the public records and keeper of state papers in Ireland 14 May 1898, Dublin, HMSO, 1898.

REGISTERS

Parish Register Society of Dublin. The registers of St Patrick, Dublin 1677 to 1800, transcribed
   by C.H. Price, ed. J.H. Bernard, Dublin, Alex. Thom, 1907.

RECORDS

Gilbert, Sir J.T., and Lady Gilbert, ed., *Calendar of the ancient records of the city of Dublin*,
   i–xviii, Dublin, Joseph Dollard; London, Bernard Quaritch, 1889–1922.

MANUSCRIPTS

See R.J. Hayes's *Catalogue of manuscript sources for the history of Irish civilisation*, Boston,
   Mass., G.K. Hall, 1965, iii, *Persons,* for additional material relating to Archbishop
   Narcissus Marsh.

In the Bodleian Library
MS Smith 52 (15, 659) (Extracts) *Letters to Dr T. Smith from Narc. Marsh 1679–1709.
MS Eng. Misc. C 23 (31, 774): (Extracts). Copies of correspondence between Abp.
   Marsh and Dr T. Smith, 1691–1709 from Bodleian MSS 15, 670 and 15, 659.
MS Smith 45 (15, 652) (Extracts) *Letters to Dr Bernard, 6 from Abp. Marsh, (1679–95)
   including observations on the comet 1680–1 and a list of Greek manuscripts in
   Trinity College, Dublin, 1680.
MS Tanner 35 (9855) (Extracts) *Letters to Abp. Sancroft from Narc. Marsh, Provost of
   Trinity College Dublin. 26 Aug. 1682. MS Tanner 36 (9856) (Extracts) *Letters to
   Abp. Sancroft from Narc. Marsh. 26 Apr. 1681.
MS Rawl C 983 (12, 813) (Extract) *Letter from Primate Marsh against the Abp. of
   Dublin's getting a queen's licence for a Convocation and having it addressed to
   himself instead of in the usual form to the Primate, 16 Jan. 1705.
Copies are on microfilm or in electrostatic prints in Marsh's Library.

In the British Library
See *Index to the catalogue of additions to the MSS in the British Museum 1854–75*, British
   Museum, 1880, p. 181.
Bouhéreau, (A), Letter to J. Ellis 1704. 28, 892, f. 30.
Bouhéreau, Elie, MD, Secretary to Lord Galway, Letters to J. Ellis, 1697–1704, Fr. 28,
   881–28, 894 passim. (I am grateful to Dr Jean-Paul Pittion for informing me about
   this correspondence.)
See *Catalogue of additions to the MSS in the British Museum 1846–47*, B.M., 1864. p. 80.
   Narcissus Marsh, Letters to the earl of Rochester, 1701–2, 15, 895.
British Museum, Additional MS. 21, 494 (Extracts). Letter of Abp. Marsh to Sir R.
   Southwell, Dublin Castle, 24 Feb. 1701.

British Museum, Additional MS. 29, 584 (Extract). Letter of Narc. Marsh abp. of
    Armagh to H. Compton, bp. of London, June 7, 8, 1703.
British Museum, Stowe MS 747 (Extract). Letter of Thomas Molyneux to — relating
    to the abp. of Dublin's (Marsh) MS Latin Dictionary, Dublin, 10 Nov. 1702.
Copies of all the above are on microfilm in Marsh's Library.
In Chetham's Library, Manchester, England
MS A 4. 26. Dr Robert Travers–Thomas Jones correspondence, 1848–75. (Xerox copies
    of this correspondence are in Marsh's Library.)

In Dublin City Library, Pearse St
Gilbert Collection. MS 192. Copy of the catalogue of MSS including many printed
    documents relating for the most part to Ireland in Marsh's Library compiled by
    Revd T. R. W. Cradock and Dr R. Travers. (This also includes newspaper cuttings
    and a copy of a letter in the Lyons Collection in Trinity College written by Dr
    Elias Bouhéreau to Archbishop William King c. July 1705.)

In the National Gallery of Ireland
Minutes of the board meetings of the governors and guardians of the National Gallery
    1855–65.
Letterbooks of Colonel T. A. Larcom, 2 vols.

In the National Library of Ireland
MS 16, 210. Narcissus Marsh. Letter-book of lord justices Narcissus archbishop of
    Dublin and Henry earl of Drogheda containing official correspondence with the
    earl of Rochester, lord lieutenant, Jan. 1701/2, March 1702.

In the National Archives
M 2453–7. Lords justices' letters, 5 vols., 1692–1701. Official correspondence (Includes
    letters signed by Narcissus Marsh, Elias Bouhéreau and Lord Galway.)

In Marsh's Library
Account books, Donations book, Visitation minute books, scrapbooks, visitors' books
    1826–33 and 1871–1977.
Archives box (This contains accounts, correspondence, 19th cent. copy of Primate
    Marsh's will and codicil, receipts etc.).
Dr Elias Bouhéreau's Diary, 1689–1719, MS Z2.2.2.
Contemporary copy of Archbishop Marsh's Diary, from 20 Dec. 1690 to 8 Dec. 1696,
    MS Z2.2.3, and a typewritten copy of this Diary, MS Z2.2.3b.

In Lambeth Palace Library
Gibson Papers, MS 929, f. 41. [Narcissus Marsh], 'State of the province of Armagh', 1706.

See H.J. Todd's *Catalogue of the archiepiscopal manuscripts ... Edmundi Gibsoni*, p. 200. This contains three letters written by Abp. Marsh regarding the Convocation in Ireland. Item no. 89 includes a complaint by Abp. Marsh about Abp. William King's refusal to agree to unite the treasurership or chantership of St Patrick's Cathedral to the library-keeper of Marsh's Library. The letter was written on 16 Oct. 1703.

In the Royal Irish Academy
MS 12/D/34. Letters from John Wallis in Oxford to Narcissus Marsh, dated 16 June and 17, 18 August 1681.

In St Patrick's Cathedral
Calendar of leases 1546–1776 no. 59 (10) 1701, Marsh's Library.

In St Patrick's Hospital
The General Board book 29 August 1746 to November 1796.
Draft minute book no. 5, 1797–1835.

In Trinity College Library, Dublin
MSS 1995–2008 a–g.
　　The Lyons collection of the correspondence of Archbishop William King (1650–1729.)
　　Abp. Narcissus Marsh to Abp. elect William King, Apr. 26, 1703, no. 1011.
　　Abp. Narcissus Marsh to Abp. King, June 24, 1703, no. 1028.
　　Abp. Narcissus Marsh to Abp. King, July 10, 1703, no. 1032.
　　Abp. Narcissus Marsh to Abp. King, March 8, 1705/6, no. 1200.
Dr Elias Bouhéreau to Archbishop King, *c.* July 1705, no 2395. (This letter is very fragile and can only be seen on microfilm. There is also a copy of the letter in the Gilbert collection, MS 192, in the Public Library, Pearse Street, Dublin.)
Dr Elias Bouhéreau to Abp. King, Dec. 1705, No. 2399.
Dr Elias Bouhéreau to Abp. King, 1705, No. 2400.
Archbishop William King's Letter–books. N3. 2b. 1489/2.
　　Abp. William King to Abp. Narcissus Marsh, 16 March 1702/3, p. 173.
　　Abp. William King to Abp. Narcissus Marsh, 23 March 1702/3, p. 181.
MS N2. 27. no. 208. Abp. William King to Abp. Narcissus Marsh, 9 October 1710. (This is copied from N3. 11 (MS 2531) N2. 27.)
MS Q5. 13 (3205). Antiquarian notebook by Dr Robert Travers, *c.*1855.
General Registry. Mun. V.5.2. from 1640.
　　See pp 202, 203, 227, 229, 233–5. (Narcissus Marsh was provost of Trinity College from 24 January 1679 to September 1683.)

Portraits and Paintings

ortraits of Narcissus Marsh can be found in Exeter College Oxford; Trinity College, Dublin; Irish Museum of Modern Art (formerly Royal Hospital, Kilmainham); the Synod Hall, Armagh; and Marsh's Library (2). The portrait in the first gallery of the library was probably painted by Hugh Howard.

Two interiors of Marsh's Library by Walter Osborne can be seen in the Hugh Lane Gallery of Modern Art.

There are drawings of the interior of Marsh's Library by Estella Solomons in Marsh's Library and a drawing of the interior by Brian Coghlan in the National Library of Ireland. There is also a drawing of the exterior of Marsh's Library and St Patrick's Close by Brian Coghlan in the headquarters of the Royal Society of Antiquaries of Ireland in Merrion Square, Dublin. Thomas Ryan PPRHA has painted the interior of the library many times in recent years, and there are numerous drawings of the library in private hands.

Keepers (or Librarians) of Marsh's

Elias Bouhéreau DD, 1701.

Robert Dougatt MA, 1719.

John Wynne MA, 1730.

Thomas Cobbe LLD, 1762.

William Blachford MA, 1766.

William Cradock MA, 1773.

Thomas Cradock MA, 1776.

Thomas Russell Cradock MA, 1815.

Thomas Russell William Cradock MA, 1841.

William Maturin DD, 1872.

George Thomas Stokes DD, 1887.

Newport John Davis White DD, 1898.

Newport Benjamin White MA, 1931.

Robert Ormes Dougan MA, 1957.

Robert Brendan McDowell FTCD, 1958.

John Gerald Simms FTCD, 1974.

John Simpson Brown MA, BD, 1979.

Muriel McCarthy MA, LLD, 1989.

Index